CHRISTMAS EVE CHARADE

"Well? Do you love him or don't you?"

Elinor stared up at him, the import of the question bursting on her like an explosion. Did she love Julian? She was suddenly beset with confusion. "I . . . I . . ." she stammered, "I suppose I—after all, I've waited five years . . ."

"That is no answer. Yes or no?"

Miles stared at her with a burning intensity for a moment before expelling an explosive breath. "Confound it, girl, you don't have to answer. I always could read your thoughts in those enigmatic eyes of yours. The answer is yes. If it weren't, you wouldn't be afraid to say so."

She had to reply somehow. "I . . . suppose that's true," she managed.

"Very well, then," Miles said, stalking to the door, "there's nothing more to be said. As far as I'm concerned, if you want the fellow, you shall have him! Wrapped, tied, and delivered. And before this deuced holiday is over!"

—From "A Sneeze on Tuesday"
by ELIZABETH MANSFIELD

A Christmas Treasure

**Elizabeth Mansfield, Holly Newman,
Sheila Rabe, and Ellen Rawlings**

B
BERKLEY BOOKS, NEW YORK

A CHRISTMAS TREASURE

A Berkley Book / published by arrangement with
the authors

PRINTING HISTORY
Berkley edition / November 1992

Contents

A Christmas Treasure

A
Sneeze
on
Tuesday

Elizabeth Mansfield

Sneeze on Monday, sneeze for danger;
Sneeze on Tuesday, kiss a stranger;
Sneeze on Wednesday, get a letter;
Sneeze on Thursday, something better;
Sneeze on Friday, sneeze for rue;
Sneeze on Saturday, God Bless you.

—From an Old Nursery Rhyme

1

WHILE precariously perched on the highest rung of a six-foot ladder, attempting to fasten the end of a long festoon of evergreens to the top of a twelve-foot-high window, Elinor Selby sneezed. It was an ordinary sneeze, only mildly explosive and accompanied by the slightest bodily tremor, but it set off an ever-widening ripple of reactions that affected not only the entire Christmas celebration but the whole direction of Elinor's life.

The sneeze occurred on a Tuesday, five days before Christmas, in the year of our Lord 1816, in the large, high-ceilinged but otherwise unpretentious (some called it shabby) drawing room of Selby Manor, Leyburn, North Riding. It was early afternoon, and from the tall windows one could see a light snow falling from a luminously gray sky. But the two occupants of the room were too busy hanging the festoon (intricately fashioned of interwoven juniper branches) between the pair of windows to take much note of the weather or the landscape that was slowly being covered with a thin veneer of winter white.

Elinor stood at the top of the ladder on tiptoe, stretching out her arms to their fullest extent in her attempt to nail one end of the festoon to the far corner of the window's cornice. Across the room at the other window, her cousin Felicia held the other end, waiting. "Oh, dear," Elinor said, pausing in the act of reaching out, "I think I'm going to . . . to . . . *ah* . . . *ah* . . . *CHOO*!"

The first effect of Elinor's sneeze was to make the ladder wobble under her. This, in turn, caused one delicately shod foot to slip from the step. For a frozen moment Elinor, arms outstretched, stood poised on the toes of her other foot like a bird about to take flight. But the ladder, refusing to right itself, swung crazily to the left, and Elinor's tentative foothold was disastrously undone.

The ladder wavered for a moment before collapsing noisily to the floor. Felicia tried to scream as Elinor flapped her arms helplessly in the air. The younger girl watched in wide-eyed horror, utterly bereft of the ability to move during that time-stopping moment before the inevitable pull of gravity would bring her cousin crashing down. Everything, even her scream, froze in that breath of time just before catastrophe.

At that very instant, however, a broad-shouldered gentleman appeared in the doorway. Though he wore no hat, he'd obviously come in from outdoors, for his hair and the shoulders of his coat were spattered with snowflakes, and a long muffler was wound about his neck. In his hand he carried a basket loaded with eggs. He'd come through his home woods and across the Selbys' east lawn on foot—in complete disregard of the light snow—to deliver them. He'd been striding past the drawing-room door on his way to the back stairs when the sound of the collapsing ladder struck his ears.

He did not freeze. Immediately perceiving the situation, the gentleman took one quick leap over the threshold in Elinor's direction and, dropping his eggs, reached out and caught her in his arms. "Elinor!" he croaked, tottering under her weight. "Good God!"

Felicia's momentarily frozen scream now rent the air. The gentleman, unable to keep his balance under the unexpected force of Elinor's fall, toppled to his knees. But this time he succeeded in doing what he'd failed to do with the eggs; he did not drop her. Instead, he managed to ease her gently to the floor in front of him, his arms still supporting her back and legs.

"*Miles!*" Elinor clutched him about the neck. "Are you all right?"

"My condition is not the question," he responded curtly, although the eyes he'd fixed on hers showed real concern. "*Yours* is."

Elinor released her hold on him, her face turning pink in embarrassment. "I'm fine, thanks to you."

Miles Endicott nodded, a frown hiding his relief. He got to his feet and helped Elinor to hers. He was the Selbys' closest neighbor, a bachelor of seven-and-thirty years, stockily built, with powerful shoulders and strong hands. His short-cropped, grizzled hair, back-belted tweed coat, and squared-toed boots made him appear to be a country squire, which indeed he was. But while country squires were usually expected to be jolly fellows, ruddy-faced, and ever ready for a chuckle, Miles Endicott could not be so described. The sardonic look in his dark eyes and a certain worldly disillusionment in the twist of his mouth gave him the appearance of a blasé London cosmopolite, despite his country clothes.

"Oh, Miles," Elinor pressed anxiously, "are you certain I didn't injure you?"

"Quite certain," he said, frowning at her, "though no thanks to you. I fail to understand why you must climb ladders and risk life and limb when your mother has a perfectly adequate staff to do such things for you."

"Miles, don't scold. You know I always do the Christmas decorating myself."

"You do everything yourself. You're the only young lady of my acquaintance who won't have an abigail to dress her."

"What need has a country girl like me for an abigail? Stop glaring at me, Miles. Since neither one of us is hurt, no harm's done."

"Some harm, I'm afraid," he said, looking down at the contents of his basket, which were now sprawled on the carpet. "The eggs I was bringing to your mother have suffered massive contusions."

"Oh, pooh, who cares about eggs!" exclaimed Cousin Felicia, dashing across the room. Felicia Fordyce was a lively girl of nineteen, with auburn curls framing a face whose perfect features and delicate coloring glowed with youth and spirit. "Oh, Mr. Endicott, you were *magnificent*!" she cried. "Your quick thinking saved the day!"

"Nonsense, child," the squire said snappishly, "don't make a to-do!" There was something about Felicia's enthusiasm that always made him testy. Although Martha Selby, Elinor's mother, had often remarked that Felicia and her daughter Elinor were as alike as two peas— "Almost like sisters in their looks," she was wont to exclaim— Endicott did not see the resemblance. Similar they might be in features and coloring, but their personalities were completely at variance. To him, Elinor had the subtlety and refinement of a Mozartean sonata, while Felicia was nothing more than a country dance played in a public house.

Elinor knelt down and, not noticing that her skirt brushed over a badly smashed egg that was oozing yellow liquid, began to gather up the still-whole eggs that had rolled hither and yon across the floor. "The contusions are not so massive," she said, looking up at her savior with a grin. "Only three have actually cracked open."

Mr. Endicott knelt beside her. "But I see that several others are showings signs of at least partial damage. Your mother will surely take me to task for—" He suddenly peered at Elinor closely. "Good God, girl, you are dreadfully pale. The fall must have upset you. Leave this clearing-up to the housemaids and lie down on the sofa at once!"

"No, truly, I'm fine," she insisted.

But he refused to pay attention to her words. Over her

repeated objections he lifted her in his arms once again and carried her to the sofa. "You do not look at all well," he told her bluntly as he laid her down.

Felicia took a stand beside him and peered down at Elinor as he was doing. "Mr. Endicott is right, Elinor. You do not look well. And, you know, you *did* sneeze."

Elinor sighed. She knew she was looking peaked. Her appetite had not been good lately, and she'd noted when she'd glanced into the mirror that morning that her nose was red and her cheeks sunken and pale. But she knew she'd recover in a day or two. There was nothing at all to make a fuss over. "It's only a mild case of the sniffles," she insisted, sitting up. "I've had it for a few days, but I'm quite over it now."

The squire pushed her back down and eyed her dubiously. He'd known Elinor Selby since birth, and he could see she was worn out. There was too much company at Selby Manor, that was the trouble. Her cousin Felicia, with her parents, her twelve-year-old sister, and her two little brothers (aged ten and eight), had come up to North Riding from London for the Christmas holidays, and the visit was probably more burdensome to Elinor than to anyone else in the Selby household. Elinor was "giving"—that was the word people used to describe her. She could never refuse to do a favor or to help someone who needed it. Generosity was a fine thing, Endicott thought, but even good qualities can be overdone.

The Fordyces, all six of them, had arrived a few days before, and the squire knew upon whom the care of the unruly youngsters had fallen. It irritated him to see Elinor used so. She was not a governess, after all! He would give her mother a piece of his mind at the first opportunity. Martha Selby should not permit her daughter to be taken advantage of. "You *must* have been overdoing things to have become so completely done in," he scolded. "It's less than a sennight since I last saw you, my girl, and at that time you were in your best looks.''

He did not exaggerate. He'd come upon her walking through the woods that edged the two estates, and he'd watched her appreciatively as she'd approached him, her pace unusually relaxed and unhurried. How beautiful she'd been that morning, smiling, at ease, and vibrant with life! Her full lips had been ripely red, and the wind had whipped bright color into her cheeks and torn her bonnet from her head so that it hung by its ribbons against her back. Her shiny brown hair had come loose from the knot in which it had been tied and had tumbled in tousled abandon about her shoulders. He remembered how long, wild strands of it had blown across her cheeks. But now that same hair was carelessly pinned back, and the few strands that had worked themselves loose in her fall hung lank and lackluster about her thin face. Even her lips were pale as death. Only her eyes—those bright, glowing eyes that always seemed to say more than her lips ever uttered—were unaffected by weariness.

''I say, Mr. Endicott,'' Felicia spoke up in brave objection (for the glowering Squire Endicott was a formidable personage to oppose), ''aren't you being a little unkind about Elinor's looks?''

''I am merely being honest,'' Miles Endicott said coldly. ''A little honesty never does ill.''

''Neither does a little kindness,'' Felicia retorted.

''It's all right, Felicia,'' Elinor put in gently, surrendering to the squire's urging and permitting herself this few moments of rest. ''Miles is like an uncle to me, you know. He can speak truth to me, if anyone can.''

''Thank you for the permission,'' the squire said dryly, turning away to evaluate the condition of his eggs, ''but I'd speak my mind whether I had permission or not.''

He *was* like an uncle to her, he realized as he bent down to collect the eggs that were not actually leaking. Acting as her uncle was a position that he'd quite enjoyed over the years. He'd been looking after her in an avuncular way ever since her father had passed on, when the child was only ten. She was now twenty-six, however, and had been betrothed since her twenty-first year to the handsome Lord Lovebourne. Shortly after their betrothal, Julian Henshaw, Lord Lovebourne, had gone to the West Indies to manage his father's estates. (It was another sign of Elinor's generosity that she'd agreed to spend five precious years of her vanishing youth in a lonely wait for his return.) But Lovebourne's five-year excursion would soon be over. Any day now he'd return and claim his bride, and when that happened, he, Endicott, would be a part of her life no longer. He was aware that this significant fact—this crucial circumstance that would deprive him of a prized relationship—had a depressing way of knotting up his stomach when he thought about it. It was, he supposed, how a father felt when giving up his daughter in marriage.

He glanced over the floor to see what eggs were left. "So . . . your mother is expecting a crowd for Christmas?" he asked absently. "Who's coming? In addition to the six Fordyces, of course."

Elinor shut her eyes, enjoying this moment of relaxation. "Mama and I make eight, and you, of course, make nine," she murmured. "And Mama sent an invitation to Julian's parents. They'll be here by tomorrow evening, so we shall be eleven at table."

"Julian's parents?" Miles looked up at the girl curiously. "Does that mean that Julian himself will be back for the holiday?"

"No, not for Christmas"—Elinor sighed—"but in his last letter he said he hoped to be back within a month of the new year."

Felicia, leaning over the back of the sofa, squealed excitedly. "*Really*, Elinor? Are you saying he'll be here in just a few *weeks*?"

Elinor opened her eyes and smiled up at her younger cousin. "Yes. Just a few weeks more."

"Well, that must cheer you," Miles said, reaching for the last two eggs and placing them gingerly into his basket. "And all the more reason for you not to exert yourself in the next few weeks. With so much excitement ahead, you can't afford to be under the weather."

"You are being much too motherly, Miles." Elinor threw him a smile that washed away some of the weariness in her face. "Hanging a few Christmas decorations cannot be called exertion."

But Miles could not agree. "Blast the decorations!" he barked in annoyance. Getting to his feet, he frowned down at the fallen festoon. "Can't we have Christmas without them?"

"No, we can't," Elinor said firmly, pulling herself up to a sitting position and swinging her legs to the floor with determined energy, "any more than we can do without the plum pudding or the wreaths or the mistletoe."

He glared at her. "Balderdash! I can do without any of them. But very well, if you insist on the importance of such folderol, I'll put up the deuced festoon for you myself . . . just as soon as I deliver what's left of these eggs to the kitchen. Your mother sent a message telling me that her need for eggs was urgent."

"Yes, Cook has run out of them, I hear. Our hens, it seems, have not been productive this month, just when Mama needs them most."

Miles picked up his basket and started toward the door. "I'll ask one of the housemaids to clean up the broken ones," he said, glancing back at her over his shoulder. "Meanwhile, promise me you'll not climb the ladder until I return."

Elinor nodded. "I promise."

But before Miles could leave, Perkins, the butler, appeared in the doorway. "Miss Elinor," he announced in tones of hushed surprise, "you've a caller. It's Lord Lovebourne!"

The squire stopped in his tracks, his face stiffening in shock.

Elinor stared at the butler in confusion.

Felicia gave a delighted gurgle in her throat. "Do you mean *Julian*?" she cried.

"No, of course he doesn't." Elinor rose slowly to her feet, her eyes wide. "It must be Julian's father. You *do* mean the Earl, don't you, Perkins?"

"No, miss," the butler said with barely concealed excitement. "It's the junior Lord Lovebourne. Says he docked yesterday and came straight here from Liverpool."

Cousin Felicia clapped her hands delightedly. "But I thought he was not expected until January!"

A pulse began to pound in Elinor's ears. "So did I!"

The words were hardly out of her mouth when Julian Henshaw himself loomed up in the doorway. The man was so tall that his head almost touched the top of the doorframe. Felicia, who'd not met him before, blinked at the sight of him. She'd never seen anyone so handsome. From the top of his sun-streaked brown curls (now incongruously sparkling with snowflakes) to the tip of his dashing Hussar boots, the man was impressive. His skin was tanned from the sun, and his light eyes twinkled. His shoulders, wide to begin with, were emphasized by the capes of a magnificent greatcoat that hung open and revealed a figure of wiry strength. To Felicia, he seemed to have walked right out of a romance. She could not help but gasp.

Elinor, however, could not gasp. Surprise had frozen her breath in her chest. But her heart pounded wildly, and her head swam in bewildered delight. For five long years she'd waited for this moment, and now all she could do was gape at him, dazed.

Endicott, too, gaped at the traveler, having forgotten what a handsome specimen the fellow was. It was no wonder

Elinor had fallen in love with him. The squire supposed that there wasn't a girl alive who could resist a man so consumately dashing.

Thus the only one who uttered a sound was the spirited Felicia. "Oh, my!" she breathed, awestruck.

Julian Henshaw, Lord Lovebourne, who'd been surveying the room from the threshold (taking only slight note of a country fellow holding a basket of cracked eggs and a disheveled woman with lank hair and a red nose), was somewhat bemused at seeing a fallen ladder and several broken eggs on the floor. But Felicia's gasp caught his attention, and he turned his eyes in the direction of the sound. His face brightened perceptibly at the sight of Elinor's lovely young cousin. "Good God!" he exclaimed. Skillfully avoiding stepping on eggs, he strode across the room to her. "I'd forgotten how very lovely you are, Elinor!"

"But *I'm* not—" Felicia began.

Julian didn't heed. Sweeping the astonished Felicia into his arms, he fixed his lips firmly on hers. "Elinor, my love," he murmured against her mouth, "I've missed you so!"

2

The turmoil and confusion that followed this startling mishap did not last long. Julian, as soon as the identities of the ladies in the room were made clear to him, was able to restore everyone's equilibrium by blaming his eyesight: the whiteness of the snow-covered landscape, he said with a self-deprecating laugh, had temporarily blinded him. His manner was so charmingly sincere, and his abject embarrassment so endearingly boyish, that he was able to convince all the observers of the incident that his error was merely amusing.

Elinor was too busy during the remainder of the afternoon to dwell on the incident. After Julian had been duly welcomed by her mother, Martha Selby (with the egg basket tucked under her arm) returned to the kitchen to continue overseeing the Christmas food preparations. Therefore it was left to Elinor to introduce her betrothed to all the Fordyces on the premises; to reassure Felicia that she was not in any way to blame for Lord Lovebourne's inappropriate greeting; to see that a bedroom for the unexpected guest was prepared; to make sure the disorder in the drawing room was set to rights; to settle a squabble that arose between the wild eight-year-old Fordyce boy and his twelve-year-old and very spoiled sister; to serve afternoon tea; and to make sure the dinner-table settings were rearranged. By the time all this was done, it was almost time to dress for dinner.

When Elinor at last found herself alone in her bedroom, the ambivalent feelings she'd pushed aside all afternoon came flooding over her. *What's wrong with me?* she asked herself. *Where's the joy I should be feeling?*

She'd waited five years for this day. She had planned it, dreamed of it, even acted it out in her mind. When one waits long years for a reunion with a beloved, it is not uncommon to create fantasies in one's mind of what that reunion might be like. Elinor had played out the scene every night, as soon as she'd blown out her candle. There in the dark she would shut her eyes and try to visualize the longed-for reunion in all sorts of settings. It might, for example, take place in the summer garden, where she (softly gowned in flowing, flowered dimity with a wide-brimmed, beribboned straw hat set beguilingly on her casually curled hair) would be cutting roses. Surrounded by the glory and aroma of the blooms, she'd look up from the rosebushes and behold him, his eyes moist with love of her. Slowly, very slowly, they'd move toward each other. "Elinor!" he'd gasp, his voice husky with emotion. . . .

Sometimes her fantasy reunion would have a winter setting. The wind would be howling in the chimney while she knelt at the fireplace, tending the fire. There would be a sound at the door . . . a commotion. She would look up, startled, and there he'd be! He would stride over the threshold but stop short at the sight of her, for she would be lovely (and so very perfectly posed) draped in a gown of dark red velvet with a neckline dashingly décolleté. The firelight behind her would cast a honeyed glow on the skin of her throat and halo her hair. And looking up into his eyes, she'd see how his undisguised adoration combined with her own reflection. . . .

But never in her wildest imaginings had she pictured a reunion in which her hero failed even to recognize her!

Yes, reality had not come close to those dreams; instead, it had brought her down with a bump. Reality! If she'd wanted reality, she could have found it right there in front of her, standing full length in her pier mirror. Her own reflection was all the reality she needed. She stared back at her reflection and laughed, a short, bitter laugh. How foolish she'd been! She should have expected real life to turn out like this. Life was not like dreams. Life was not a rose garden or a gown of red velvet. Life was a case of the sniffles, life was a basket of broken eggs, life was a room full of visitors who, of course, had to be present at precisely the wrong moment.

A closer look at herself in the glass made her laugh again, for her appearance was positively ludicrous. Her hair hung round her face in a neglected straggle, her nose was red, her eyes rheumy, her cheek streaked with soot (and how *that* had happened she had no idea!), and—oh, God!—there was an ugly smear of dried egg across the bottom of her skirt! What a vision of romance she was, indeed! No *wonder* Julian had embraced someone else!

But the laugh died in her throat, replaced by a choked sob. Her own true love hadn't even recognized her! She knew she was not at her best, but did she truly look as terrible as *that*? As dearly as she wished to believe his laughingly offhand explanation, she could not prevent this attack of very painful doubts. Was she truly so much changed in the five years since Julian had last seen her?

The question smote her spirits with devastating force. She sank wearily down on the chair before her dressing table and stared at her face in the smaller mirror. The face that stared back at her was—she had to admit it—no longer youthful. Her cheeks, her hair, her lips—they were all faded and lusterless. She looked so wan and weary—so different from the youthful girl who'd waved goodbye to him—that Julian *must* have been confused. She could scarcely blame him. Poor Julian! she thought, tears filling her eyes. Poor disappointed—

A tap at the door interrupted her. "It's Miles, Elinor," came a voice from the corridor.

With a quick sniff and a hasty rub at her cheeks with the back of her hand, Elinor got up and went to the door. Miles stood on the threshold, trying to mask the concern in his eyes with a polite smile. "I just stopped by to make certain, before I took my leave, that you were finally going to rest."

"Yes, thank you, Miles," she replied, trying to keep her voice steady. "I have an hour before I must dress for dinner. You *are* coming tonight, aren't you? I've set a place for y—"

"Good God, girl," he interrupted, his smile fading as he peered at her closely, "you've been crying!"

"No, I haven't," she denied. "It's just this blasted cold. It makes my eyes runny."

"It's not the cold. I know how you look when you cry." He lifted her chin and made her look up at him. "Has that blasted Lovebourne made *another* blunder?" he asked, outraged.

The suggestion brought a hiccupy laugh up from her chest. "Isn't the f-first blunder enough?"

"I suppose so, but . . ." He released her chin and made a helpless gesture with his hands. "But I thought you accepted his explanation. You seemed so perfectly sanguine all afternoon."

"I was. It's just that . . ." She hesitated, embarrassed to reveal to Miles the depth of her shameful self-pity.

"Yes? Go on," he prodded.

She turned from the door and sank down on the bed. "I took a look at myself in the mirror just now, and I suddenly saw what Julian saw."

"Oh? And what was that?" he demanded.

"A hag."

He stalked to the bed and glared down at her. "What utter nonsense is this?"

"It isn't nonsense. You yourself said I look hagged."

"*I*? I *never*—"

"Yes, you did. It was when you first saw me this morning."

"I said, ma'am, that you were not in your best looks, which you may take my word is a very far cry from—"

At that moment Martha Selby appeared in the doorway. Having heard whisperings of the day's doings all the way down in the kitchen, she'd come up, still wrapped in her apron, to learn for herself what had occurred. Hearing Miles's raised voice, she paused on the threshold and raised her brows. "Am I interrupting a quarrel?" she asked bluntly.

"You might say that," Miles snapped. "Your daughter is behaving like a foolish child."

"Is she? What about?"

"About—of all the idiotic notions—her looks! If there is anything in the world less worthy of concern, I don't know what it could be. What she *should* be concerned about is her *health*!" He threw the girl one last, fulminating glare and strode to the door. "But I leave *you*, Martha, to deal with her. I've run out of patience."

After he slammed out, Martha approached the bed. "Aren't you feeling well, my love?"

"I'm fine, Mama," Elinor answered, not meeting her mother's eyes. "Just a bit tired."

Martha, lips pursed, studied her daughter closely. "What's this I hear about Julian kissing Felicia?"

Elinor threw her mother a worried look. If there was anything she didn't wish to endure, it was going over the Julian matter with her mother. The two women were so close that each could feel the other's pain, and pain was not something Elinor wished to inflict on her mother.

But Martha Selby could not easily be put off. A plump, energetic woman with a round, open face topped by a head of wiry white hair, she was as unpretentious as the household she ran. She cared nothing for elegance or show and was happier spending hours in the kitchen kneading dough than sitting like a lady at her embroidery frame working small stitches in fine silk. She had a warm heart that embraced all the people in her world down to the lowliest scullery maid. But the center of that heart was kept inviolate, possessed solely and completely by her only child—her daughter, whom she loved beyond all else. If anyone or anything threatened her daughter's happiness or well being, she, like a lioness defending her cub, would rise in wrath, ready to do battle.

"It was nothing worth speaking of, Mama," Elinor said, hoping her mother would not do battle over this. "I'm surprised you heard of it."

"Heard of it? Everyone's heard of it, from your uncle Henry to Samuel in the stable. They're all whispering about it."

"But why? There was nothing to it. Julian merely mistook Felicia for me at first glance. Merely a little misunderstanding, that's all."

"Then why are you crying?" Lady Selby cocked her

head at her daughter with a look that combined suspicion with concern.

"I wasn't! I . . . d-didn't—!" Elinor insisted bravely, but, quite against her will, her chin begin to tremble, a certain sign that she was about to cry again. She turned away so that her mother might not see.

But her mother could always sense her pain. "Oh, my poor, sweet Elinor!" she murmured in heartfelt sympathy, sitting down beside her on the bed and throwing her arms around the girl. Elinor dropped her head on her mother's shoulder and surrendered to sobs.

Elinor was not the sort, however, to indulge herself in waterworks for very long. After a few moments she lifted her head and wiped her cheeks. "You m-mustn't make too much of this, Mama," she said, gulping down what remained of her tears. "I'm only c-crying for Julian, not myself."

"For *Julian*? Why on earth—?"

"Because he's spent five lonely years dreaming of coming home to a lovely young betrothed, and now he finds himself faced with a faded *hag*!"

"*Hag*?" Martha Selby cried, outraged. "My beautiful daughter a hag?"

Elinor shook her head. "Look at me, Mama. Really look at me. Not as a mother, but as a man might see me who remembers me as I was five years ago. Then you'll see that I'm . . . I'm"—it was hard for her to say the word—"unrecognizable."

"What balderdash!" Lady Selby rose to her feet in magisterial dignity and, taking her daughter's face in her hands, tilted it up and studied it. "No wonder Miles lost patience with you. I admit you're looking a bit peaked— after all, you've been troubled with a head cold all week— but anyone with normal eyesight and a grain of sense can see beyond the pallor of illness to the beauty in this face!"

"Oh, Mama, really!" the daughter objected, blowing her nose. "Beauty, indeed."

"Beauty I saw, and beauty I mean! If you ask me, Julian Henshaw is a fool."

"Well, he's the fool I love. And I'm afraid he's disappointed in me."

"In that case, my love, we must do something about it. If you think I'll permit His Lordship Lovebourne—or any other man, for that matter—to think my daughter a hag, you're out in your reckoning. Get up, child, and let's brighten you up a bit. If Lord Lovebourne needs to be reminded of the girl he fell in love with, we'll remind him."

3

By the time Elinor went down to dinner, she was indeed "brightened up." Her mother had pinched some color into her cheeks and, against the girl's objections, had blackened her eyelashes with soot. "It makes you look less sickly," Lady Selby had argued. And she'd brushed the girl's hair till it glowed, then braided it and wound it round her head like a coronet. Finally, she'd chosen a pretty new dinner gown for Elinor to wear—a jade-green peau de soie, with a low décolletage and a graceful flounce at the bottom. Elinor had intended to save the gown for Christmas Eve, but, as her mother had declared, "Desperate circumstances call for desperate measures."

Julian, waiting at the drawing room fire for the dinner party to assemble, beamed at the sight of his betrothed. He crossed the room to her in four strides, smiled down into her eyes, and lifted her hand to his lips. "I've dreamed of this so often," he murmured. "I knew I'd find you as lovely as ever."

The words were soothing to her ears, although she

couldn't help wondering if they were sincere. "Butter sauce, my love?" she asked, smiling.

"Never. You, my dearest, are not the sort to require flattery, nor shall I ever need to offer it to you." He slipped an arm about her waist and led her to a chair. "When I speak to you, nothing but the truth shall pass my lips."

Instead of making a proper response to those lovely words, Elinor had to pull a handkerchief from the bosom of her gown and sneeze into it. The cold she'd caught—blast it!—was refusing to disappear. She felt her eyes become teary and her nose sore. As she dabbed at her eyes with her handkerchief, she saw a streak of black appear on the white linen. The eyelash blacking! She'd undoubtedly smudged it!

At that very moment, when Elinor's spirits were plummeting from the feeling that, besides looking pathetic and sickly, her eyes were smeared with soot, Felicia came in with her parents. The girl was a vision in her blue gown. Her cheeks glowed, her eyes danced, and her hair was brushed up in a charming topknot, with tiny curls escaping and framing her face. In fact, she was utterly adorable. Julian stared at her with a look that seemed to Elinor very much like longing. The look made Elinor's breath catch in her throat.

Julian caught the sound. At once he turned away from the vision at the door and knelt down beside his betrothed's chair. "Your cousin is a charming child," he whispered in her ear. "In time she may be almost as lovely as you."

Now that, Elinor thought ruefully, is butter sauce if ever I heard it. But it was cleverly done—a smooth, practiced cover-up. The Julian she'd known five years ago could not have done it. So, she thought in surprise, Julian, too, has changed. Five years ago she would not have questioned his sincerity; he would have been too youthfully ingenuous. Now, however, his manner was worldly and sophisticated, as if, among other things, the years had given him a great deal of experience in the art of dalliance.

Miles arrived shortly afterward. Elinor went up to greet him at the door. "I hope you're not still angry with me," she murmured as she handed his hat to the butler.

He merely eyed her coldly. "I see you've taken pains to prettify yourself," he remarked. "You'd have done better to stay in bed."

"Really, Miles, must you be so churlish?" she chided with a smile. "You could at least have said my prettifying showed some success."

"I don't have to say it. You are perfectly cognizant of how well you look. Even with a smudge of soot under your eye."

"Oh, dear,"—Elinor sighed in embarrassment—"I was *afraid* I'd smudged that blasted lash blacking."

"Lash blacking!" Miles shook his head in disapproval. "I wouldn't have believed you'd be so foolish as to think you needed such embellishments. But here, let me fix it." He removed a large handkerchief from his pocket and wiped away the smudge.

"Thank you, Miles," she said gratefully. "You're the kindest fellow in the world."

"For a churl," he retorted.

She laughed. "Yes, for a churl."

Dinner was announced at that moment. Elinor was glad of it. Perhaps doing something as mundane as eating dinner would keep her mind from dwelling on the discomfort of her head cold and the worry about what Julian was thinking of her.

The seven adults who took their seats round the table made an intimate, friendly gathering. Conversation flowed easily. Elinor's Uncle Henry, Lord Fordyce, encouraged Julian to relate some of his adventures overseas, which Julian was delighted to do. Most of the stories he told were colorfully amusing, like his account of his elderly native butler who insisted on wearing a pair of spectacles from which the lenses had been removed (the fellow explained to

Julian that his eyesight was perfect but that wearing the rims made him look distinguished enough for his high post). The lively way he related another tale—of how he'd reacted to the first meal prepared by his native cook (the dish had contained hot peppers) by leaping from his chair with a cry of agony at the first bite—made the room ring with laughter.

All but two of the diners at the table were charmed. One of the two who found the dinner less than delightful was Elinor, who noticed how often Julian seemed to be directing his words to Felicia. The other was Miles, who spent the meal studying the speaker with an enigmatic expression that any perceptive observer would have interpreted as intense dislike. But with Julian taking center stage, no one, perceptive or otherwise, took notice of Miles.

The gentlemen did not linger very long over their brandies; a mere quarter hour after the ladies had excused themselves, the gentlemen joined them in the drawing room. Lord and Lady Fordyce, always partial to passing the time in modest gambling, organized a game of silver-loo with Elinor and Julian, while Miles buried himself behind the London newspaper, and Martha Selby took the armchair near the fire and busied herself with knitting. Felicia, not greatly addicted to cards, wandered over to the pianoforte and tinkled the keys absently.

Fanny Fordyce looked up from her cards. "Why don't you sing for us, my love," she said to her daughter. "I know your aunt Martha would enjoy hearing 'The Thorn.'" She turned to Julian and explained, "It's a ballad we dearly love, Martha and I. We could listen to it forever."

Felicia blushed. "I don't wish to distract you from your cards," she said shyly.

"You won't distract us," her father assured her. "We can listen to your singing and still concentrate on the cards."

Felicia good-naturedly began to sing. She had a soft, unexceptional voice and considerable talent at the keyboard.

In this informal, unpretentious setting, her modest perfor-
mance was appealing. Her music made a pleasant background for the other activities in the room. Martha tapped in
rhythm as she knitted, Fanny hummed along happily as she
sorted her cards, and even Miles put down his *Times* to
listen. As for Elinor, she was glad that the music kept
everyone from noticing her own too-frequent need to sniffle
into her handkerchief.

At the card table Henry Fordyce led with his trump,
followed by Elinor, with another. Then there was an
unexpected pause. Lord Fordyce looked up from his hand.
''Your play, Lovebourne,'' he prodded.

But Julian didn't seem to hear. Elinor raised her eyes
from her cards curiously, to discover Julian staring at the
singer. Even Madame Neroli, the acclaimed coloratura from
Italy, would not have warranted so enraptured a response.
Lord Lovebourne was so riveted by the girl at the piano that
he hadn't even heard Henry's reminder. What was particularly disturbing to Elinor was her betrothed's expression. It
could only be called adoration. Oh, my heavens, Elinor
thought with a sinking heart, Julian is really smitten!

4

By the next morning a bright sun shone down from a sky
miraculously cleared of clouds. But the sunshine did not
miraculously help poor Elinor to recover from her case of
the sniffles. She came down to breakfast with eyes red-
rimmed, nose sore, and throat tight. Nevertheless, she
greeted her guests with a warm smile.

The brilliant sunshine also failed to melt the veneer of
snow that covered the landscape, for the air was icy cold.
Everyone remarked on it. Julian, however, did not think the
weather too cold for riding. ''It's been five years since I last

had a winter-morning canter,'' he said, peering out of the morning room window longingly.

"Then, by all means take out one of the horses," Lady Selby urged. "Samuel will mount you. I'm sure that both horse and rider will benefit from the exercise."

Julian happily accepted the offer and rose from the table. But before departing to change to his riding clothes, he asked Felicia and Elinor to accompany him. They both refused, Elinor explaining that she still had too many tasks to perform before his parents arrived that evening.

"But *you* have no such excuse," Julian said to Felicia. "Why won't you come with me? A bit of fresh air is bound to do you good."

In the end Felicia succumbed to his urging. Later, Elinor, who was watching from an upstairs window as the two of them made their way to the stables (leaving a trail of matched footsteps across the white lawn), found herself overwhelmed with a feeling of chagrin. Her betrothed hadn't spent half as much energy trying to convince *her* to ride with him as he had her cousin. No, she admitted to herself, she was more than chagrined. She was jealous, hurt, and angry.

But these were ugly feelings, feelings that were quite new to her and that she'd always considered beneath her. Giving way to them was not up to her standard of conduct, and the knowledge that she'd done so made her feel small.

The situation was depressing. She'd spent several sleepless hours that night trying to face the fact—and with every passing moment that fact was becoming more obvious—that Julian was infatuated with Felicia.

Painful as it was, Elinor was at last ready to accept the truth. The problem now was what to do about it. She could, of course, pretend not to notice that her betrothed no longer cared for her. She could close her eyes and mind to Julian's faithlessness and simply go ahead with the wedding. She would not be the first woman to take herself a reluctant bridegroom. But she had too much pride to choose that option. Besides, her nature was too generous and giving to wish to make him unhappy. For the sake of *her* pride and *his* happiness, she had to release him.

To that end, after luncheon that very day, she drew him into the upstairs sitting room and asked him to sit down. "Julian, my dear," she began, seating herself on the edge of the chair facing his and twisting her fingers together nervously, "I think we should . . . er . . . reconsider our situation."

"Situation?" His brows lifted uncomprehendingly. "What situation?"

"Our arrangement." She dropped her eyes to her clenched fingers. "Our . . . betrothal."

"Our *betrothal*?" He seemed to stiffen. "What are you saying? What is there to reconsider?"

"A great deal. We haven't laid eyes on each other for five years. That is a very long time, and . . . and we were so much . . . younger then." Here she couldn't keep her voice from trembling. "We c-could not have realized . . . I mean—"

"Are you saying you wish to break our troth?" he asked bluntly.

"Yes," she admitted, not looking up.

He stared at her bent head for a long moment and then got slowly to his feet. "This is because of what happened yesterday, isn't it? Because I didn't see you at first and mistook your cousin for you?" He knelt beside her chair and took her hand. "Please, Elinor, don't refine on the incident too much. I'm sorrier than I can say about spoiling our reunion. I can't imagine what came over me. But it was a *foolish* mistake, not a significant one."

"It's not only that, Julian." She lifted her eyes and gave him a level look. "What *is* significant is that we've both changed."

"Not in our feeling for each other!" he insisted.

"Especially in that," she replied, more blunt than he.

He rose from his knees and began to pace about the room, his brow furrowed and his lips pressed together in a worried frown. "What have I done, other than that one slip, to make you believe such foolishness?" he demanded. "Have I been distant, or cold, or withdrawn? Have I offended you in some way?"

"You've behaved in every way the proper betrothed." She threw him a quick glance. "Perhaps too proper."

"Too proper?"

"Lovers should, I believe, feel a greater sense of . . . of intimacy than we've been able to show toward each other." To her embarrassment, she had to blow her nose at this point. The sniffle into her handkerchief made her statement seem pathetic, and pathos was not at all the emotion she wished to convey.

Julian put a helpless hand to his head. "Perhaps we're suffering a strain because of having been separated for so long. But we'll recover that feeling of intimacy in time. After all, I've been back less than two days."

"There was more intimacy between us during the two days after we first met, when we were comparative strangers, than there is now, after months of closeness and five years of frequent correspondence."

"Damnation, Elinor, you know that correspondence is no substitute for propinquity. We need time *together*!"

She waited for a moment before speaking. The silence made him pause in his pacing and peer at her. She met his eye. "Be honest with me, Julian," she urged. "If we had met this week, instead of five years ago, would you have been attracted to me?"

"Yes, of course I would!"

She lowered her head. "I think not. And certainly not enough to offer for me."

"That is silly supposition. I *have* offered for you!"

"Yes, years ago, when I was twenty, with the bloom of youth still glowing on my cheeks."

"Do you really believe me to be such a dastard as to wish to renege on that offer now, just because that bloom has go— I mean, because the bloom has ripened into lovely maturity?"

She laughed, for she rather liked his little stumble into honesty and the embarrassment that followed it. But at the same time she was abruptly struck with an understanding of the reason why he seemed reluctant to accept her offer of release: *accepting it would make him a dastard in his own eyes!*

She was both touched and amused by his naive sense of honor. He truly believed that a manly man could not accept such self-sacrifice from a woman to whom he'd pledged his word. "It would not be dastardly," she explained gently, "to admit that our feelings are not what they were. We are only betrothed, after all. We are not wed."

"My feelings *are* what they were," he said stubbornly.

She took a deep breath. It was obvious that she would have to take stronger measures. "Well, mine are not," she lied, bravely going to this extreme for his sake, to ease his guilt.

He stopped in his tracks. "I don't believe you! I haven't seen a single sign of change in your feelings—"

"Women are good at dissembling."

"Elinor!" he gasped. "You can't mean it! Are you saying that . . . that there's *someone else*?"

"Yes."

He peered at her as if he'd never seen her before. "Who?"

"I hardly think it matters who—"

"It matters to me. Is it someone I know?"

She shifted awkwardly in her chair. Lying was something she never could do easily. "I believe you may have met him."

"Tell me his name."

"I don't see why. What difference will—?"

"I shan't be able to believe a word of this until you tell me his name."

"You are behaving like a jealous lover, Julian," she declared, drawing herself up proudly. "It's a role that ill becomes you. Suffice it to say that there's someone to whom I believe I'm better suited, just as, I suspect, there is someone to whom you feel *you* are better suited."

His face immediately tightened into an expression of complete denial. "There is *no one* to whom I—!"

She faced him squarely. "I am speaking of my cousin Felicia."

"Oh." His eyes fell. "Was I—? Have I . . . er . . . shown interest in that direction?"

"I think you know the answer better than I."

Lowering his head like a guilty schoolboy, Julian took a quick turn about the room. "It was only that she is so like my memory of *you*," he mumbled at last.

"I know, Julian," she said gently. "I feel no bitterness. Perhaps we were fortunate to have been separated all these years. If we hadn't, we might have wed and spent all these years being miserable. Now, however, you'll be able to make a more suitable match and live happily ever after."

Something in her tone arrested him. "I will *not* live happily ever after," he declared suspiciously, "if I suspect you are doing this for *my* sake rather than your own."

"I've already assured you that it is for my sake, too."

"Then why will you not tell me his name?"

"Because there is nothing fixed between the man and me. My being betrothed, you see, prevented—"

"I understand that, of course. I assure you, Elinor, that I'll not say a word to anyone else. But if I knew who he was and truly believed he would make you happy, I could go my way with a freer conscience."

"Drat your conscience," Elinor snapped, feeling cornered by her lie. "His name is . . . is Endicott," she burst out, rising from the chair and turning her back on him, unable to face him. "Miles Endicott. There! I've told you! I hope you're satisfied."

"Endicott?" Julian blinked, trying to place the name that had a familiar sound. Then his eyebrows rose in amazement. "I say, it's not that fellow with the eggs, is it? He's a bit old for you, isn't he?"

She wheeled round to face him. "Haven't you just admitted that I'm a bit 'ripe' myself? Miles Endicott is the *perfect* age for me!"

"All right, you needn't bite my head off." His face relaxed for the first time since this interview began. "Endicott, eh? He seems a good enough sort." A smile, broad and charming and full of happy relief, made a slow appearance on his face. "All I can say, Elinor, is that I wish you happy."

His conciliatory smile made her anger die. "Thank you," she mumbled awkwardly. "And I wish you the same." But she could not manage a matching smile.

5

Elinor could not imagine why she'd told a falsehood merely to provide Julian with a name. She'd been a weak-kneed jellyfish to have surrendered to his urging. And why had she named Miles, of all people? Miles, who was a friend and neighbor and who would be spending much of the Christmas holiday with them! If she had to name someone, why hadn't she had the good sense to choose someone far away—someone like Jeremy Hallworthy, her cousin from New York who was traveling abroad, or Sir Lionel Nethercomb, who'd been one of her suitors during her come-out year and was now living in India? She had no talent as a liar, that was the trouble.

And how she would ever again be able to look Miles in the eye she did not know!

What she *did* know was that she didn't want Julian to be forever watching her when Miles was in their company. How very awkward it would be if Julian kept watch for signs of love in Miles's eyes, or for the exchange of secret little glances, or for blushing cheeks and palpitating breasts. Good God, she would die of shame! What had she done?

Upset and disgusted with herself, she wanted nothing more than to retreat to her bed. Not only was she ill in spirit but in body: her throat was sore, her nose was stuffed, her head throbbed, and all her muscles ached. But she could not retire to her room, for there was still much to do to prepare for the arrival of Julian's parents, who were expected in time for dinner. She tried to dismiss from her mind the matter of Julian and the aches of her body as she ran about busily assisting in the preparation of two more guest bedrooms, arranging for the extra places at table, and completing the hanging of the Christmas festoons.

The Earl of Lovebourne and his Lady, having received word that their son had returned from abroad, were so eager to see him that they arrived several hours early. In fact, the others had just sat down to tea when the Earl's two carriages (one devoted solely to carrying their many trunks and bandboxes) trundled up the drive. Tea was forgotten as Lady Selby and all her guests hurried to the wide, high-ceilinged entry hall to greet them.

Lady Lovebourne, a very tall, imposing female wearing a huge feathered hat and fur-lined cloak, swept over the threshold in the manner of visiting royalty. She was trailed by her husband, Maurice Henshaw, the Earl of Lovebourne, an unassuming man of average height, who was quite accustomed to following in his wife's wake. Lady Lovebourne's eyes at once fell on her son, and she threw herself upon him with a cry of gladness. Meanwhile, as the other guests pressed round the new arrivals, Perkins and the footmen set about unloading luggage, and housemaids began to run up and down the stairs with cloaks and overcoats. Loud voices and shrill laughter rang in the air, combining with the sound of hurrying footsteps clacking on the marble floor. To add to the din, the Fordyce children, excited by the stir, took to dashing in and out among the adults, their shouts and hoots echoing in the rafters and making the scene more riotous than it already was.

In the midst of this commotion Miles Endicott appeared in the doorway. "I thought I was invited to a quiet family tea," he remarked to Lady Selby as he surrendered his hat to a harried footman.

"We're quite at sixes and sevens"—Martha Selby laughed, her good nature undisturbed by the tumult—"but don't worry, my dear. We shall soon settle down and have a lovely tea."

Julian, who'd noted Endicott's arrival, extricated himself from his mother's tearful embrace and drew Elinor aside. "Does Endicott know we've broken our troth?" he asked her in a whisper.

Elinor tensed. "No, of course not. When could I have—?"

"Then don't say anything yet, please, Elinor. It has just this moment occurred to me that my mother may be very put out about this. She's so fond of you, you know."

"But, Julian, we'll have to tell her sometime," Elinor pointed out.

"Yes, of course, but can't we put it off? You know how overbearing Mama can be. She might very well make a scene. We don't want to spoil Christmas. Perhaps we should wait to make the announcement after the holiday."

Elinor glanced over at the group still milling about near the door. The Earl and Lady Lovebourne, having embraced Henry and Fanny Fordyce and complimented Felicia on her blooming womanhood, were now greeting Miles, who was quite well known to them. The sight of Miles reminded

Elinor of the embarrassing situation she'd created for herself, and it occurred to her that it would be to her benefit to agree to Julian's suggestion. If the breaking of her troth were not announced until after Christmas (or, better still, just before everyone went home), Miles might never have to learn about her dishonest use of his name. "Very well, Julian," she murmured. "Our news can wait."

She turned away to search for Perkins, for it was clear that the tea service would have to be moved from the sitting room to the drawing room to accommodate the expanded number of guests. That chore accomplished, she left it to her mother to usher the guests to the tea table. Meanwhile she collected the noisy children and led them off to the nursery. There, after calming them and setting them to playing a game of spillikins, she sat down to catch her breath. Her throat burned, her head ached, and she felt dizzy. She knew she was feverish. She yearned for bed. But she was determined to make an appearance at the tea table to keep her mother from becoming concerned about her health. This was not the time to be ill—she could not let a little head cold spoil the holiday. So, with a determined effort, she got to her feet, straightened her tucker, smoothed back a tendril of hair that had fallen over her forehead, blew her nose, and made her way down to join the tea party.

At the drawing room door she found Miles waiting for her. "Elinor, my dear, you look terrible," he said bluntly.

She threw him a rueful glance. "Thank you, Miles. I needed only that to make my day perfect."

He ignored her attempt at witticism. "You are obviously more ill than when I saw you last. Why aren't you in bed?"

"You know why. Nine guests—ten, counting you."

"Your mother and the servants can take care of the guests," he pointed out sourly. "I think it's time I gave your mother a piece of my mind."

"No, Miles, please don't make a to-do! It's only a little cold. Come in and let's take some tea."

He eyed her worriedly, shaking his head in disapproval, but knowing how she abhorred being fussed over, he finally shrugged, took her arm, and led her to a chair. As soon as she was seated, Elinor looked up to find Julian's eyes on her. He'd taken note of her entrance on Miles's arm. Despite her dizziness and a growing feeling of sickness in the pit of her stomach, she felt herself blush. What was Julian thinking? Had Miles's fatherly attention appeared to be loverlike affection to the onlooker?

The room was beginning to spin around. If a sip of tea failed to steady her, she would have to excuse herself and go upstairs; she couldn't keep up this smiling demeanor for long. She hoped no one was watching her, but almost immediately Felicia, who was sitting alongside her, leaned over to her and whispered, "Are you well, Elinor? You look so tired."

Before she could answer, Elinor heard herself being addressed by Lady Lovebourne. "Don't you think, Elinor, dearest, that April will be a perfect time?" the countess asked.

"Perfect time?" Elinor echoed stupidly.

Felicia came to her rescue. "For the wedding."

"Oh," Elinor murmured. "Yes."

"April is indeed lovely here in North Riding," her mother said, "but perhaps you and Julian would prefer to have the nuptials sooner."

Elinor's color deepened, and her eyes flew to Julian. He merely smiled and stirred his tea. "What is an eager bridegroom to say?" he remarked smoothly. "Whatever Elinor wishes, of course, but I must admit that I prefer March. Or February, if that is possible."

"February is quite impossible," his mother declared firmly. "Since so many guests will be coming up from London for the ceremony, we must choose a time when the weather will not make travel too difficult. Prinny himself has said he'd make an effort to come—didn't he say that, Maurice, my love?''

"Yes, my dear," the Earl said obediently. "The Prince did say that."

"So you see, it must be April," the Countess insisted.

"If that is what Elinor wishes, I have no objection," Martha said. "The garden and lawns will be greening then. April is a lovely time."

Lady Lovebourne nodded in satisfaction and sipped her tea. Then she looked about the room with a change of expression. "You intend, I hope, Martha, to refurbish the public rooms."

Martha Selby, in the act of popping a triangular cucumber sandwich into her mouth, stayed her hand. "Re*furbish*—?"

"Yes, indeed, my dear. Your furnishings are well enough, I suppose, for an ordinary country seat, but this house is, fortunately, a good deal better than ordinary. It has space and a certain rustic dignity. Even Maurice says so, don't you, my love?"

"Yes, my dear," the Earl said.

"It might even be considered fine," her ladyship went on, "if it were properly decorated. I admit that you'll have difficulty doing it over in only three months. If only Elinor had agreed to be wed in London, in our town house, you wouldn't have needed to bother, which is not to say that I don't respect Elinor's wishes to be married in her family home. But since you will be hostess to the cream of the *ton* for the affair, you must agree that we wouldn't wish them to be entertained in a setting that some might find . . . well, to be frank . . . shabby."

"Shabby?" Martha cried, reddening furiously. "*Shabby*?"

"I mean no offense, of course," Lady Lovebourne proceeded heedlessly. "These furnishings were probably quite fashionable when you came here as a bride. But tastes have changed, you know, and those unadorned country-style tables and sideboards are decidedly outdated. New furnishings in the *Haute Egypte* style would do wonders for this room, wouldn't they, Maurice, my love?''

The Earl sighed. ''Yes, my dear.''

''And your lovely windows would show to more advantage if those faded draperies were replaced,'' the Countess continued. ''The sofas and armchairs might be saved, I suppose, if they were properly reupholstered, but an Aubusson carpet would make all the difference to these floors. . . .''

On she prattled, ignoring or unaware of the effect her words were having on her listeners. Fanny Fordyce, who hated scenes but who knew her sister-in-law was capable of a formidable show of temper when irked, exchanged a nervous look with her husband. Elinor, although aware that the entire argument was moot (since there would be no wedding), was too feverish to think of something useful to say. But Miles Endicott was under no such inhibitions. ''It seems to me, your ladyship,'' he said curtly, ''that everything in this house is pleasing to the eye just as it is. It's designed for the comfort of inhabitants and guests, and no one should ask for more.'' He turned to the Earl and asked in a tone of unmistakable mockery, ''Don't you agree, Lord Lovebourne?''

The Earl looked from Miles to his wife and merely shrugged.

Miles rose from his chair and put down his cup. ''Furthermore,'' he told the Countess as he started toward the door, ''I can't for the life of me understand what possible difference new draperies would make to the prospects of the bride and groom, nor how standing on an Aubusson carpet could affect the sincerity of the vows they will be taking.''

''Hear, hear!'' Henry Fordyce muttered under his breath.

''Perkins!'' Endicott shouted into the hallway. ''Get my hat!''

''Well, *really*!'' gasped Lady Lovebourne, who was not

at all accustomed to being scolded. "I must say, Miles, I am surprised at you. Don't you care what the prince might think?"

"Not in the least," Miles retorted, "though I have no doubt he will find these surroundings perfectly satisfactory."

"If you think that," her ladyship snapped, "you've never been to Carleton House."

"Enough, Mama," Julian said, getting up. "Cut line! The furnishings in this house are not your affair. You must permit Lady Selby to make her own decisions about her household." With that he turned to Miles, who was just taking his hat from the butler. "Wait for me, Endicott," he said, crossing the room. "I'd like a word with you. I'll see you to the door."

Elinor, flushed and dizzy with fever, nevertheless sensed that she shouldn't permit Julian to have a private conversation with Miles. "Wait, Julian!" she said, rising unsteadily. "I'll see him out myself."

But the two men had already left the room. She hurried out after them, but by the time she reached the entry hall, she was so wearied from the exertion that she had to lean against the wall. The two men did not see her in the shadows. Julian was occupied with shaking Miles's hand. "I must congratulate you for your courage," he was saying. "There aren't many men who could take my mother on that way."

"Hummmph!" Miles snorted, clapping on his hat. "It didn't take courage. Only temper."

"I must admit, old fellow," Julian went on, "that I didn't really approve of Elinor's choice when she told me of it, but now that I know you a little better, I fully understand why—"

"Julian!" Elinor gasped, but her cry was too weak to be heard in the huge hall.

"Elinor's choice?" Miles asked, bewildered. "What on earth are you babbling about, Lovebourne?"

"It's all right, old fellow," Julian assured him. "You needn't hide your feelings from me. Elinor and I won't announce it for a few days, but we've agreed to sever our connection. So you see, the way is cleared for—"

With the greatest effort of will, Elinor took a few steps into the hallway. "Julian, for heaven's sake, stop!" she tried to say, but her voice emerged from her constricted chest in an unrecognizable croak. She put out her hand to stop the world from spinning so crazily about, but it would not stop. The ground shifted beneath her feet, and then, with Julian and Miles staring at her in horror, she did what she'd never in her life done before—she fainted dead away.

6

Elinor was only dimly aware of being brought round by a sniff of sal volatile, of being carried up to her room, examined by the doctor, dosed with James's Powders and lemon-and-barley water tisanes, and treated with cold compresses on her forehead. She had no real sense of time's passage. She only knew that, after a while, the thickness seemed to clear from her head, and she was able to turn on her side, snuggle into her pillows, and surrender to a deep, deep sleep.

She awakened to the sound of clicking needles. She opened her eyes and discovered her mother sitting beside her bed, calmly knitting. Elinor sat up gingerly, expecting to feel dizzy, but her head was quite clear. And the pain in the throat was gone!

From the way the rays of the sun were slanting in through the windows, she deduced it was afternoon. "Mama," she exclaimed, "you shouldn't have let me sleep so late!"

"Elinor, my love," Martha Selby cried, throwing aside

her knitting and jumping to her feet in delight, "you're awake!"

"Yes, and feeling so much better. I knew that I only needed a few hours of good, sound sleep."

"A few *hours*?" Martha gurgled with laughter as she sat down on the side of the bed and enveloped her daughter in an ecstatic embrace. "My dear, you slept the clock twice round!"

Elinor's face fell. "What? Twenty-four hours?"

Martha grinned at her. "More than that. Your fever broke yesterday morning, and then you simply turned on your side and went to sleep."

"I don't believe it. Are you saying that almost two days have passed? Then today is . . . good *heavens*! Friday! Tonight is *Christmas Eve*! I must get up at once—there's so much to do!"

She tried to throw off her blankets, but her mother held her back. "You will *not* get up! Whatever has to be done will be done by the staff and me. You will not leave this bed for another day at least. Those are Dr. Ogilvy's orders."

"But, Mama, that's silly. I feel fine. Quite recovered."

"Nevertheless you will remain abed. If you are very good, if you rest quietly and drink your barley water and hot soup—which I shall go down and prepare for you forthwith—you may come down for Christmas dinner tomorrow. But you will not set foot on the floor until then."

"Not until Christmas dinner *tomorrow*? Mama, you can't mean it!"

"But I do. You had a fever from a respiratory infection, which Dr. Ogilvy said could have been pneumonia if you'd had a less healthy constitution. Fevers tend to leave one weak, and I shan't permit you out of bed until your strength is fully restored." She got up from the bed, rescued her knitting from the floor, and started out of the room. "Besides," she added over her shoulder, "Miles has already given me a tongue-lashing for neglecting to order you to bed sooner. I don't wish to receive *another* scolding from the fellow.''

The mention of Miles's name brought back to Elinor's mind a vivid recollection of the scene in the entry hall. Her cheeks reddened in shame, and she sank back against the pillows. ''Mama, did Miles say anything else? Or Julian?''

''Anything else?'' Martha, her hand on the doorknob, turned and studied her daughter curiously. ''About what? What do you mean?''

Elinor shrugged. ''Nothing, Mama. Never mind.''

Martha frowned at her daughter suspiciously. ''What's amiss, Elinor? Has something happened between you and Julian?''

''Why do you ask?'' Elinor countered cautiously, surprised at her mother's astuteness.

''Because of your manner. It's a bit evasive, isn't it? But you don't have to explain anything to me if you don't wish to. I pride myself that I am not the prying sort. However, my love, don't think I haven't noticed that your Julian is behaving very peculiarly.''

''Is he?''

''Indeed he is! He hasn't asked more than twice to come up to see you—which Miles asks every hour on the hour—and, what's worse, he's been flirting with Felicia quite brazenly.''

''Well, don't let that trouble you, Mama. I myself requested that he . . . er . . . entertain her.''

''Did you really?'' Martha shook her head in bewilderment. ''I don't understand you young people.'' She sighed. ''When I was betrothed, your father and I carried on in a much more romantic style. However, if you're not concerned about Julian's behavior, I won't trouble myself about it, either.''

''Good.''

Martha Selby opened the door. ''Shall I let Miles come up, my dear? He's waiting so anxiously.''

Elinor shuddered fearfully. If Miles wanted to see her, his motive was surely to berate her for her lie. She supposed she would have to endure a tongue-lashing sooner or later. But not yet, she prayed in cowardly silence. "No, Mama, no!" she said hastily. "Tell him I'm still asleep."

"Elinor!" Martha exclaimed in surprise. "Are you asking me to *lie*? To *Miles*, of all people? He's as worried about you as if he were your *father*! What on earth has gotten into you?"

Elinor winced. She was a sorry creature indeed, wishing to avoid a reprimand that she fully deserved. "I'm sorry, Mama," she muttered, shamefaced. "Let him come up, if he wishes."

"*If* he wishes?" Martha threw her daughter an enigmatic smile. "Oh, yes, my love, that is most certainly what he wishes."

7

Two minutes later Miles stood before her. He was somewhat disheveled, his thick, graying hair tousled, his brows knit, and his lips tight. The lines around his mouth seemed to be etched more deeply than before, and there were circles under his eyes. The man looked as if he hadn't slept for days. It was true, then, as her mother had hinted, that he'd stayed awake during all the hours she'd been sleeping, worrying about her. How kind of him! He was such a loyal friend; he did not deserve to be used as she'd used him.

She managed a hesitant smile. "Hello, Miles," she said softly.

He did not smile back, but his eyes made a close examination of her face. "So you *are* better," he said gruffly. "You almost look like your old self. I'm much relieved."

"Thank you. You are kind to be concerned."

"I am not kind," he declared, coming to the foot of the bed and glaring down at her. "Now that I see you almost restored to health, I would like very much to wring your *neck*! Whatever did you mean by making Julian believe you and I are secret lovers?"

Elinor swallowed. "I must say, Miles, you don't mince words. Are you very angry?"

"That depends. Why did you do it?"

"I don't quite know. I had to conjure up a beau to convince Julian to agree to break our troth, and your name was the first to come to my mind." She twisted the edge of her blanket with nervous fingers. "Did you tell him it was a lie?"

"No. Since you are not usually given to falsehoods, I knew you must have had a reason, so I waited to speak to you." He walked slowly round to her side and looked down at her. "Why did you wish to break your troth, Elinor? Don't you care for Julian anymore?"

"He doesn't care for *me*. I've grown too old for him."

"*Old*? What utter balderdash!" His eyes darkened in fury. "Did he *say* that?"

"Almost in those words. He's taken with Felicia, you see, who seems to him a younger version of the girl I once was. But his sense of honor made him unwilling to accept the freedom I offered him, so, to relieve his guilt, I said I loved another."

"Me."

"Yes."

"I see." He turned to the fireplace and stared down at the glowing coals. "He must have found that a ludicrous choice for you to make," he remarked dryly.

"Why ludicrous?"

"I'm too old for you, for one thing. You've always thought of me as an uncle."

"You're only thirty-six, Miles. Not quite an ancient."

"Thirty-seven. And much too old to enjoy this sort of game." He punctuated his statement by kicking angrily at the coals with the toe of his boot, sending up a shower of sparks.

Elinor felt her throat tighten with tears. "I'm s-sorry, Miles. I was very . . . foolish."

"Yes," he agreed, "very." With an effort he turned away from the fire and came back to her bedside. He stood silent for a moment, looking down at her. Then, rubbing the bridge of his nose as if massaging away a headache, he sighed deeply. "I'd prefer it, Elinor, if the fellow knew the truth. With your permission I'll tell him this afternoon."

"Yes, of course," she said in a small voice. "If you must."

"Of course I must," he snapped, suddenly angry. "What else is there to do?"

"There *is* another option."

"What option?"

She lowered her head. "I'm afraid to suggest it to you."

"Have I suddenly become an ogre? Suggest it!"

She eyed him with wary unease. There followed an awkward pause. At last she said hesitantly, "We could keep up the pretense."

His black eyebrows rose. "You can't mean it! What on earth for?"

She looked down at the bit of blanket she was twisting between her fingers. "I'm afraid Julian may insist on wedding me after all, if he believes me to be . . . unattached."

"What's *wrong* with his wedding you? Didn't you say, not a moment ago, that you still care for the deuced dunderhead?"

"Not enough to wish to wed him if he feels reluctant."

"*Damn* his reluctance!" Miles stomped back and forth across the room to ease his disgust. "And as for you," he growled, turning on her, "you are speaking sentimental claptrap. If you care for him, marry him! No man with a grain of sense could fail to see what a prize you are. The fellow's a gudgeon, but not such a gudgeon that he wouldn't think himself the luckiest man alive after a mere month . . . a *week*—no, a *day*!—of being wedded to you.''

"Oh, *Miles*!" His words took her breath away. For a moment she gazed up at him awestruck. Then, afraid to take him too seriously, she lowered her lids and smiled wryly. "Spoken like the fond uncle you are," she said lightly. "It's too bad Julian can't look at me with an uncle's eyes."

"I wish you'd remember, Elinor Selby," Miles snarled, "that *I'm* not your uncle, *either*."

"Nevertheless, Miles, since Julian does not see me in that way, I'd rather *not* wed him." She sat erect and peered at the stern-faced squire curiously. "Would it be so hard to pretend to be in love with me? It would only be for a few days."

"Hard?" His dark eyes glittered in sardonic amusement. "No, my dear, not hard. *Impossible*."

His tone, self-deprecating and bitter, confused her. "But why?"

"Why? *Why*?" He laughed and shook his head. "Can you truly be so damnably, naively blind? *This* is why!" And he reached down, pulled her up on her knees, and into his arms.

To her complete astonishment she found herself being passionately kissed. Her bewilderment was so encompassing that it utterly froze her thoughts. She could only *feel*—the bruising pressure of his lips, the grip of his arms against her back, the pinching pain on her breasts of the buttons of his coat. That was all she was conscious of. Yet she had a sense that there was more to her feelings than the pressure of buttons—that there were stirrings so deep inside her she could not for the moment fathom them. But before she could begin to get hold of herself, before she

could even make herself *think*, he lifted his head. "There!"
he muttered. "I've wanted to do that for years."

"*Miles*," she gasped, still befuddled, "you'll catch my
cold!"

He burst into a startled laugh. Then, eyeing her as if he
didn't know quite what to do with her, he shook his head,
swore "Damnation!" and kissed her again.

Though still astonished, Elinor's brain came whirling to
life. What was the meaning of this? it asked her. And why
was her pulse pounding so hard in her ears? Moreover, a
stern voice at the back of her mind demanded to know if she
realized that she was wearing nothing but a thin
shift . . . that, while almost naked, she was being enveloped in a man's arms and not doing a thing to drive him off?

As if he'd heard the same question, he let her go. They
stared at each other for a moment, catching their breaths.
Then Elinor, without taking her wide-eyed gaze from his
face, slipped down under her blankets and drew them up to
her neck. "Good God!" she breathed in a hoarse whisper.

"I'm *not* going to apologize," Miles said in his normal,
reproving voice. "You deserved that."

"I *did*?"

"Yes. For your willful ignorance."

"My ignorance was not willful," she retorted. "And I'm
still ignorant. What did you *mean* by that, pray?"

"If you can't guess, I shan't tell you. However, I admit
that I played the fool just now. You have my word I won't
do so again." Without further ado, he strode out the door
and slammed it behind him.

Elinor lay against the pillows, staring at the door, the
fingers of one hand pressed against her mouth (where she
could still feel the pressure of his lips) and the other against
her breast (where she could still feel the mark of his
buttons). The message he'd given her was quite clear: He
loved her. Miles Endicott loved her! Miles, the squire of the
neighborhood, to whom everyone for miles around turned

for advice or assistance when in trouble. But the idea was impossible. Ridiculous. He *couldn't* really love her! He was the kindest, wisest, most generous man in the world, and in recent years he'd been, even more than her mother, the person to whom she'd confided her feelings. In truth, he was her best friend. But he'd always kept an avuncular distance between them. She'd always thought of him as a superior being, too superior even to be *considered* as a suitor. Above her touch, as a Londoner might put it. The idea that he could love her was too flattering to be believed!

She slipped out of bed and pattered barefoot across the floor to her dressing table. Sitting down, she peered at her face in the glass. Was this the face that Miles Endicott loved? Her cheeks were flushed, though not from fever, her eyes were shining, her tousled hair seemed electrically alive, and her lips were full and red from their bruising. Heavens, she thought, amazed, can it be that there is something beautiful about me after all?

There was a tap at the door. Her mother was back with the soup, she thought. "Come in, Mama," she said.

"It's not Mama," Miles said, coming in.

She wheeled around. "M-Miles!"

"I've changed my mind," he said. "I'll do it."

She gaped at him stupidly. "Do it?"

"I'll act the lover role for you. Just tell me what you want me to do."

8

Being forced to remain in bed was not as unpleasant as Elinor thought. Everyone in the household paid her a visit that afternoon, even the Fordyce children (who were permitted to stand just inside the door to express their good wishes, but who'd been warned not to step too far into the "sick room"). Then, in the evening, each of the adults

called on her again just before dinner, some to show off
their evening clothes, some to cheer her up for having to
miss the lighting of the yule log, and all to wish her a joyous
Noel. Felicia, looking particularly charming in a red Chinese silk round gown, hugged her and said with tremulous
sincerity that she missed Elinor's company and that her
absence from the festivities was felt by everyone. Then
Julian (breathtakingly handsome in his formal attire) came
in with an armload of winter mums that he'd gone all the
way to Harrowgate to procure. He must have found her
appearance much improved, for his eyes lit up at the sight of
her, and he repeated so often how remarkably well she was
looking that she almost believed he meant it. Staying abed
was turning out to be not unpleasant at all.

It was not until later that night, when she heard the sound
of the carriages arriving at the front door to take the
assemblage off to the midnight service at St. Michael's in
Leyburn, that Elinor began to feel lonely. Going to the
midnight service was a family tradition; this was the first
time ever that she would miss it. She ran to her south
window, the one that overlooked the drive, and watched the
guests as they gathered round the carriages. Since the
conveyances only sat four, two were required for the trip.
The Earl and Lady Lovebourne with their son and Felicia
headed toward the first carriage, and Henry and Fanny
Fordyce with their hostess, Martha Selby, meandered toward the second. Only Miles Endicott was missing from the
group. Elinor wondered where he could be; he'd always
gone to the Christmas midnight service in their company in
former years.

The night was cold, and the travelers' cloaks and greatcoats flapped in the wind as they climbed into the carriages,
but they all seemed to be laughing merrily. The only one of
the group not smiling was Elinor's mother, who at that
moment, remembering her daughter alone upstairs in her
bedroom, looked up at the window where Elinor stood

watching. Elinor saw her mother pause on the coach step and wave. "Go back to bed!" Martha mouthed.

"Yes, Mama." Elinor sighed and turned away to do her mother's bidding. She lay abed listening to the laughter, to the clunk of the coach doors closing, to the shouts of the coachmen starting up the horses, and to the crunch of the coach wheels on the gravel. But the noises of departure soon faded away. The only sound remaining was the howling wind, a gloomy whine that made the house seem suddenly very, very still. It's not fair, she thought. No one should have to be alone on Christmas Eve.

She shivered, sighed more deeply than before, and was just about to succumb to a few tears of self-pity when there was a tap at the door. "Yes?" she asked, surprised.

Miles poked his head in. "May I come in?"

"Miles!" Elinor's spirits lifted at once. "Of course. Why aren't you with the others, on the way to St. Michael's?"

He stepped over the threshold. "If I'm to play your lover, ma'am, I may as well do a good job of it. I'd be a poor sort of lover, wouldn't I, if I went off with the crowd while my beloved lay imprisoned in her room all alone on Christmas Eve?"

"I suppose you would," Elinor answered, touched.

"Of course I would. So I made my excuses to your mother and her guests, and here I am."

"How very thoughtful of you," she murmured, torn between feelings of gratitude for having found a companion for Christmas Eve and feelings of embarrassment at the close presence of the man who'd kissed her a few short hours ago—shocking behavior that neither of them would easily forget.

"Nothing thoughtful about it," Miles said casually as he crossed the room to poke up the fire. "And I needn't stay, if you'd prefer going to sleep to making conversation. My mission was accomplished merely by dropping out of the party."

"Of course I wish you to stay." She kept her voice as calm and steady as his. If he could be casual, so could she. "How could you believe I would rather sleep than converse with you? Pull up the rocking chair and sit near me. But what do you mean by your 'mission'?"

"The mission that I undertook for your sake. To play your lover for the edification of Lord Lovebourne." He pulled the rocker to the bedside and sat down. "I do believe, Elinor," he added cheerfully, "that your Julian looked a bit put out when I announced my intention to stay behind and to keep you company."

Elinor's expression changed. "See here, Miles, you're off the mark. I didn't ask you to do this to make Julian jealous. I suggested this masquerade merely to convince him that the rupture of our troth is not his fault but my own selfish desire."

"Well, ma'am, that may have been *your* aim," he said with a tinge of annoyance, "but it isn't mine."

She eyed him warily. "Are you saying that you *want* him to be jealous? I didn't think you capable of engaging in such . . . such devious strategems."

"Be truthful, my girl. Isn't that what *you* want?"

"Of course not!" she declared vehemently. "I don't want to win him by chicanery."

"Damnation, ma'am," he growled, "it isn't chicanery. It's . . . er . . . clarification."

Her eyebrows rose. "*Clarification*?"

"You said before that you wished Julian could see you through my eyes. Well, this is how we'll get him to do it. Clarify his vision, so to speak."

"But that was not at all my intention when I . . . when I . . ."

"When you named me as your lover. I know. But when I agreed to play this game, I did it with intentions of my own."

"What intentions?"

"To make that idiot Lovebourne see the error of his ways."

"His ways are not in error. All he did was fall in love with someone else."

"That's the whole point. To be fool enough to choose the empty-headed Felicia Fordyce over you is error of the worst sort."

"Well, whatever you wish to call it, Miles, he's smitten with her. Moreover, it's unethical, immoral, and . . . and . . . *humiliating* to me to have you *trick* Julian into changing his mind."

"Unethical and immoral indeed!" Miles snapped, rising and glowering at her in impatience. "See here, woman, there's no need to be so overly scrupulous. I've told you once, and I'll tell you again, what I'm doing is not trickery. It's merely restoring the fellow to his senses."

Elinor blinked up at him, confused. This behavior was not what she expected from a man who had almost confessed to being in love with her himself, and not more than ten hours before. "I don't understand you, Miles," she muttered, her voice quivering. "I thought . . ."

"You thought what?"

She colored. "I mean . . . didn't you tell me that you . . . when you kissed me . . . didn't it mean . . . ?"

He turned his back to her. "It didn't mean anything."

"Didn't it?"

"No! It was just a . . . a momentary aberration."

"Oh." She felt a definite sinking feeling in her chest. "A momentary aberration. I see."

"No, you don't see," he barked, wheeling round to her. "You're muddling things up, bringing up trickery and chicanery and questions of the ethics of this. Let's not get ourselves muddled in ethics. Your claim to ethical behavior went out the window when you lied about loving me. As for *my* ethics in this matter, I excuse my dishonesty by the purity of my motive. The ends justifying the means, and all that.''

"What ends? What motive?''

"Your *happiness*, of course. To help you win your heart's desire. What other motive would I have?''

"Do you think I can be happy if I win my heart's desire by trickery?''

"Yes, you can, if that is truly your heart's desire. If you truly love the fellow.'' His eyes burned into hers. "Well? Do you love him or don't you?''

Elinor stared up at him, the import of the question bursting on her like an explosion. Did she love Julian? Did she? She was suddenly beset with confusion. Wasn't the answer a simple yes? Yesterday the answer would have been yes without a moment of doubt. She'd taken her feelings for Julian for granted for so long, it hadn't, until this moment, occurred to her to question them. "I . . . I . . .'' she stammered, "I suppose I—after all, I've waited five years . . .''

"That is no answer. Yes or no?''

She suddenly found herself bereft of voice. Something within her was making it impossible to answer him.

He stared at her with a burning intensity for a moment before expelling an explosive breath. "Confound it, girl, you don't have to answer. I can see it in your eyes. I always could read your thoughts in those enigmatic eyes of yours. The answer is yes. If it weren't, you wouldn't be afraid to say so.''

She had to reply somehow. "I . . . suppose that's true,'' she managed.

"Very well, then,'' he said, stalking to the door, "there's nothing more to be said. As far as I'm concerned, if you want the fellow, you shall have him! Wrapped, tied, and delivered. And before this deuced holiday is over!''

9

Christmas morning dawned crisp and clear. The motes of the air, frozen into tiny crystals of ice, sparkled in the sunlight. Elinor, enlivened by the restoration of her health and by the brilliance of the morning, threw open her window and breathed deeply. She was well, her head was clear, and she would be free to leave her bedroom by the afternoon. It was going to be a glorious day.

Before she'd breathed her fill, there was a knock at the door. Expecting the caller to be her mother (who was certain to berate her for standing barefoot at an open window), she hopped quickly back into bed and drew up her covers. But it was not her mother. Her first visitor of the day was Cousin Felicia. The girl burst into Elinor's room with an eager step and eyes alight with excitement. "Did you hear what happened last night?" she asked, perching on the side of Elinor's bed. "One of the carriages skidded on a patch of ice and the two right wheels sideslipped into a ditch."

"Goodness!" Elinor exclaimed, sitting up abruptly. "Was anyone hurt?"

"No, but the Earl and Lady Lovebourne had to squeeze into the other coach with Mama, Papa, and Aunt Martha. There was no room for anyone else, so Julian and I waited inside the tilted carriage while the coachman went for help. It took so long for the livery men to come and right the coach that we missed the entire church service."

"That *is* too bad. You must have been freezing!"

"No, I had a lap robe, and Julian gave me his muffler. We had a lovely chat, he and I. All about you."

Elinor was taken aback. "About *me*?"

"Yes, he told me about your courtship, about how he met you at an assembly ball while visiting a school friend at

Leyburn, and how he drove his phaeton up from London every week thereafter to woo you.''

"Goodness, is that all he could find to speak to you about?'' Elinor asked, astounded. "How very dull for you!''

"No, I truly enjoyed it. You are very fortunate in your betrothed, Elinor. He's not only the handsomest creature on God's green earth, but he's utterly charming.''

"Yes, he is.'' Elinor studied her younger cousin curiously. Felicia's manner was so open and free of guilt that it was clear the girl had no designs on Julian at all. But even more astonishing, it appeared that Julian had taken no advantage of the opportunity the accident had provided to try to attach her. What was the matter with the fellow? Why, if he was smitten with Felicia, did he spend those precious moments of privacy reminiscing about a romantic involvement with someone else? He'd seemed so proficient in the art of dalliance a few days ago; why was he suddenly behaving like a clod? "Didn't he spend any time talking about *you*, Felicia?'' she asked.

Felicia shrugged. "Perhaps at first, to be polite. But it was you he had on his mind.''

"I'm quite surprised. I had the distinct impression he found *you* delightful.''

"Me? Why do you believe that? He thinks of me as your silly little cousin, that's all.''

"No, that's not true. I believe he's quite taken with you. Would you not like it if he were? After all, you did say you find *him* charming and 'the handsomest fellow on God's green earth.' ''

Felicia blinked at her in puzzlement. "Yes, I did say that, of course. And he is.''

"Don't you like him, then?''

"Yes, very much. As a partner for *you*.''

"Only in that way? But, Felicia, let us suppose for a moment that Julian and I were not betrothed. In those circumstances, wouldn't you have the slightest urge to attach him to yourself?''

''As a *suitor*, you mean?'' Felicia's eyebrows rose in amusement, as if the mere suggestion were a ridiculous impossibility. ''Good *heavens*, no! Your Julian may be handsome, but he's much too old for me. Besides, I'm madly in love with Bertie, you know.''

''Bertie?''

''Bertie Duffield. You know whom I mean. I've told you of him dozens of times. My friend Sarah's brother.''

''Oh. That Bertie. I see.'' Elinor did remember hearing of a Bertie, but she hadn't paid mind to the name. Felicia had such a tendency to babble that it was sometimes difficult to sift the meaningful details from the dross. ''And is this Bertie madly in love with you, too?'' she asked, fascinated.

Felicia smiled in naughty delight. ''Of course he is, though we haven't told a soul. Papa doesn't like him above half. We're waiting until Papa becomes used to him. In a few months, when Papa is softened up sufficiently, Bertie will ask for my hand. We have it all planned. Meanwhile, you won't give me away to Mama or anyone, will you, Elinor?''

Elinor assured her that her lips were sealed. But she couldn't help feeling very sorry for her once-betrothed. Before Julian could plead his cause, it was already a lost one. Poor Julian, she thought. He never had a chance.

After Felicia took her leave, it occurred to Elinor to wonder what would happen next. Would Julian, having been so quickly deflected from his amorous objective, now wish to reinstate the betrothal? Would he come to realize he loved Elinor after all? And if he did, would she be pleased? She *had* to be pleased, she supposed, for it would mean she could resume her life as she'd been planning it for the past five years. Wasn't that what she wanted?

But she knew, with a certainty that came from deep within her, that the answer was no. No, it was not what she wanted. In these few days since Julian's return, she'd learned to understand herself. Julian had been a girl's dream, but she was a woman now. And the woman she'd become had suddenly recognized her deeper dreams, dreams that in girlhood she'd pushed aside as impossible. But perhaps they were possible now. Miles Endicott had kissed her. That had made all the difference. She could now admit the truth: It was Miles she wanted, Miles she loved. No one else, not even the "handsomest creature on God's green earth" would do.

10

Miles Endicott, having no knowledge of this latest development, was determined to make good his promise to drop Lord Lovebourne—lock, stock, and barrel—at Elinor's feet. To that end, he appeared at the Selby house on Christmas Day at midmorning. He had no plan, other than to point out to Julian—with what he hoped would be a sufficient degree of subtlety to seem not to be doing so—the obvious superiority of Elinor Selby's character and person over those of that silly chit, Felicia Fordyce.

He'd made up his mind to accomplish his objective before they all sat down to Christmas dinner. Thus he wasted no time in bibble-babble with his hostess or the other guests but set about at once to find his quarry. He searched the breakfast room, the front and rear sitting rooms, and the drawing room before coming upon Lord Lovebourne in the deserted library. His lordship, dressed in riding clothes, was standing before the fireplace, his elbow resting on the mantel and his head lowered. He was staring down at the flames and absentmindedly hitting at the fender with his riding crop. From the condition of his mud-spattered breeches and boots, it was clear that he had just returned from a bruising ride. "Good morning, Lovebourne," Miles said from the doorway.

Julian glanced over his shoulder at him. "Oh, it's you, Endicott," he said sourly. "You're not looking for me, are you?"

"I was, but you don't seem in the mood for company," Miles answered, deciding the time was not propitious. "I'll see you later, after you've imbibed more of the Christmas spirit."

"You may as well come in now," his lordship muttered. "I've no indication that the Christmas spirit will visit me at all this year." He turned and beckoned Miles to a chair. "I'm not as fortunate as you, you know."

Miles stepped over the threshold. "Fortunate as I?" he asked curiously. "In what way?"

"In your marital prospects, of course. You are a lucky dog, Endicott. Your Elinor is a pearl beyond price."

Miles kept a puzzled eye on Julian as he sank down on a chair. "Yes, she is. But I was given to understand that you had your eye on another pearl."

"More fool, I," Julian muttered, turning back to stare at the fire. "I was blinded by the glow of youth."

"Were you, indeed?" Miles, unable quite to believe that his task had, by some miraculous chance, already been accomplished, leaned forward in his chair and peered at Lovebourne intently. "But Felicia *does* have a glow," he pointed out cautiously. "It hasn't worn off overnight, has it?"

"Miss Felicia Fordyce's glow has worn off for me. I was forced to spend two hours in her sole company last night, and it took no more than the first fifteen minutes to discover that the chit is a complete bore."

"You don't say."

"Talking about nothing but gowns and dancing shoes and the trouble her hairdresser has taken with her coiffure. Then she went on and on about her success at her come-out ball. A bit too taken with herself, Miss Fordyce is.''

''Is she, indeed?'' Miles murmured, thinking that the same criticism could be made of Lovebourne as well.

''I tell you the chit's a glib-tongued pittle-pattle!'' Julian declared firmly, turning from the fire to face his listener. ''Finally, in desperation, I directed the conversation to myself. I must have been as great a bore as she, going on as I did about my courtship with Elinor. I tell you, Endicott, it was an unbearable two hours. I've been asking myself ever since how I could have been so besotted as to believe I preferred her company to Elinor's. Why, comparing Elinor to Felicia is like . . . like . . .''

''Like comparing a Mozart concerto to a dance tune?'' Miles offered.

''Yes!'' Julian nodded in heartfelt agreement. ''Exactly so!'' He crossed the room and sank into a chair. ''What a muddle I've made of my life, Endicott,'' he groaned, dropping his head in his hands. ''What a deuced muddle!''

''Not necessarily,'' Miles suggested carefully. ''All may not be lost.''

Julian's head came up abruptly. ''What do you mean? Aren't you and Elinor—?''

''We are not. Perhaps the time has come for complete honesty, old fellow. But first, there is something I must know. If your feeling for Elinor true and sincere, or are you the sort to lose your heart to every pretty female who comes into your line of vision?''

Julian, his brows knit, stared at Miles intently. ''I've loved Elinor for more than five years, without once being tempted to infidelity. Except for this one stupid mistake.'' He rose slowly from his chair. ''What is it you're trying to tell me, Endicott?''

''Elinor lied to you. It's you she loves, not I.''

Julian stood for a moment transfixed. ''She doesn't love you?'' he asked suspiciously. ''Is that really true?''

"I promised you complete frankness, didn't I?"

Julian blinked down at him, afraid to believe what he'd heard. "But . . . I don't understand. Elinor is not the sort to tell falsehoods. Why did she lie to me?"

"To free you," Miles responded. "To free you to court Felicia without guilt." He rose and strode to the door. "That's the sort of selfless generosity she is capable of."

Julian ran after him. It took three quick strides to catch Miles and grasp his arm. Julian's eyes glowed with hope. "Do you mean Elinor would really consider renewing our betrothal? That she would forgive me?"

"Just ask her." Miles shook off Julian's hold and went quickly to the door. But at the threshold, he paused, turned, and glowered at the other man. "But I warn you, Lovebourne, that if at any time in the future you play her false, you'll have to answer to me."

Julian took no notice of Miles's sudden glower. He was too elated to pay mind to anything but the delightful news he'd just been brought. His prospects were suddenly bright, and so was his mood. The Christmas spirit had overtaken him at last.

The fact that the Christmas spirit had completely disappeared from *Miles's* heart troubled his lordship not at all.

11

The sun was setting in spectacular majesty when the guests assembled in the drawing room for the traditional drink from the wassail bowl before Christmas dinner. The kissing bough, hanging over the drawing-room door, had already worked its magic on the assemblage, the gentlemen having taken their places early at the side of the door and kissed each lady as she arrived. Now, wassail cups in hand, they awaited Elinor's arrival. On this occasion, her first appearance downstairs since she'd been taken ill, they all were eager to welcome her.

While they waited, Martha Selby paced the room. It was not her daughter's arrival that worried her, for she'd helped Elinor to dress and had seen that the girl's health was truly restored and that, in addition, she was in her very best looks. It was Miles Endicott who troubled her. "I don't understand Miles," she complained to Fanny, her brow wrinkled in concern. "He found me in the kitchen this morning, announced that he wouldn't be with us for Christmas dinner in a voice that made poor Cook jump with fright, and then stalked out without another word. I must have offended him in some way, but I can't for the life of me imagine how."

Elinor was just coming down the stairs at that moment. She was still a trifle pale from her recent bout of illness, but her mother was quite right about her appearance. She looked utterly lovely. She wore a green velvet gown cut low across the shoulders and embroidered with silver-threaded festoons of geranium leaves at the décolletage and the hemline. Her hair was pinned up in loose curls at the top of her head, with a few tendrils permitted to escape and frame her face. But the features that gave her appearance its greatest charm were her eyes; they positively sparkled in happy anticipation of this event. Unfortunately, however, the guests were not to see that sparkle, for the girl overhead her mother's words, and the glow in her eyes died at once. *Miles was not coming.* "Oh, Mama, *no*!" she cried in disappointment as she paused in the doorway.

The gentlemen, taking no note of her little cry, surrounded her at once. Holding her prisoner under the kissing bough, her uncle Henry kissed her right cheek and the Earl her left. No sooner had they released her than Julian bowed them aside and took her into his arms. "Merry Yuletide, my love," he whispered in her ear. "I've never seen you look more beautiful."

"Thank you," Elinor answered absently, wishing those words had been said by someone else.

"Endicott told me everything," Julian went on. "The whole truth."

Elinor gaped at him. "Everything?"

He grinned down at her, quite sure of himself. "I can only be thankful that I still have your love. Now we don't have to announce the end of our betrothal at all." With that he pulled her to him and kissed her with brazen fervency.

While the others watched the little scene, smiling in benign approval, Elinor tried to wrench herself from his embrace. "No, Julian, no!" she gasped. "You don't underst—"

But Julian, holding her tightly round the waist with one arm, had already turned to the others. "Let's drink to *next* Christmas," he said proudly, picking up a cup of steaming ale with his free hand and holding it high in a toast, "when Elinor and I shall be husband and wife."

"Hear, hear," chortled the Earl as the others drank.

"No!" Elinor cried, pulling herself free. "No! Julian, stop! Mama . . . everyone . . . don't—! I'm so sorry. Julian, my dear, I *can't*—!"

Julian at last took note of the dismay in her voice. "*Elinor*!" he exclaimed, shocked. "What are you *saying*?"

"Don't look at me that way, Julian, please! It's not so dreadful to break one's troth, really it isn't. One soon gets over it. You'll find yourself a much more suitable bride in London. After all, you are the handsomest creature on God's green earth." She took one last glance at all of the shocked faces looking up at her, winced, turned, lifted her skirts, and fled from the room.

Ignoring the hubbub behind her, she ran down the hall. Halfway to the entry hall, she came face to face with the butler. "Perkins!" she cried. "My cloak, please, quickly!"

The butler stopped in his tracks. "Miss Elinor!" he

exclaimed. ''Where are you *going*? You can't leave now. I was just about to announce dinner.''

''Please, Perkins, go ahead and announce it. Don't let them wait for me. Tell them I'll . . . I'll explain later. But first, my cloak.''

A brief moment later she was out the door. The Endicott manor house was not quite two miles away. Elinor took the shortcut through the Selby south field, through the home woods, and up the rise that led to the squire's west lawn. By the time she'd crossed the lawn and knocked at his front door, she was completely out of breath. As she waited for Miles's man to admit her, she put a shaking hand to her now-tumbled hair. She must look a fright, she realized—wild-eyed, red-nosed, and windblown.

But Farrow, Miles's elderly houseman, did not show surprise at her appearance. ''Good arfternoon, Miz Elin'r,'' he said in his up-country brogue. ''Murry Christmas to ye.''

''Thank you. And a Merry Christmas to you, Farrow. Where is he?''

''In the liberry, ma'am. But 'e said 'e ain't to be disturbed.''

''I don't doubt it,'' she retorted brusquely, marching past him.

''I wouldn't go in, ma'am, if I wuz ye. In a turrible temper 'e is. Wouldn' eat no dinner nor nothin'.''

''Then don't come with me,'' she threw over her shoulder. ''I'll announce myself.''

''Yes, ma'am,'' he said stoically. ''It's yer funeral.''

She strode down the corridor with a determined step, but her courage faltered a bit when she reached the library. However, knowing that Farrow was watching her from down the hall, she squared her shoulders and threw open the door.

Miles was slumped in an easy chair, his neckerchief hanging untied round his neck, his booted feet resting cross-legged on the hearth, and a book lying open but unread on his lap. "Go away, Farrow," he growled without turning his head. "I told you not to bother me about dinner."

"Who cares about dinner?" she said lightly, pausing on the threshold. "But did you intend not even to wish me a happy Christmas?"

He wheeled about, half rising from his chair. A look of astonishment crossed his face and quickly disappeared. If there was a hint of gladness in the look, she did not see it. He stared at her for a moment, speechless, and then returned to his former position, legs extended. "You've come a long way for a rather commonplace greeting," he muttered sullenly, "but if you must have it, here it is. Happy Christmas. Now go back to your guests."

"Heavens, you *are* in a 'turrible temper,'" she said, closing the door and crossing to the hearth to face him. "Is it because you feel guilty for betraying me to Julian?"

"Betraying you?" He raised his eyebrows coldly. "How can you call it betrayal? I dropped him in your lap, just as I promised."

"Yes, so you did."

"If you've come to thank me, you may save your breath. Go back to him and live happily ever after. Just leave me out of it."

"Why should you be left out after doing so much to bring us together? Don't you want to *see* the result of your efforts? Why didn't you come to dinner to hear his romantic declaration?"

He glowered up at her. "I've had quite enough of you and Julian for one day."

She untied the strings of her cloak and let it fall. "Your efforts were wasted, you know. I've refused him."

"*Refused* him?" Miles's booted legs came down from the hearth with an angry stamp as he sat bolt upright. "Why on *earth* did you refuse him?"

She met his eyes bravely. "I had my reasons."

"I'm *damned* if I understand you! You told me you loved him, didn't you?"

"No, I didn't tell you anything of the sort. You said you read it in my eyes. Perhaps you don't read them as well as you think."

He stared at her a moment, brows knit. Then, holding his breath, he got slowly to his feet. "I'm in no mood for word games, Elinor," he said, grasping her by her shoulders. "Are you trying to tell me you no longer care for the fellow?"

"I'm trying to tell you much more than that," she said softly, dropping her eyes from his burning glare. "I'm trying to tell you that I . . . that it's *you* I love."

His grip on her shoulders tightened. "What nonsense is this?" he demanded angrily.

She blinked up at him, her heart pounding in fear. This wasn't the reaction she'd expected. She wanted to run away, but she'd gone too far to stop now. "I know this all seems too sudden to be believed," she murmured awkwardly, "but you see, ever since you kissed me yesterday, I—"

"When I kissed you yesterday," he cut in scornfully, "your only reaction was to caution me that I'd catch your deuced cold."

"That was *not* my only reaction. Honestly, Miles, you are making this very difficult for me."

"Sorry," he said brusquely. "Go on."

"The truth is that my reaction was quite . . . overwhelming." This confession made her blush, but she went bravely on. "Ever since you kissed me, I . . . I haven't been the same. I began to realize that I've loved you for a very long time, but I didn't believe until yesterday that you could love me."

Something softened in his expression. His eyes searched her face hungrily. "Are you telling me the truth, woman?

This isn't one of your self-sacrificing acts, is it? Giving up Julian in order to make *this* old fellow happy?''

A little gurgling laugh bubbled up out of the turmoil inside her. Everything was going to be all right after all. ''You gudgeon,'' she said, her lips curving into a tremulous smile, ''do you think I'm as self-sacrificing as all that?'' She stepped closer to him and slipped her arms about his waist. ''I know how to put your doubts to rest, my dear. Why don't you kiss me again, just as you did yesterday? I was too startled then to let myself respond. But now I'm quite ready.''

He expelled his pent-up breath slowly, and his eyes took on a glow Elinor had never seen before. ''My God, woman,'' he said hoarsely, taking her face between his hands, ''I've loved you for so long I can't remember when it began.'' Then he lowered his head to hers and kissed her gently.

It was she who changed the tenor of the embrace. With a joyful cry, she flung her arms about his neck and, pressing herself tightly against him, kissed him with all the passion that had been pent up in her. He needed no more evidence than that to be completely convinced of the sincerity of her declaration.

Later, seated on his lap in his large wing chair, she lifted her head from a most satisfying embrace and reminded herself that there was one unpleasant task still ahead. ''Miles, my love,'' she sighed, reluctantly breaking the silence, ''I'm afraid I've stayed too long. I must go home and face the others. I left matters in a terrible turmoil.''

''We'll both face them. Together.'' But instead of making an attempt to rise, he gathered her into his arms for one more embrace. ''I promise we'll go,'' he murmured in besotted content, ''in a little while.''

But just as he was about to kiss her again, he stiffened, stopped short, pulled a handkerchief from his pocket, and raised it to his nose barely in time to meet a very hearty sneeze. ''Dash it all,'' he muttered after the explosion, ''I *have* caught your blasted cold!''

''But, my dear,'' she murmured, nuzzling his neck, ''you can't blame me. I did warn you. . . .''

The
Rocking
Horse

Holly Newman

BAYNEVILLE Castle estate ahead, miss!'' called out the jehu.

Miss Jocelyn Maybrey drew aside the heavy leather curtain covering the coach window. Beside her, Lady Maybrey stirred and looked over her shoulder, each woman seeking her first glimpse of the legendary estate.

Just ahead, massive stonework marked the entrance to the property.

Lady Maybrey touched her daughter's hand and gently squeezed it. Jocelyn turned her head and smiled. For all her London *beau monde* savvy, her mother was excited. Well, Jocelyn wryly admitted, so was she.

Christmas at Bayneville! Memories for a lifetime!

The coach turned right to pass between cream stone walls surmounted with snarling lions that overlooked the roadway. Dry, ash-brown leaves swirled upward as they passed, sailing into the air. Chiseled in the Roman style into the stone wall below the lions was the legend BAYNEVILLE, stark and arrogant. Reading it, Jocelyn felt a shiver of anticipation. She turned her head and stared down the drive and across a half-mile expanse of scythed winter-browned grass to the massive stone structure known as Bayneville Castle, seat of the Marquess of Tarkington, scion of the Bayne family.

Bayneville Castle—for all its size and name—was not a true castle. The current structure had been built over the long-ago ruins of an earlier, smaller building more deserv-

ing of that sobriquet. Nonetheless, Bayneville was more
than a country estate with pretenses to importance. So vast
were its holdings and outbuildings, its tenantry and craftsmen, that the estate was a self-sufficient village.

But as impressive as the entire estate was, all agreed it
was the house and its immediate grounds that commanded
attention. From a guidebook she'd purchased at Hatchard's
Bookshop, Lady Maybrey had learned that the main building was constructed around three separate courtyards. At
either ends of the house wings jutted away from the main
body with each wing ending in a tower topped by a cupola.

". . . And," she told her daughter as their carriage
bowled down the long drive, "there are two formal gardens,
a maze, a topiary garden, and an orangery. All worthy of
investigation, it says in the guidebook, as the finest exam-
ples of their kind,"

"In December?" Jocelyn asked absentmindedly as she
rocked gently with the carriage.

"Yes, even in December. Imagine. It does sound too
fantastic to be real. . . . And to think your Charles stands
heir."

Jocelyn frowned at her mother's presumption of a betrothal between her and Mr. Bayne, and at her consideration
of Mr. Bayne's position as Tarkington's heir. "Only if his
cousin does not remarry and sire sons," she carefully
reminded, "and I think it macabre to dwell on that possibility."

"Well, naturally one does not wish ill for Tarkington, but
they do say the marquess has not been himself since his
wife's death. Why, I don't believe he's visited his London
house at all!"

Jocelyn sighed. Her mother considered all events in light
of London society. "Mama, the gentleman has been in
mourning the past year. It would not do for him to have
lived a social life. And, as you have often stated to me, if

one cannot go to London entertainments, why be in London at all?''

Lady Maybrey nodded, the tall apricot plumes in her bonnet swaying. "But don't forget Lord Tarkington's involvement with politics. That should not have been disrupted by mourning. Maybrey says he was extremely active and vocal prior to his wife's death. His presence has been sorely missed in the House of Lords—by his peers *and* by those in the House of Commons who saw him as a peer for the people.''

"Perhaps his notion of what is proper for mourning is stricter than most,'' Jocelyn suggested.

Lady Maybrey nodded and stared at the manor, a pensive expression on her finely drawn features. She worried her lower lip between her teeth for a moment, then: "I do hope overly circumspect behavior does not put a damper on the festivities. What a dreary visit we should have, and how unfortunate it would be for dear Lady Mary.''

Jocelyn laughed. "Lady Mary is the liveliest of creatures. I cannot imagine her easily acquiescing to sober entertainments—especially as the Christmas Eve ball and the subsequent house party are to celebrate her betrothal to Lord Killingham. No. Whatever her elder brother's disposition, she'll run her way, as shall all the guests. Mark my words.''

Lady Maybrey took her eyes away from the manor house and leaned back against the velvet squabs. "If that is true, this may well prove the social event of the year. And prove your highlight as well if Charles should come up to scratch. . . . Wouldn't that be lovely? I can think of a few mamas whose noses would be good and tweaked,'' she finished with relish.

"Oh, Mama,'' Jocelyn gently chided, shaking her head in loving exasperation though a faint blush of embarrassment tinted her cheeks.

Sir Jasper and Lady Maybrey more than enjoyed the social milieu. They thrived upon it. It was their life. The

Maybreys were invited everywhere. Jocelyn could recall very few times when their house wasn't filled with guests. Her parents had always been socially active and socially conscious. Consequently they had not been surprised when Jocelyn was readily accepted into society as she made her social bow. Though her fortune was only modest and her appearance pleasant rather than beautiful, she quickly found herself with a handful of dedicated, worthy suitors.

Her favor fell upon Mr. Charles Bayne, for she felt the most at ease with him. They became friends, and Jocelyn supposed that was adequate for a good marriage. She knew her parents smiled and nodded approval. Charles Bayne was socially active, well connected, interested in government, possessed a modest though adequate competence, and stood heir to a marquess. What more could a young woman require in a husband? And, though she may blush at her mother's verbalization, Jocelyn *did* expect Mr. Bayne to solicit her father for her hand in marriage during their visit at Bayneville Castle. What a suitable finale that would be to her first season. Everyone said so. She could be serene in the knowledge that her life was secure and mapped out to continue in the mold created by her parents. Hers would be a familiar and comfortable existence.

But how could she account for the little mental gremlin who wouldn't leave her alone, the imp of mischief that searched for something else than an ordered existence? In the lonely hours of the night when she lay abed, sleepless, staring at the shadowy folds of the bed hangings, Jocelyn wrestled with a sense of deep disquiet. It felt like an itch that had no source and therefore could not be scratched.

Something was wrong. Desperately wrong. She was not content and she did not know why. She wanted to dismiss the odd feelings as hesitancy to leave her family, to commit to marriage; but somehow that explanation was too simplistic. Nonetheless, she wouldn't—couldn't—guess at an answer. She had to *know*.

She hoped this trip to Bayneville, away from familiar, everyday events in London, would help her grasp what this odd feeling might be and therefore help her discover a cure, or at least an acceptance.

She sighed and turned her head to look at Bayneville again. The nearer the carriage came, the grander the estate's appearance seemed. It went on forever, a formidable beauty. Odd to even consider finding simple answers in such an ornate backdrop. Looking at the vast property, Jocelyn felt an odd prick of curiosity for the man who held it, the eighth Marquess of Tarkington. She'd yet to meet him, even though he was the elder brother of her best friend. She did know him by sight, though, for she'd seen him from a distance at the theater and about town.

Lady Mary's mother preferred London to the country; consequently after the requisite mourning period following her widowhood, she took up residence at the Tarkington London house, bringing Lady Mary with her. The marquess and marchioness remained at Bayneville for most of the year, coming to London for the height of the season and when Parliament sat.

It was only now, after Lady Mary's betrothal, that the dowager marchioness came to spend any time in the country. There was curiosity in London as to why the Lady Tarkington deemed it necessary for Lady Mary's betrothal party to be at Bayneville Castle. Still, society did not complain, for when invited they were not averse to journeying to the country to visit legendary Bayneville Castle.

According to the letter Jocelyn received from her friend, the house would be full by Christmas. Looking at the bucolic peace of Bayneville in its pastoral setting, Jocelyn felt a surge of joyous relief in the knowledge that she and her mother were arriving before the press of London guests bringing London society with them. Her eyes sparkled in anticipation, and her pulse quickened.

As the carriage drew up before the entrance to Bayneville, Jocelyn was delighted to see her friend coming out to greet them, a hastily donned shawl thrown about her slight shoulders. Lady Mary skipped down the wide stone steps, eager for the waiting footman to open the carriage door and set the steps. Jocelyn's anticipation matched Lady Mary's.

Behind Lady Mary, descending the broad manor steps in a sedate manner, came an elegant gentleman dressed in a soft pigeon-gray suit. His dark hair waved back off a high brow, though one recalcitrant lock curled forward. Studying his confident, settled demeanor, Jocelyn was surprised that his hair dared to fall out of place. She recognized the man at once. Here was the eighth marquess of Tarkington, Simon Charles Froborough Bayne.

It struck Jocelyn that his mien—while in high contrast to his lively sister's and his amiable cousin's—was not the somber, morose aspect she'd expected. Nor was there the arrogance one often found in a man of his portion. His was a hard face, true, full of angles and planes with a stubborn, square-cut jaw. Nonetheless there was a welcoming smile on his lips, and he radiated a calm contentedness. Here was not a man with ghosts to dispel, a mask to wear, or hidden goals to achieve. He was as he was.

Fascinated at this divergence from idle supposition, Jocelyn stared at him until her attention was recalled by the feel of Lady Mary's arms about her shoulders in enthusiastic greeting. She blushed at her preoccupation with the marquess—and not a little for the realization of the rudeness in her stare. Flustered, she fixed her eyes firmly upon Lady Mary and vowed not to let them stray again in the marquess's direction until they were introduced. She grasped her friend's hand, kissed her cheek in gentle salute, and exclaimed on how good it felt to see her again.

"And I you! I swear I have been driving poor Tarkington to distraction with my pacing and wondering when you'd arrive! I'm so glad you and Lady Maybrey could come early," Lady Mary said, turning to greet Jocelyn's mother. "Mama's in the parlor anxious for all the London news."

"*After* your guests have had a chance to rest and freshen up," interceded Tarkington in a calm, surprisingly low voice that rumbled along Jocelyn's spine. She gave a tiny, involuntary shiver.

"Well, yes," Lady Mary agreed with her brother. "Oh, dear, and I have been most shatter-brained again, haven't I? I haven't yet made you known to Tarkington!"

"Ah, I was wondering when you would recall that trifle," Tarkington faintly drawled.

"I do apologize, but excitement and happiness overwhelm all thoughts!"

"Odd, I thought that an everyday occurrence," murmured her brother.

"Beast!" Lady Mary exclaimed, laughing. "Now please hush, I'm trying to do this right." She drew her shawl closer about her shoulders, cleared her throat, and drew herself up. "Tarkington, may I present Lady Maybrey and Miss Maybrey?" she said solemnly—and promptly sneezed.

Everyone laughed, Lady Mary pouted, and Jocelyn clapped a hand over her mouth, apologetic blushes for her laughter running high.

When the laughter quieted and the smiles settled, Lord Tarkington greeted Lady Maybrey easily, for they were known to each other from London's political circles. Then he turned and, quite to Jocelyn's surprise, winked at her. Her blushes soared again, and she could only hope that as she ducked her head and curtsied he would not notice.

To her relief he merely acknowledged her greeting before turning back to her mother and offering his arm to escort her into the house.

"We have so much to talk about and to do before the ball!" Lady Mary said as she and Jocelyn linked arms and followed behind. "When will your father and Charles arrive?"

"Not until Christmas Eve, I'm afraid. They would have come with us, but there was some meeting or other on the twenty-third they needed to attend."

Lady Mary pulled a handkerchief out of the cuff of her dress and dabbed at her nose, which was turning bright pink in the cold outside air. "Aunt Bayne has not been happy that Charles delayed his arrival. She lives in the Dower House, you know."

"Yes, Mr. Bayne told me."

"Mr. Bayne?" Lady Mary teased archly.

"There has been nothing formalized between us," Jocelyn said carefully.

"*Yet*. . . . But I should not tease you. I know how uncertain I was before Edward approached Tarkington for my hand in marriage. Even when I knew he meant to! I miss him. I wish he were here now. Unfortunately he arrives with the rest of the Killinghams in the very midst of the Christmas Eve rush!" She sneezed again, jamming her handkerchief against her nose. "Oh, Jocelyn, I am so happy! I would you were, too! As I would everyone share in my joy."

She paused as she watched her brother bow over Lady Maybrey's hand before he consigned her to the care of Mrs. Penneybacker, the housekeeper. "But I believe I should forfeit it all just to see my brother the way he was before Diana died," she whispered, "so involved with society and politics. Active, running hither and yon on a moment's notice. Giving speeches, writing papers. It's as if that part of his light that burned so brightly was snuffed out with her death. I don't understand it." She shook her head, then sighed. "But this is not the time for regrets, is it?"

"No, not at all. This is the time for *your* future! Though I should say I think the more of you for your concern."

Lady Mary smiled mistily, then she sniffed and brusquely gathered her composure. "Well, I've delayed you long enough, and you must be anxious to shed that heavy cloak and wash up after your long journey. I swear I have become a goose of late with my run-on nonsense. Emmie here shall show you to your room. It is quite one of the nicest, even if it is seemingly in the back beyond. I hope you like it. We can talk more—"

"And more and more!" Jocelyn interjected.

Lady Mary laughed, her ebullience returning. "Yes, and more and more, after you rest. We shall be having an early country dinner tonight. Four o'clock. Shall I see you an hour before downstairs?"

Jocelyn easily agreed and turned to follow the maid. Emmie led her up the wide marble staircase to a broad landing. From the landing there were slightly narrower marble staircases at either end that continued upward. Emmie took the right-hand staircase to the first floor, where tall triple windows looked out across the front lawn and the long drive that approached the house. She led Jocelyn down a wide, oak-paneled hall past innumerable rooms and two side halls. Finally Emmie stopped where the hall ended and another branched off to the left. She opened a heavy oak door with shiny brass fittings that was more reminiscent of a castle door than a modern bedroom door. But once Jocelyn went inside, she understood and cooed with delight. It was one of the circular tower rooms her mother had told her about after reading the country house guidebook.

Three large and separate windows dominated the opposite wall, each covered with heavy dark green velvet drapes swagged back and held with gold cord. Between each window hung jewel-toned tapestries. On the floor lay an intricately patterned Oriental carpet. The bed, hung with the same velvet as the windows, stood on a dais in the middle of the room. The fireplace was on the same wall as the entrance door. In the hearth a fire was burning brightly, warming the room.

Jocelyn crossed to one of the windows to study the view beyond. Bayneville Castle itself and its surroundings fasci-

nated her. It was so big, the expanse of land so vast! And so
other-worldly to her, a city-bred woman. To the south the
winter-browned grass undulated gently down to a narrow
river lined with tall, bare-branched trees etched against the
hillside. Beyond, up the sloping hill, were green hedges and
dark pine set against a pale blue-washed sky.

She went from window to window. To the east stood a
village of estate buildings, to the north a small dower house,
a church, and greenhouses with orchards beyond. Emmie
came up beside her to quietly point out and name the
landmarks. Jocelyn was touched by the young girl's
thoughtfulness and silently vowed to procure a small
Christmas token for the maid.

Just as they were about to turn away, a tall, hatless figure
in a worn coat and stained leather breeches crossed the
ground from the house toward one of the smaller whitewashed outbuildings. Jocelyn recognized the figure as the
marquess and said as much aloud.

"Yes, Miss. He be going to the carpenter's," the maid
said. She turned away to hang up Jocelyn's coat.

"The carpenter's?" Jocelyn asked before she could stop
herself. Silently she cursed her wayward curiosity, the bane
of her existence. It did not do to appear nosy before
servants, especially when one had just arrived.

Emmie didn't seem to notice. "Aye." She paused to
smile and glance toward the window. "'Tis for his little
ladyship, don't y' know."

Jocelyn laughed, entirely confused. "No, I'm afraid I
don't."

"Och, that's right. You'll not have met her yet," Emmie
said as she shut the armoire door and crossed the room to
turn down the bed. "'Tis a rocking horse he makes for her.
Her one desire, she says. Poor wee one."

She shook her head, though her gentle smile remained.
Finished with the bed, she removed a large kettle from a hob
on the fireplace and poured hot water into a basin beside

which she laid out a small scented soap and a towel. "There ya be, miss, hot water to wash with, a warm fire to take the chill from ya bones, and a bed turned down for a nice nap. Will there be anything else?"

Yes! Jocelyn wanted to shout, surprised at the questions and feelings consuming her. Tell me more of rocking horses, little ones, and the marquess! Tell me of vast expanses of land, of clear blue skies, and country living! Her soul thirsted.

But she only laughed, the questions going unasked. She was too well bred. Inwardly she sighed and chafed at the social restraints that demanded a curb on curiosity. The feeling joined the niggling mental discomforts she'd felt of late but did not understand. She brushed it aside. "No, Emmie, nothing else," she said on a wistful sigh. "I thank you for your care. You may be sure I shall mention your efficiency to the housekeeper."

"Thank ya, miss," Emmie said, beaming as she backed out of the room, leaving Jocelyn alone.

Jocelyn looked once more toward the building the marquess had entered; then she walked toward the basin to wash away the travel dust and compose her mind.

By two o'clock Miss Amelia Barnes, Jocelyn's abigail, had arrived with all her baggage. The redoubtable little woman set immediately to unpacking, pressing wrinkled clothes, informing Jocelyn on how fortunate she was to be an extended guest at such an exalted establishment, dressing Jocelyn's luxuriant dark hair with combs and velvet ribbons, and otherwise pushing and prodding her young mistress into fashionable formal attire. Jocelyn's protests that they were dining *en famille* fell upon deaf ears. After all, this was the house of a marquess! insisted Miss Barnes. Proper form must be maintained. Her young mistress would be best guided by her. Without argument.

By three o'clock Jocelyn found herself attired in yellow

figured silk complete with pearls—Miss Barnes would have preferred the yellow topaz with diamonds—gloves, fan, filmy shawl, and reticule, as if she were attending a London soiree. Moments later a beaming Miss Barnes gently pushed Jocelyn out of the room, then closed the door.

Bemused, Jocelyn stared at the closed oak door. A puff of quiet laughter escaped her lips, and she shook her head ruefully. Even here, in the country, this attention to society was the same. Somehow she thought it would be different. Perhaps the expanse of land she'd seen from her tower window, the number and types of buildings upon the land, or simply the worn coat and stained leather breeches the marquess wore when he passed under her window made her think of differences. Perhaps, in truth, there weren't any, and therefore she should be touched by her maid's interest in her—in her—

What?

Her mind stumbled, and her bemused smile faded into a pondering frown. Interest in her social exposure? Success? Presence?

Why? To what purpose? Must this attention exist every moment of her life?

Slowly she turned away from the door and walked down the long corridor, her pace slow and measured. This time she scarcely noticed the richly oiled and immaculate wainscotting, the paintings hung between windows out of the sun's fading glare, the carpet runners woven with the Tarkington heraldic device. Vaguely she realized this was a long walk, but it felt right, for it gave her time to gather her wits, to leave behind "silly ponderings that had no meaning or purpose," as her mother often said in exasperation when Jocelyn questioned her on society's unwritten rules.

Somewhere nearby heavy footsteps rang staccato on marble. She heard them as one hears city background sounds and ignores them. Jocelyn's teeth worried her lower lip as her mind slid steadily toward considering what Miss Barnes's interests might be.

Jocelyn turned the corner toward the main staircase and scarcely saw the dust-encrusted boots before she collided with their owner, her downcast head bouncing off a broad chest that smelled of sawdust, sweat, and leather. She stumbled backward. Strong, work-roughened hands caught her bare arms where her shawl slipped down. She found herself staring at those hands.

"I beg your pardon, Miss Maybrey. Are you all right?"

That voice! Deep, solemn, and threaded with an ingrained sincerity. Jocelyn's gaze flew upward to meet soft gray eyes. "What? Oh, my lord! Oh, yes—yes—thank you very much. I was woolgathering, quite my fault. I do apologize, my lord."

"Nonsense, Miss Maybrey. It is for me to apologize." He smiled, and a spark of mischief lit his eyes. The expression transformed his face and took Jocelyn's breath away. His hands slid away from her bare arms, their roughness sending shivers down her spine. "*I* was running. Something I was told from childhood—as I'm certain you were—not to do in the house." He winked at her. "So I do not think you need apologize."

Jocelyn laughed. "You are too kind, sir." Her breathing calmed from that first flush of fear and surprise, though her voice remained high and breathy. There was something about the marquess that fascinated, and her fascination embarrassed her. She stepped away, embarrassed both by her clumsiness and her breathless responses. Firmly she dropped her society mien into place.

"Kind? Scarcely, Miss Maybrey. Or as lately my mother would have it, not at all. But I beg you to excuse me. I have been too long at my work when I specifically promised my lady mother that I wouldn't do this, your first day with us."

"Oh! Please do not rush on my account," she said,

lightly dropping a hand on his arm. "I daresay I would not be ready if I weren't so well managed by my maid!"

"You, too, eh?" An odd expression—both mocking and humorous—twisted his lips.

"I beg your pardon?" she asked. She still had her hand on his arm. The realization flustered her. Her hand fell awkwardly away.

"Nothing. Is the room to your liking? Mary would have it that you'd be enchanted by one of our drafty towers."

"I am! It's wonderful. It has— It has—oh, I don't know. Character, I guess you could say."

He laughed at that, a rich, warming laugh. "Character. Yes, I do believe that is apt."

Emboldened, she added, "It really is quite a romantic room."

He crossed his arms over his chest. "Romantic?" he asked, one eyebrow quirking upward in wry, questioning humor.

In another man the expression would have been sardonic and would have reduced Jocelyn to silence, but she sensed that while his amusement was genuine, it was not mocking.

"A room for dreaming," she clarified, blushing at what her description had implied.

"Ah, and what would Miss Maybrey dream in a tower room? Of knights and shining armor?"

She laughed with him this time. "More like castles and kings," she said.

His humor faded, and a somber mask cast his features into quite another aspect. "There are no kings in my castle. Please excuse me, Miss Maybrey. I must be off," he said pleasantly enough, though with a hint of strained crispness in his voice.

Jocelyn's jaw slackened open. She snapped it up and stared at him, bemused by his sudden change.

"Before I came up the stairs, I believe I saw my sister in

the music room. That's the first door on your left at the foot of the stairs.''

Numb, she thanked the marquess and edged around him to descend the stairs, her head high and her pace measured. Inwardly she quaked, for now she saw he could be as hard as he looked. What could have caused that terrible swift change? She felt as gauche as a country-bred young woman at her first London society function. Worse, she knew he watched her until she rounded the bend in the stairs and looked up at him, standing tall and now strangely formidable at the top of the stairs, his shoulders squared and his hands braced on lean hips as if he expected an argument. Their eyes caught and held, brown versus gray. Quickly Jocelyn tore her gaze away. She lifted her skirts and ran the rest of the way down the stairs.

When she reached the music room door, she paused in her headlong flight and forestalled the footman, who stood ready to open the door. Her hand drifted to the vicinity of her heart—as if that would still its pounding thunder.

Why should the marquess affect her in this giddy manner? Gracious, she was in an odd humor this day. Perhaps as much as a country girl felt gauche at her first city function, so she, a city girl, felt gauche in the country.

How absurd!

Thoughts of absurdity brought a smile to her lips and the color back to her cheeks. Probably the long carriage ride that morning left her more tired than she knew. She should have napped before her dresser arrived. Fatigue was the villain.

She bade the footman open the door.

"There you are, Jocelyn!" Lady Mary exclaimed, jumping up from her seat on the sofa to grab Jocelyn's hand and pull her down to sit beside her. "I was hoping for a comfortable coze before dinner. Mama, I know, will not be down until nearly dinner. She thinks four o'clock unseemly for dinner, but acquiesces for Tarkington's sake. She has

been so agreeable to all he says. It quite has me wondering
if fairies take more than infants, and if changelings come in
all ages!''

Jocelyn laughed. ''More than likely she has favors to ask.
Or merely curries favor for the sake of your coming
wedding.''

''Oh, there would be no need for that. Tarkington
suggested the wedding be here. And the Christmas betrothal
house party!''

''Really? I thought—I mean, all London thought . . .''
She blinked and shook her head. Why was it that everything
she learned of the marquess surprised her? ''Well, that *will*
be meat for the groaning boards of the London gossip
tables! All have been full of curiosity.''

Lady Mary laughed. ''I can well imagine. But in fairness,
Mama thought of asking. She has been worried about
Tarkington, you see, for he's withdrawn since Diana's
death. He rarely laughs, and his smiles don't have that spark
of life or that mischievous humor that lurked in his
expression no matter the gravity of the discussion.''

''Curious,'' Jocelyn murmured softly, remembering his
expression when she met him at the top of the stairs. ''But
if he is still in mourning, why would he suggest this
betrothal house party?''

''Tarkington is no longer in mourning, Jocelyn. That's
not the problem. He *has* let Diana go. It was not easy, I'll
agree; but he came to terms with Diana's death for Anne's
sake. . . . At least, that is what he told me, and I believe
him. Oh, Jocelyn, Anne is the dearest child who delights in
each discovery!'' Lady Mary laughed, though her eyes
glistened with unshed memories. ''I took her with me when
I had my last fitting for my gown. The seamstress let her
play among the baubles.'' She shook her head in rueful
memory. ''Soon she demanded the seamstress put all
manner of odd beads and ribbons on the dress. I had a time
convincing her otherwise! We had to promise to make her

up a dress with a certain blue bead as part of the decoration and miles of trailing ribbon. That is to be her play ball gown, she told me.''

''She sounds incorrigible.''

''She is. But she has not become snide, like so many children do. She merely knows her own mind quite well. Tarkington is awed by her, I believe,'' she mockingly confided, her blue eyes dancing with humor.

''Awed? By his own daughter?''

''Well, he says prior to Diana's death his London activities kept him from home too much. Consequently he's lost track of the time from when she was an infant until now. She's grown without him noticing. When did she stop being an infant in arms? When did she learn to talk? To walk? he says. He's lost a part of his child's life that he can never recover. It is for Anne that he remains at Bayneville, you know. He doesn't want to miss a moment again.''

''Gracious. That sounds rather morbid.''

''Hmm, I suppose, but Anne is such a joy—one wants to be near her. Still, though I do understand, I fear he is making a grave mistake. He was born and bred to take his place in society. I fear he is using Anne merely as an excuse to shun society.''

''The maid who escorted me to my room, she mentioned something about a rocking horse . . . ?'' Jocelyn ventured.

Lady Mary nodded. ''He's building one for her.''

''Building a rocking horse?''

''Yes. And doing much of the work himself.''

''Himself?''

''Tarkington says doing the work himself will give the present more meaning. Making the rocking horse will represent his love for her.'' Lady Mary shook her head. ''I asked him for whom—himself or Anne—but he didn't give me an answer.''

''Probably didn't dare to! And I suppose that accounts for

his work-roughened hands,'' Jocelyn said, then blushed at the admission she'd noticed his hands.

''True! And though I disagree, I do understand a bit of what he's saying. Christmas at Bayneville has always been a marvelous and very special time. For everyone.''

''How do you mean?''

Lady Mary smiled. ''The house is a beehive of activity. For two days before Christmas, the smells of baking sweetcakes and breads permeate the kitchens.'' Her voice increased its speed and enthusiasm. ''Throughout the house everything is dusted and shined. The day before Christmas a yule log is chosen, and pine, boxwood, holly, and ivy are gathered for garlands to lavishly decorate the house. Afterward, mistletoe is gathered by footmen and—with giggling help from the maids—is hung from kissing boughs throughout the castle. With the advent of night, candles are lit everywhere until the house is a blaze of light as brilliant and warm as the sun.'' She paused and shook her head as she considered the work involved. ''They shall probably prepare the entire estate for the holiday better than they do for my wedding! Of course, I cannot say I blame them. Last year Christmas at Bayneville was bleak. Mama and I were here, and every time one or the other of us would do something that Diana normally did, everyone would burst into tears. Not even our traditional gift line brought laughter.''

''Gift line?''

Lady Mary enthusiastically nodded, her color high. ''On Christmas Eve the servants gather and we give them two presents each. The first is useful, like a new pair of boots or a shawl. The second is always fanciful or funny, and the household rings with merry laughter when those are passed out.''

''What an enchanting tradition!''

Lady Mary sneezed as she nodded. ''Excuse me. . . . It is, isn't it?'' she said, her eyes watering. ''My grandmother began the tradition. She was the tiniest of creatures, but she possessed the heart of a lion.'' Sneezing again, she dabbed at her nose with her handkerchief.

"Gracious, Lady Mary, don't say you're becoming sick! It only wants days until Lord Killingham arrives!''

"No, no. . . . It's nothing—a trifle.''

"Perhaps, my dear, but one can't be too careful,'' Lady Maybrey said gravely.

Jocelyn and Lady Mary turned to see Lady Maybrey in the doorway followed by Lady Tarkington.

"What is this? Is my Mary ill?'' Lady Tarkington's naturally high voice shrilled with concern.

Lady Maybrey's skirts softly rustled as she crossed the room. She stopped in front of Lady Mary and laid a cool wrist against her brow. "My dear, this is no trifle. Your brow is warm and damp from fever!''

"No . . . I can't be. . . . I tell you I'm all right!'' Lady Mary pulled away, panicked denial in her voice and face.

"Oh, you are! You are ill!'' shrilled Lady Tarkington, coming up by her daughter and repeating Lady Maybrey's actions.

"Oh, Mama,'' Lady Mary protested. She sniffled, then straightened to bestow her sunniest smile upon her mother. "It's nothing,'' she insisted again until her body betrayed her with an involuntary shiver.

"No!''

The harsh, single word startled the ladies. They turned to see the marquess standing rigidly while myriad emotions chased across his face.

"Tarkington!'' exclaimed his mother.

He spun away from them to shout at footmen in the hall: "Joseph! Fetch Dr. Linden. Matthew, tell Lady Mary's maid to turn down her bed!'' He turned back to the room and crossed to the couch. Unceremoniously he picked up Lady Mary, holding her high against his chest.

"Tarkington! Put me down!" She squirmed in her brother's arms.

Looking at Tarkington's clenched jaw, Jocelyn knew he wasn't going to listen to his sister. Swiftly she gathered up Lady Mary's shawl from where it had fallen on the floor and ran ahead of the marquess to open the music room door wider.

Lady Mary began weeping softly, muttering denial. Jocelyn followed the marquess and her friend as far as the stairs. From the base of the staircase she watched him carry her upstairs. Lady Tarkington followed behind, calling out further instructions to the servants as she went.

Lady Maybrey came up behind Jocelyn and laid her hand on her shoulder. Jocelyn turned her head to look at her mother and smile wryly. "I am beginning to feel this will be one very long day."

Thirty minutes passed. The butler had supplied Jocelyn and Lady Maybrey with sherry and had informed them in solemn tones that dinner would be set back an hour. They heard a flurry of activity when the doctor arrived; otherwise silence ensued, leaving them with only each other's company. For a time they exchanged prosaic remarks on the house and Lady Mary's illness. Still, time crawled, and Jocelyn paced the room like a caged animal. Finally she stopped at the beautiful gold-inlaid white harpsichord and let her fingers idly play over the keys, listening to the rich, unique, bell-like pinging sound. She sat down on the bench before the instrument, and her left hand joined her right in chords to accompany simple melodies, then to intricate patterns, and finally to songs. She sang softly, her eyes drifting shut as she allowed the music to fill her soul.

Lady Maybrey leaned back against a nest of pillows on the sofa. "I'd almost forgotten how well you play the harpsichord," she said when the last note of a song faded away. "You haven't played the instrument in months!"

Jocelyn shrugged slightly, a soft, almost sad smile on her lips. "When has there been time? We have been so busy the last months, I scarcely have time for myself. And, too, the time I have devoted to my music has been spent practicing the pianoforte for some soiree or another, learning songs others can sing as well." She sighed. "The harpsichord is not as favored an instrument as it was in the past. Reminiscent of hooped skirts and heavy brocades, I think. It is, you must admit, Mother, considered old-fashioned and therefore boring in the *bon ton*."

"And, of course, one must accommodate the *ton*," the marquess said from the doorway, his voice a deep, mocking drawl.

"Well, naturally."

"Why?"

"Why? I'm afraid I don't understand."

"Jocelyn, the marquess is teasing you!" Lady Maybrey said with a laugh.

"Am I?"

"Of course you are! Now come and sit down and tell us of Lady Mary. What has the doctor to say?"

He raised an eyebrow at her sweeping summation of his action but did as she requested. "He believes it to be just a grippe that will pass in a few days if Mary remains in bed and takes the medicine he prescribes." He turned toward Jocelyn. "I'm afraid, Miss Maybrey, that this shall put a damper on your visit. I apologize. We shall try to compensate."

"Please, there is no need. I find Bayneville so fascinating that I vow I shall be well occupied in exploring your marvelous estate. That is, if I may?"

"Of course, Miss Maybrey. You are most welcome. And should you desire to ride, I shall arrange a horse for you and one of my grooms to accompany you."

"That will not be necessary, my lord. I am a city-bred girl

and not given to riding. However, I should be grateful of a pony cart if there is one available.''

"Yes, of course. I have one that we take Lady Anne about in.''

"Well, then, perhaps Lady Anne and I could go about together!''

"As you wish.'' He looked at her quizzically.

"Dinner is served, my lord.''

"Ah, about time. I'm certain you ladies must be famished.'' He rose and offered Lady Maybrey his arm.

"No, though we thank you for your concern. We are actually accustomed to eating much later,'' Lady Maybrey answered.

He nodded wryly. "My mistake. I had forgotten how different London time is kept from the country. We shall begin immediately to accommodate our timetable to that of our London guests.''

Though his words were bland enough, Jocelyn could not help hearing an underscore of mockery. She looked at him curiously as she followed her mother and him out of the room.

Late rising was another London tradition. When Jocelyn rose the next morning, the sun was almost at its zenith. She stretched and yawned, feeling that she'd compensated for the atrociously early start they'd made from London the previous day. She rose from her bed, rang the bell to summon a servant, found her wrapper, opened the drapes, and settled down in a chair by one of the windows where she could look out across land and buildings.

Jocelyn reveled in the openness of the scene cast before her. From the windows of her home in London, and from her boarding school in Bath, all she'd ever seen was a city of stone and brick layered in soot, and perennial dirty fog. Here, though the day was cloudy, the landscape was mantled in a dull silver light—a presage to winter pewter when damp winds would pierce the thickest bundling. But there was a beauty to this scene that the city lacked. These late morning clouds resembled a thick down-filled tick, all warm and cozy.

For all of Bayneville's grandeur, it remained a working estate, not a rich man's toy. White curls of smoke rose from estate buildings, attesting to their usage and utility. She watched two maids carry between them a large wicker basket laden with soiled linens, a young lad in a leather apron sweeping the stone flagway leading to one of the outbuildings, a weather-beaten man in a slouch hat carrying a rake, and an old woman dressed in black carrying a covered basket. Grooms exercised horses, dogs raced across the open ground, and a cat stalked a fat winter wren resting on a low wall. There scarcely could have been more activity in the yard of the busiest London coaching inn.

The knock of the maid at her door roused her from her absorbed interest. "Come in!"

Emmie backed into the room bearing a large tray.

"What's this?"

"Breakfast, miss."

"Breakfast! All this!" Jocelyn exclaimed, waving her hand at the array of covered dishes and pots on the tray.

"Yes, miss. I didn't know what you'd like, so I brought a bit of everything, I did. And as soon as you've eaten, Miss Barnes will be up to dress you, she says."

"How is Lady Mary this morning?"

Emmie shook her head. "Poorly, she is. Up most o' the night, I hear, sneezin' and snifflin'. Wouldn't take no laudanum, nor the medicine the doctor left, until my lord wur called. He made her sure enough. " She shook her head. "My lord, he wur that determined. Fearful lest he lose his sister as he done his wife. But my Lady Mary, she's sleepin' now, her maid says. And what would ya like, miss? Coffee or hot chocolate?"

"Hot chocolate," Jocelyn said slowly, her mind engaged

in considering all the maid said. Then she recalled herself and smiled at the maid. "And thank you, Emmie. I promise I shall not inconvenience you again in this manner. All this food, and the size of that tray!"

"No bother, miss. 'Tis a blessed change it is to see visitors again at Bayneville, y'know. And my lord said to let ya sleep late after yur travels yesterday."

"What time is breakfast normally served, Emmie?"

"Nine, miss."

"Nine!" Jocelyn burst out, then laughed. "I see this is another difference with which I shall have to accustom myself between the city and country. At home I seldom rise from my bed before nine. No one does."

"I've heard tales, miss."

Jocelyn laughed again. "I'm sure you have. Only don't believe half of it," she said, winking. "Mmm, this chocolate is delicious. I'd been noticing before you arrived how busy the estate is," she said, glancing back out the window.

Emmie laughed. "We're not busy, miss. 'Tis winter. Not like it be in summer—or at harvest! Lud, miss, it's an anthill, we are. But pardon, miss, I shouldn't be standin' jawin' with ya like this."

"Why not? I enjoy it. And with Lady Mary ill I must take my enjoyment where I can. Or shall you be missed belowstairs?"

"No, miss, that I won't be. Until t'other guests arrive, I'm assigned to ya."

"Splendid! Can you tell me more of the estate? As I shall be left to my own devices until Lady Mary recovers, is there anything I should particularly see?"

"Oh, yes, miss!" Emmie said, her eyes gleaming. "The boxwood and yew garden. 'Tis most amazin' the shapes the gardeners cut everything. 'Tis artists they are to be sure as well as good gardeners. In their glass gardens—greenhouses they call 'em—they grow flowers and fruit in winter! And visit our chapel, beautiful it be with paintings and carvings—for all of us, my lord says. Reverend and Mrs. Stemple live in the whitewashed cottage just on the far side of the chapel. Happy they'd be to show it to ya, I'm thinking.''

Jocelyn laughed. ''I've met few men of the cloth who didn't want to share their church with guests. I think that is an excellent idea. Thank you, Emmie.''

Emmie blushed scarlet, so she busied herself straightening the room in order to hide her pleasure.

Two hours passed before Jocelyn had an opportunity to leave her room. After Emmie removed the breakfast dishes, Miss Barnes descended upon Jocelyn like the headmistress of a boarding school upon a new midyear student whose parent was a wealthy, influential peer. Not even for London entertainments was Miss Barnes ever so exact and demanding of her mistress. When she learned of Jocelyn's plan to explore the estate, she outfitted her in a red-and-white-striped moire walking dress with a red pelisse trimmed in swansdown and insisted she wear her red kid half boots and gloves. Jocelyn's protests that the outfit was not conducive to brisk walking fell upon deaf ears. No lady should ever walk briskly, Miss Barnes told her. Jocelyn wondered why she'd never noticed Miss Barnes's managing manner before. She did not protest, for she was not certain the woman was wrong. A relaxation of standards between city and country could, Jocelyn supposed, have detrimental effects on the impressions of others. That would not do. And she had yet to meet Mrs. Bayne, Charles's mother. She did not know why, but she was not eager to meet Mrs. Bayne. No one ever spoke badly of the woman. Then again, no one ever spoke well, either. Charles's own attitude confused Jocelyn. He rarely came to Bayneville to visit and when he came, he kept his visits brief. And she knew he had no intention to remain at Bayneville long past Christmas Day while she was to remain another week. Was his reluctance aimed at his mother or his cousin? After meeting Tarkington she could not see how he could discommode Charles.

If she were to become engaged to Charles—as everyone supposed would be a result of her visit at Bayneville—then it was best she do nothing that might give her future mother-in-law, or Tarkington as head of the family, a distaste of her. She must remain worthy of Charles; after all, he was destined for great notice and deeds in government, and he was—as her mother mentioned—Tarkington's heir.

Now, why should that last thought depress her?

Sedately she descended the house's rear terrace steps to the courtyard that separated the Bayneville outbuildings from the main house. Asking a young groom to point her in the direction of the topiary garden, she sauntered in that direction, her enthusiasm for exploring dimmed by etiquette and society rules. She felt hemmed in and constrained. While she realized her circumstances were no different than she experienced in London, she felt ill at ease. She hoped the cold, brisk December air would blow through her beleaguered mind and bring respite.

How odd, she mused, her lips curving up into a gentle smile. Even before she arrived at Bayneville she'd been looking for it to offer some medicine, some remedy for her jumbled thoughts.

The sounds of a child's laughter drew her eyes up. There, not ten feet away, crouched the marquess behind an intricately molded bush resembling some exotic bird. She almost spoke, but a quick wave of his hand and conspiratorial wink silenced her. She smiled and audaciously winked in return before continuing forward, this time pretending to examine the bushes in great detail.

"I'm coming, Papa!" rang out a high, young voice from behind a baby elephant-shaped bush. The voice was followed by the appearance of a little girl with large brown eyes and thick, wavy brown hair falling free of its ribbon and threatening to hide her tiny heart-shaped face. A bonnet hanging by its neck ribbon bounced on her back as she ran.

She and Jocelyn both stopped and stared at each other, solemnly considering. The little girl popped a thumb in her mouth, her fingers curling around her nose as she stared at Jocelyn. Then the child dropped her hand to her side and smiled. "Hello. What's your name?"

Jocelyn's smile answered the child's. "Jocelyn Maybrey."

"I'm Anne," the child said forthrightly. "Have you seen Papa?"

Jocelyn squatted down by the child, pulling the bonnet back into place and retying its ribbon. "Well, I don't know. I might. What kind of animal is a papa?"

Gales of childish giggles burst out of the little girl. She fell backward on the ground, rolling from side to side.

"Oh, please. Mustn't do that or you'll get sick like your aunt Lady Mary." She pulled her up and brushed the loose grass and leaves from her dark blue coat.

"No, I won't. You're silly."

"I am? Now, why would you say that?"

"Papa's not a'mal."

"He's not! Well, tell me what he looks like, then."

"He's bigger than that," she said, pointing to the parrot-shaped bird. "And strong, and my papa knows everything! My papa's a *mar-kiss*!"

"Well, he certainly sounds like an interesting person. You shall have to introduce us."

The little girl nodded, her thumb disappearing again into her mouth.

"So, are you playing hide-and-seek with your papa? Shall we look for him together?"

The child nodded again, a grin breaking out from around the thumb stuck in her mouth. Shyly she offered her free hand to Jocelyn. Together they circled a bush cut to resemble a giraffe, then Jocelyn led her new companion toward the parrot-shaped bush. She encouraged Lady Anne to go before her around the bush.

"No. Not here!" Lady Anne declared, then ran back to grab Jocelyn's hand to pull her toward another bush.

"Not here? But—" She pulled away from the child to peek around the bush herself. There was no marquess. In confusion she quickly looked around to see if there were other parrot-shaped bushes about. There were none.

"Come on!" encouraged Lady Anne, pulling on Jocelyn's skirt.

"I'm coming," Jocelyn told her, hurrying forward and cursing the stiffness of her skirts that made quick movements feel like running in sand.

Lady Anne scampered on toward the lion-shaped bush. "Papa! Papa! I got a new friend, Papa! Come see!"

Jocelyn followed, wondering if the child could get lost. "Lady Anne! Wait for me!"

Too quickly the child disappeared from view.

"Lady Anne! Lady Anne!" Jocelyn called, panic seeping into her voice. She lifted her skirts above her ankles to quicken her pace. "Lady Anne!" she called out again as she searched behind pyramids and circled other animals. "Lady Anne!"

"Are you looking for us?" inquired a low voice colored with laughter.

Jocelyn whirled about, her breath catching painfully in her chest. Behind her stood Tarkington with Lady Anne in his arms. The little girl had one arm looped around her father's neck, while the other was clamped over her mouth as she tried to stifle her giggles. Jocelyn sagged backward against a bush in relief, only to jerk upright at the feel of sharply cut branches piercing her back.

"Don't do that!" she admonished, frowning at them. She rubbed a spot on her shoulder that had received a particularly sharp poke from the branches.

"Do what? Don't you like playing hide-and-seek?" the marquess teased, his eyes laughing.

"I do, but it's not fair to put me in the game when I don't know the playing field," she returned sharply.

Tarkington laughed, and Jocelyn was again struck by the thought that this was not the gentleman Lady Mary had described. Her fascination grew.

"Well, my lady," he said, addressing his daughter, "shall we show Miss Maybrey about our garden playground?"

Lady Anne nodded. She pushed away from her father's shoulder and squirmed. "Down. Down, please."

When she was on the ground, she trotted off on sturdy little legs to another sculpted bush and turned to wait for the adults to follow.

"You joined in the game quite readily. For my daughter's sake, I thank you."

Jocelyn glanced up at Tarkington's suddenly solemn face, surprised by his comment. "Why? I enjoyed myself. At least until Lady Anne disappeared from sight. I was afraid lest she come to harm. I haven't any experience with very young children, you see, so I do not know their capabilities, let alone what I should do or say to them. My experience has been limited to those I've seen in the London parks with their nursemaids and governesses."

Tarkington looked about to speak, but a shrill "Come on, Papa!" interrupted him.

"We're coming right now," he called out to her, then offered his arm to Jocelyn. "You surprise me, Miss Maybrey," he said as they approached Lady Anne.

"In what manner, my lord?"

"Where are your languid manners? Your ennui?"

Jocelyn laughed. "I fear it is too cold and brisk out here for that. Much more fitting for hot weather or overly warm and stuffy ballrooms. Besides, I must confess I do not have the constitution to be, nor the appearance for, a hothouse flower.''

''I cannot say regarding your constitution, but I believe you do yourself a disservice regarding your appearance, Miss Maybrey,'' Tarkington said solemnly, then dropped her arm as thirty pounds of petticoats and little girl hurled themselves into his arms. ''What's this, now?''

''You're too slow, Papa. Let's show the lady—''

''Miss Maybrey.''

''Miss *May-brey,*'' Lady Anne dutifully repeated, drawing out the syllables. ''Let's show her the fox and rabbit!''

''Fox and rabbit?''

Tarkington laughed. ''More sculpted bushes, Miss Maybrey.''

''I can see why the guidebooks say not to miss your topiary garden! What clever people you have!'' she exclaimed as she walked around and examined a scene of a rabbit running for a hole in the hedge to escape the fox.

''Not me. The estate. I merely inherited them. Allow us to show you another. . . .''

The next hour was one of the most enjoyable hours Jocelyn thought she'd ever spent. She was enchanted by the vast artistry of the garden, by Lady Anne and her childish delight, and by the marquess for his humor, sensitivity, and obvious love for his daughter. The last brought a tight lump in her throat, which she had to swallow hard to dispel, and surreptitiously she wiped away tears of happiness at seeing and appreciating their joy.

She never imagined a father and daughter could be so close. She had always considered her own father loving, but never in her memory had he ever taken the time to play with her when she was very young, as Tarkington did with his daughter. What astonished her was his enjoyment of his daughter. He did not begrudge her his time or find any question she asked too trivial to be answered. He almost seemed disappointed when she yawned and he realized it was time for her nap. Jocelyn accompanied them back to the house, found herself agreeing to a pony cart outing for the next morning, and parted with them at the staircase that led to the nursery wing. Tarkington even intended to see his daughter to bed!

Jocelyn wandered toward the front of the house where a footman took her outdoor garments and told her where she could find Lady Tarkington and her mother.

"Ah, Jocelyn, there you are!" exclaimed Lady Maybrey. "I was told over an hour ago that you went outside. What have you been doing all this time?"

"Lady Anne and Lord Tarkington graciously gave me a personal tour of the topiary garden. I must say, Mother, it is every bit as wonderful as the guidebook said."

"It is unusual, isn't it?" Lady Tarkington said. "We have been most fortunate in Edwin, who is in charge of that garden."

"But how is Lady Mary? The maid, Emmie, said she had a poor night last night."

"Jocelyn, do not tell me you have been gossiping with servants!" Lady Maybrey exclaimed. She grimaced at her daughter and glanced quickly in Lady Tarkington's direction.

"One may always trust a servant to know everything," Jocelyn said. "Besides, I like Emmie. She is very good."

Lady Tarkington smiled. "She is young, but she tries very hard. I hear from Mrs. Penneybacker that it is her desire to rise to the position of housekeeper. So refreshing to see aspirations and willingness to work. Or perhaps I am just jaded by the sullenness of my London servants. But as for Mary, I'm afraid Emmie was correct. She did not pass a good night, but she is sleeping now. Perhaps before dinner you may visit her. I'm sorry, my dear, that you must be so at loose ends."

"That is quite all right, Lady Tarkington. I have not been bored. I was wondering, however, if I might spend some time practicing the harpsichord. I rarely have the opportunity to play it anymore.''

''Of course, my dear! And I shall see you have refreshments sent in to you.''

Two hours later Jocelyn came out of the music room, tired but exhilarated. She met Lady Tarkington in the Great Hall. The dowager marchioness wore an expression of chagrin as she stood indecisively, gnawing on one fingertip.

''Is there anything the matter, Lady Tarkington? May I help?''

''No, I don't think so, my dear. It's that blasted woman. . . . Oh, dear, I did not mean that, of course. Only . . .''

''Yes?'' Jocelyn prodded, intrigued. Guiltily she looked about for her mother. Lady Maybrey would frown and scold if she heard her curiosity.

''Clarice Bayne sent round a note saying she'd join us for dinner at five, only I've ordered Cook to set back dinner to seven, more in keeping with London hours, and I told Tarkington he would not be required until six-thirty. I completely forgot, what with Mary's illness and plans for our coming guests, that she would of course want to meet you! It only wants three now, so I suppose I can tell Cook of the new arrangements and still enjoy a passable dinner, but it is Tarkington I am concerned with. If he is not present, she shall take it personally, you know.''

''No, I'm afraid I don't.''

Lady Tarkington blushed and looked guiltier yet. She grabbed Jocelyn's wrist. ''Oh, I beg your pardon, my dear. That was ill done of me. I swear Mary's illness has made a dreadful shatterbrain of me. Pay no attention to my rambling.''

''No, please, Lady Tarkington. Don't you think it is only fair that I be forewarned, if forewarning is needed?''

''Yes. No. Oh, I don't know. It is sometimes so dreadfully difficult to avoid offense. Clarice Bayne is—well, different. She can be a difficult woman,'' Lady Tarkington said slowly, carefully watching Jocelyn's face for her reaction. ''She has not been pleased we are having a house party here for the holidays. Unseemly, she calls it. Christmas, she believes, is for pious, solemn observance. A time for meditation and prayer. Sometimes I do believe she would be happier in a convent,'' she finished morosely with a sigh. ''She and Tarkington do not get along. Not that they argue, mind you. He tries as best he may to ignore her. That includes avoiding her company. Well, her own son does that,'' she said righteously.

''Even as he encouraged me to come early, I thought Mr. Bayne's excuses to delay his arrival were spurious,'' Jocelyn said wryly.

Lady Tarkington nodded, the tight curls that framed her face bouncing with the movement.

''And, if I understand you correctly, it would be best for peace withal for Tarkington to be here,'' Jocelyn said.

''That's it exactly.''

''Where is he? Is he at the carpenter's?''

Lady Tarkington looked up at her in surprise. ''How did you know that?''

Jocelyn grinned. ''Servant gossip, of course.''

Lady Tarkington clucked her tongue.

''Why don't you go handle the cook to see that dinner is ready on time, or at least by five-thirty. I am in need of some exercise after sitting for two hours, so I will endeavor to tell the marquess of the change in dinner plans,'' Jocelyn offered.

''Oh, would you, my dear? I would be ever so grateful. Under the circumstances, knowing what his reaction is liable to be, I am loath to send a footman. As you said, servant gossip. Clarice Bayne is particularly attuned to it. I swear she has spies in this household.''

Jocelyn laughed and winked. ''Don't worry. We shall thwart her this time.''

* * *

Jocelyn tried to peer through the diamond-shaped panes of grimy, slightly green glass set in the old oak door of the carpenter's workshop. From inside she heard an odd rhythmic sound, something like *clip-clatter, clip-clatter, clip-clatter*. She knocked on the door and waited, but there was no response, no cessation of the strange noise. She pushed down on the latch, and the door opened smoothly with nary a squeal or screech from its old hinges. Tentatively she poked her head in the doorway.

"My lord? My lord Tarkington?"

Across the room she could see the marquess standing before a strange-looking device. His foot worked a treadle on the floor that was connected to belts and wheels to two iron pins which held a piece of wood between each tip. The wood spun around. Beside him stood a squat man with large square hands. Dust obscured the glasses on his red nose, so he looked over them in order to observe the marquess's progress.

"Easy, my lord. Not too much pressure. . . . Let it slide easily. . . . Yes, that's it, my lord. Very good!"

A gust of wind came in through the open door, swirling sawdust into the air. The marquess's eyes flickered upward. "Kindly close the door, Miss Maybrey. I am creating enough of this confounded dust without your stirring up more."

Jocelyn blushed bright red but hurried to do as he requested. Then she came farther into the workshop to see what the marquess was doing, her eyes darting about, taking in the unpainted carved horse lacking a tail, mane, rockers, and handle. It leaned against a wall, out of the way, a small rug tossed over its back, to protect it, Jocelyn presumed. Two rockers, shaped and sanded, were also propped against the wall. A pile of multicolored horse hair—likely culled from the tails and manes of estate horses—lay on a nearby table. Hanging from a peg on the wall was a small leather bridle and two small stirrups with leather straps attached.

To her amazement Jocelyn realized the truth. The marquess *was* making a rocking horse for his daughter—and doing the work himself, not overseeing it. Somehow, though she'd been told he was doing the work, the idea of his total involvement had never penetrated her understanding. She'd never known any nobleman to labor in this manner.

She stood agog. She was delighted!

It appeared that Tarkington now worked on the handle destined to be inserted in the horse's head.

"So what brings Miss Maybrey to a carpenter's workshop? Are you slumming, Miss Maybrey, or did you have some purpose?"

His caustic tone distressed Jocelyn for a moment. She'd not thought that to be his normal manner. Perhaps he just did not care to be caught at his manual labor? Or had she disturbed his concentration?

"My lord, the countess wishes you to know that Mrs. Bayne is joining us for dinner."

"Bound to happen."

"At five o'clock."

"Five!" The device faltered in its rhythm. "But it wants but four now!"

"Careful, my lord!" implored the carpenter.

The marquess released the treadle, stopped the lathe from turning, and stepped back. "No. I cannot do more." He scowled at the wood, though Jocelyn knew his scowl was more for the information she gave.

"It is my fault."

Tarkington looked up. "How do you deuce that?"

Jocelyn colored again. "It is because of Mr. Bayne's interest. I presume I'm to be examined like a horse at a fair: good teeth, sound of limb, no sway back or jarring paces."

The marquess laughed loudly, which brought out the light

Jocelyn had come to look for in his eyes. "For someone who does not ride much herself, you have an understanding of the nature of horses."

She shrugged. "I'm a good listener."

He studied her a moment. "Yes," he said slowly, "I believe you would be. . . . But, Miss Maybrey," he continued in a brusk fashion, "I shall never be able to finish this rocking horse before Christmas if I am continually interrupted!"

Jocelyn cocked her head. "Why not? From what I've seen, you have enough craftsmen. Together could they not make the toy in a day?"

Tarkington turned away, the set of his shoulders speaking eloquently of his disappointment in her response. Jocelyn clasped her hands together, not clearly understanding what she said that again had him turning from her in a cold manner.

"Why can I not make my family, my peers, understand? What have we as a society become? A clamor of vain fribbles that must have everything done for us? Can we not enjoy laboring for others? Or is this some damned sin against society?" he railed.

"I beg your pardon, my lord?" Too late Jocelyn heard the shrill self-righteousness in her own voice.

The marquess's face became still and coldly empty of expression. She might as well have just received a direct cut at the most fashionable social event of the season. It was as if the coldest winter wind had blown through the small carpenter's workshop. Jocelyn hugged her arms tightly against her body to ward off the chill. Nevertheless it seeped into her heart and lay there like ice on a lake, growing, threatening to cover all.

She turned quickly to grab the door latch, her eyes blurring too much to see clearly. A sob caught in her throat. She swallowed hard, determined to hide her distress. Please let him believe it anger!

She yanked the door open to escape, but the marquess was faster than she. He caught her arm, halting her flight on the flagstone steps outside the workshop.

"Please, my lord!" She kept her head averted as she twisted her hand within his grasp, struggling to get free.

He pulled her toward him, anchoring her arm against his side, then with his free hand he grabbed her chin and forced her to turn toward him. He looked down at her tear-streaked cheeks, and his own expression twisted, cracking free of that cold stillness to reveal remorse. "I have made you cry," he said softly. "I forget too easily."

Jocelyn did not like him staring down at her like that. She was not comfortable with his nearness or the rapid pulse that throbbed in her neck. She searched her mind for some way to break the odd spell that surrounded them, to return each to their place. Another gust of wind blew one of her bonnet ribbons across her cheek. As she pushed it aside with her free hand, she realized the marquess had come after her without his coat.

"My lord! Your coat!"

"Damn the coat!"

"But you could take a chill!"

"Perhaps that would be fitting punishment for my insensitivity, Miss Maybrey," the marquess said wryly, letting go of her arm.

Jocelyn stepped back. "Oh, no, my lord!"

"Miss Maybrey, I warn you, do not toady! Rank is no excuse for bad manners. Do not excuse it on that basis."

"It is merely, my lord, that I am confused. All the years a young girl is growing up at home she is taught by her parents about society without experience of the actuality. Then when one goes to school, other more stringent society rules are taught."

"By old maids who have only observed from the chaperon couches at the closest—some not even that close."

"Yes, my lord, and my own heretofore limited experience in the city has not taught me differently. But you—I beg your pardon, my lord, but you do not act as I have been taught or have observed a member of society to act. I freely confess I am fascinated by this difference. I'm not certain why.''

The marquess laughed and tucked Jocelyn's arm in his as he led her across the courtyard toward the manor house. ''I believe I begin to see what attracted my cousin to you, Miss Maybrey. You are a delightful mixture of honesty and naïveté that is refreshing. For all the inculcation you have received, how is it you are not jaded and full of ennui?''

''I'm not certain I understand your direction, my lord. However, my mother says one of my most besetting faults is my curiosity.''

''Faults? Nay, Miss Maybrey. I should call that one of your most shining traits. Next you shall be telling me she disapproves of your sensitivity toward others.''

''She does say I am too soft-hearted.''

''Nonsense, and you may tell your mother a marquess said so.'' He winked at her. ''That is bound to get blessings.''

Jocelyn laughed.

At the house she parted from the marquess with a curious sense of regret and hurried to her room, where Miss Barnes awaited.

''Enough! Enough! I swear if you twitch another fold into place, straighten another bow, or pat another curl, I shall scream! My toilet is complete. You have—as always— outdone yourself, Miss Barnes,'' Jocelyn told the woman with laughing exasperation as she attempted to edge toward the door. ''I must go. I wish to visit with Lady Mary before going downstairs, and I don't have much time.''

''But you would allow me no time!''

''Nonetheless, you rose to the challenge. I thank you,''

she assured the woman before closing the door and hurrying down the hall.

A light tap on Lady Mary's door was greeted by a cheerful croaking. A maid answered the door and showed her inside.

"Jocelyn! I despaired of seeing you today!"

"Every time I asked someone of your condition, I was told you were sleeping."

"Sleeping! As thick as my head feels? Not bloody likely! What we have, my friend, is a conspiracy."

"A loving conspiracy, I'll venture."

Lady Mary waved her hand in offhand agreement, the handkerchief she clenched fluttering with the movement. "To be sure. And I will admit I did sleep some today. Especially after old Mrs. Morrison—the estate herbalist and midwife—prepared an infusion of boiling water and herbs that she had me inhale. Whatever it was, it eased my breathing."

Jocelyn sat on the edge of the bed. "Now you must concentrate on getting better. Don't think of anything else, and do take the medications you are given."

Lady Mary plucked restlessly at the sheets. "Resting here is difficult to do. The longer I lay here, the more I am filled with remorse that you are left solely to my brother's less than cheerful company."

"Nonsense. The marquess and I have dealt admirably together. Tomorrow I might even ask if I may help with the rocking horse. . . . No, the person I fear most is Mrs. Bayne. Have you heard she *announced* she would be coming to dinner tonight?"

"She is known for that. I often wonder if her actions are deliberate or blindly inconsiderate, as we've always assumed."

"In the interest of not burning my boats *à la Caesar,* I'd best keep my visit to you brief and go downstairs to meet her."

Lady Mary chuckled. "'Tis a wise woman you are, Miss Maybrey."

"Sometimes I wonder," Jocelyn said as she rose from the bed and said goodbye.

She could not seem to shake the image of Tarkington from her mind. Why should his sister bear such an unflattering impression of him? Jocelyn saw little in his behavior that she would deem symptoms of melancholy. Quite the contrary! There was a reserve to the gentleman, which was to be expected around a stranger and one who was his younger sister's friend. He probably did not consider Lady Mary an adult. That was obvious by his behavior when she was discovered ill! Was it any wonder he should treat his sister's friend in a similar manner? But he was not always reserved—she found herself often thinking of the time spent in the topiary garden with Tarkington and Lady Anne.

But was it wise or politic to spend one's time considering the marquess? Such tenacious thoughts as she seemed to possess worried her. She did not understand the interest the marquess roused in her, or the way a curious fluttering invaded her stomach when he was nearby, causing her to talk and act like a veritable ninnyhammer! She allowed she was touched by his love and concern for his daughter, but that would not solely answer for the feelings she had long before she met Lady Anne or came to know of Tarkington's devotion to his daughter.

It was delightful to watch him and the child together. He was truly a man who deserved a large family. A houseful of children! Well, the estate certainly had the space and resources. It would be tragic should he not remarry and father additional children. Perhaps that was disloyal to Charles, but quite frankly Jocelyn could not imagine Charles as a marquess. He had not the essence—whatever that was—of a marquess. The fine spirit, the oneness with one's land and people. Tarkington possessed those qualities, but Charles was too much the city man. Bayneville needed and deserved attention, more attention than a political and social gentleman like Charles was bound to give.

But didn't Lady Mary claim that Tarkington once possessed the same attributes that Charles had? And didn't she lament their disappearance?

Jocelyn was confused. Through it all, nonetheless, one thing was becoming manifest for her. She must decide what life she preferred, for she'd just discovered there were alternatives to her parents' and Charles' life!

That idea shook her. It frightened her. It made her realize she knew nothing of life. It made her realize she had choices in life. And it made her determined to learn.

"Miss Maybrey, you look in a brown study. Is something the matter?"

Jocelyn looked up, her frown easing into a weary smile. "I beg your pardon, my lord. I was away a bit with my thoughts. Please forgive me."

Tarkington walked toward her. "There is nothing to forgive, Miss Maybrey. We are all at times given to private thought. No, I was merely concerned lest you have some fear or problem."

Jocelyn laughed. "What young woman does not? Or think she does not?"

"Touché, but I would have thought that a gentleman's line regarding a woman."

"And why is that, my lord? Do you not think a woman capable of self-examination?"

Tarkington laughed. "Acquit me, Miss Maybrey. Mine was more a cynicism against gentlemen. But there is much to say of the way a woman bursts into flames at the least crossing." They began to walk together down the hall toward the main stairs.

"I shall cry craven at that, my lord, for you have me."

"A man could only wish, Miss Maybrey."

"I beg your pardon, my lord?"

"Nothing. More of my cynicism. A blight upon my being, or so Mary tells me."

"Nonsense! What can be seen as wrong in plain speech?"

"Much. You have a great deal to learn, my dear, for all your grave nature."

"Grave?"

"We had best join the others before Aunt Bayne takes it upon herself to look for us."

"Yes. But a moment, my lord. I have a boon to ask of you. I know you are set upon making the rocking horse entirely by yourself, but I was wondering if you would allow me to assist. I have some measure of talent with a paintbrush, I am told, and I have painted many a piece of furniture with dioramas of historical events that Father wished to preserve. I should like to make that my gift to you and Lady Anne for this Christmas visit. Despite Lady Mary's illness, I am enjoying myself."

"In what way?"

"The peace of the estate. The observation of life. The relaxation of appearance. Oh, I don't know that I can completely explain it to you, my lord. It is merely part of the warm and quite strange feelings I have experienced since being here. This morning I sat in a chair by a window in my room and looked out across your estate. I looked at the land rolling away toward the river, I watched the people coming and going on estate business, I listened to the silence." She sighed, then self-consciously laughed. "I have not had experience with the country, my lord. Perhaps it is merely the novelty."

Tarkington looked at her thoughtfully, then a slow smile pulled on his lips and crept into his gray eyes, burnishing them to a silver gleam. "Perhaps indeed, Miss Maybrey. Perhaps indeed. And asked in that pretty fashion, how might a man refuse? Truly I should relish your talent, should you be serious. Time is short. But come," he said, taking her arm as they descended the stairs. "To your next novelty . . . Mrs. Bayne!"

"Ah, here they are. You see, Clarice? I *told* you they would be here momentarily," Lady Tarkington said brightly. Her expression directed toward Tarkington and Jocelyn was the antithesis of good humor, however. Frustration and anger sparked like steel on flint in her blue eyes. But as quickly as it appeared it disappeared, so that the mien she turned toward her sister-in-law remained determinedly cheery.

Clarice Bayne nodded ponderously. "Tarkington, I was just telling your mother that I do not believe in gossip and I do not care to receive it. In your case, however, I have of late seen that it is more than gossip. It is truth."

"And what is that truth?" Tarkington asked, strolling over to the burl-veneered credenza to pour himself a preprandial drink. He looked inquiringly at Jocelyn. She shook her head.

Mrs. Bayne pulled her wool shawl closer about her gaunt form, then puffed out her narrow chest like a bantam hen. "It is my sorrowing duty to point out to you your mental deterioration. Of late you've lacked the proper understanding of your duties as head of the family."

"Clarice!" gasped Lady Tarkington.

"I'm sorry, Martha, but it must be said—and I hold you responsible for allowing this situation to persist. Tarkington is not the man he was prior to Diana's death."

"And that is to the bad?" Tarkington asked quietly, not looking at her, his attention ostensibly centered on the glass he rolled between his hands.

Lady Maybrey reached out from the small sofa where she sat to grab Jocelyn's hand and pull her down to sit beside her. Jocelyn looked quizzically at her mother. Lady Maybrey shook her head, warning Jocelyn against curiosity.

"It is lamentable, particularly as you have a young

daughter to coach in the ways of society and her proper place in it. This morning I saw you running about the garden with her like a peasant with his child.'' She shook her head sadly. ''Most distressing. You have your station to consider.''

Jocelyn could scarcely countenance what she was hearing, or that the dowager countess and her mother should remain so silent!

''And my station would suffer from giving my child some small moments of laughter?'' Tarkington asked quietly.

''Yes. Such things are cumulative. You *must* realize that, Tarkington. When your people see you without your dignity, they lose respect for you and fail to do their proper duty.''

Tarkington laughed. ''If that were all it took to reduce their opinion, then I'd say their opinions are well past redemption, for I've done more than play in the garden, Aunt Clarice.''

''This levity of yours is unseemly,'' she said severely. ''You are a widower, after all.''

''And I should still be in mourning? If that is your contention, Aunt Clarice, then I will have you know, and be done with it, that I disagree. It is nearly Christmas! This is not the season for morose introspection. But what of you?''

''Me?'' Mrs. Bayne looked up at him, and Jocelyn thought she saw a fleeting expression of hate cross her pinched features.

''Yes. Is it proper, since that is what you think I should be, that you should ignore the guest who entered the room with me, not encouraging an introduction?''

She laughed. '''Twas not necessary. I know who she is. She is the woman my Charles is to marry,'' she said with great complacency.

''I beg your pardon, Mrs. Bayne, but nothing has been

voiced to that effect,'' Jocelyn burst out, thoroughly annoyed with this woman. Lady Maybrey frowned at her.

Mrs. Bayne smiled, her narrow face now condescending in its expression. She nodded toward Lady Maybrey. "A most proper observation, Lady Maybrey. You are to be commended for your daughter's delicacy of spirit. It is regrettable that Charles did not accompany you. My son is a man of great responsibility, else I am certain he would not have let you come here alone. *He* understands responsibility."

Tarkington slammed his glass down on the credenza. "Does he, Aunt Clarice? Does he know what responsibilities a father owes his daughter? Does he know what a landlord owes his tenants? Does he know what it is to have a thousand souls dependent upon him? Does he know what it is to be so consumed with politics that family and estate are forgotten? Does he knew what it is to miss seeing his daughter take her first steps, say her first words? Does he know what it is to arrive at his wife's deathbed only in time to say goodbye? *Does he know what it is to love?''*

"You are overwrought, Tarkington," Mrs. Bayne snapped, all semblance of kind patience flying away. "I suggest a laudanum dose. You are exhibiting proof that you are no longer capable of running this family."

"Ah, I see how it is. You think as Prinny has become regent for his father, so Charles could for me? Perhaps you had rather I be assigned to Bedlam?"

"There is no need for an emotional display, Tarkington. That will be quite enough," Mrs. Bayne declared. "Really, Martha, you are entirely too weak. To allow him to digress to this extent! Have you called in Dr. Linden to consult? Well, I hold myself accountable as well. I should have insisted on removing Lady Anne from his influence as soon as I detected this change in him."

"No!" Jocelyn cried out. She surged to her feet, her body quivering with anger.

Three pairs of eyes swiveled in Jocelyn's direction.

"I have spent time with Lady Anne and Lord Tarkington. Theirs is a loving relationship! That we all should be so fortunate. How much time have you spent with either of them, Mrs. Bayne? You say you do not countenance gossip, yet I perceive it is the gossip *you* are creating that guides you!"

"Jocelyn!" protested Lady Maybrey.

"No, Mother, I shall not be hushed. I understand from all I have seen and heard here that the marquess is not the same man he was prior to his wife's death. He has changed. But not, to my observation, for the worst!"

"Young woman, how dare you speak to me in that manner! I shall have to talk to Charles!"

"Do that!" Jocelyn countered, burning with anger.

"Er, my lord, dinner is served," intoned the butler from the doorway.

"I'm sorry. I find I cannot join you for dinner. I seem to have developed a splitting headache!" Jocelyn said, twirling around to run from the room.

"Miss Maybrey!" the marquess called after her.

She ignored him, fleeing up the stairs and down the long carpeted corridor to her room. She slammed the door closed behind her and collapsed into the chair before the fire, feeling suddenly and inexplicably chilled.

The next morning oppression lay heavily on Jocelyn. Listlessly she allowed Miss Barnes to dress her, voicing no protest when the woman added more jewels to her toilet than was seemly for day attire. She stood like a doll, her mind whirling from her previous evening's idiocy. She wished she could spirit herself back to London, back to the world she understood, to the formal rules, the little plays, the shallowness of communication. It was not a world that required—or even liked—sincerity and love. It was a safer world. She could see that now. With leaden feet she left her room and went downstairs for breakfast. And that was nearly beyond her ability. It was only the knowledge that her mother and Lady Tarkington would still be abed and that Mrs. Bayne would be back at her home that gave her the strength to venture down to possibly face the marquess and her own folly.

To her relief, the breakfast room was empty, one setting already removed with only a trace of a drop of coffee on the white tablecloth to show anyone had sat there. The realization that the marquess had already eaten and left felt like a weight leaving her shoulders. With a lighter heart she filled her plate, for this morning she was sharp-set.

She was finishing a second rasher of ham when she heard a sound behind her. She turned to find large brown eyes looking up at her from under a plain, dark blue bonnet.

"Hurry!"

"Hurry?"

The little head bobbled, and a tiny gloved hand reached for hers. "Papa's getting my pony cart."

"That's nice, Lady Anne, but what—" Then Jocelyn remembered. She had promised to accompany Lady Anne today. But she couldn't. Not now, not after the way she'd made a fool of herself last evening. She wished she had fallen victim to Lady Mary's malady so she could keep to her room until after the holidays and it was time to leave. She could not face Tarkington. What he must think of her! Her cheeks burned in memory.

"Oh, my dear, I can't . . ." Her voice trailed off helplessly as she stared into Lady Anne's guileless young eyes. A promise had been made. Lady Anne was too young to understand casually made and casually broken promises. Jocelyn would not begin her education.

"I forgot to bring down my outdoor garments. I shall have to fetch them first," Jocelyn told the child as she rose from her chair. She would use the time to gather her wits and secure some mask that could see her through the day.

"Emmie brung them."

"Brought them," Jocelyn corrected without thought, then started. "She did?"

Lady Anne's head bobbled again as she pulled Jocelyn out of the breakfast parlor. "See?" She pointed at Emmie standing near one of the pier glasses that flanked the front entrance. Worse, she was speaking with the marquess.

Jocelyn felt her heart descend into her stomach. There would be no reprieve, no chance to order her mind or adopt any mien that could see her through her embarrassment. She stared at him, vulnerable to the slightest look or word.

"Miss Maybrey, you should not have let Anne take you away from your breakfast."

Jocelyn blushed and looked wildly around, searching for inspiration, for the right words to say.

"We would have waited," the marquess finished.

Jocelyn whipped her head back to look at him. He was smiling only slightly, but the expression reached his eyes. She blinked, bemused.

"That's quite all right. I was finished. Really."

The marquess nodded, took her cloak from Emmie, and held it out for her. Numbly Jocelyn walked toward him and allowed him to put her cloak around her. She only woke from her dazed state when it appeared he would take her hat from Emmie as well. The thought of his hands placing her hat on her head and tying the bow under her chin galvanized Jocelyn to action. She dived under his arm to seize the hat first, then turned toward the pier glass to settle it on her head. The marquess stepped away, but through his reflection in the glass Jocelyn saw the odd way he compressed his lips and the light in his eyes glow brighter. He was laughing at her!

"Well, Lady Anne," she said briskly, "shall we go for a ride in your cart?"

"I'm afraid we won't be using the cart," the marquess said as they descended the stone steps before the manor.

"But, Papa!" protested Lady Anne.

"Hush. This is much better. See? I instructed the grooms to harness one of the small estate wagons. How else can we bring home the Christmas greens your grandmother wishes us to gather?"

"You, my lord?" Jocelyn heard herself ask.

Tarkington laughed. "Yes, Miss Maybrey. It seems the house servants are considered to have more important matters to attend to. I, as the most frivolous of the lot, am free for garland and boxwood and mistletoe gathering."

Jocelyn smiled despite herself. "Frivolous, my lord?"

"Decidedly frivolous." He stopped by the wagon. "You first, Miss Maybrey."

"What? Wait—"

The marquess's hands were firm about her waist. He lifted her high as if she weighed no more than Lady Anne. Instinctively her hands grabbed his forearms for security. He set her on the worn padded wagon seat. He would have dropped his hands immediately if it were not for the firm grip Jocelyn maintained. Guiltily, and flushing once again, she released her grip, her hands sliding self-consciously away.

Jocelyn's breath clouded against cold morning air, but inwardly she felt a new glowing warmth almost like banked coals. It was a curious feeling, not altogether unpleasant, though the thought of what might fan those banked coals to flames unsettled her.

Their eyes held a moment longer, then the marquess turned to lift his little daughter for Jocelyn to settle between her and where the marquess would sit on the wagon bench seat. Afterward, Jocelyn's breathing felt tight, as if a band constricted her chest. She turned her attention toward Lady Anne, seeking some solace in the child's bright chatter as the marquess turned the wagon down a trail paralleling the river.

Remnants of the night's frost glistened on the north face of rocks sheltered from the sun's warmth by the tangled briar from summer's berries, clumps of pine, and evergreen shrubbery. Winter wrens flew up before them to settle on branches overhead. Their feathers puffed out against the cold, and they cocked their heads from side to side, their bright dark eyes watching them pass. Once they saw two male wrens fight over a large red berry, so preoccupied with their war they scarcely had time to fly out of the horse's way. Lady Anne laughed at their antics. Her laughter eased the tightness in Jocelyn's chest, and she laughed at the child's delight.

When they crossed a narrow wooden bridge over the river, Jocelyn instinctively clung to the side of the wagon, fearful they'd come to mischief on so narrow a structure. She disliked bridges. They always made her nervous. Once on the other side the marquess stopped the wagon and told her she could relax her grip. She meekly apologized, color rising in her cheeks.

"Do not apologize, Miss Maybrey. It is not necessary. That was a narrow bridge and to one unfamiliar with it or without control of the reins, crossing can seem daunting. I myself do not like others to drive me across. I prefer to be in control on such a structure."

"Thank you, my lord, but I confess I do not like bridges at all. An inexplicable failing of mine, I'm afraid," she said with a shaky laugh and offhanded gesture.

"Miss Maybrey! I wish I had known! There was no need for us to go to the wood across the river for greenery. I merely thought to take you to this wood because of its high vantage point. In my vanity I wished you to see Bayneville from the top of the hill ahead that borders the wood."

"Please, my lord, do not overly concern yourself. I'm fine."

"But will you be fine when I confess there is no way back to Bayneville lest we cross the river again?"

"I gathered that, my lord," she said dryly. "Rivers this wide and deep don't vanish in the next mile or so."

"True, but I can at least ensure that your crossing not be disturbing in quite that manner."

Jocelyn laughed. "Nothing can make a bridge less disturbing."

The marquess smiled as he lifted the reins and urged the estate horse on. "We'll see, Miss Maybrey."

Jocelyn was touched by Tarkington's concern. It was relaxing in a manner she'd never experienced.

"Are we almost there, Papa? Are we almost there?"

The marquess laughed. "Almost, poppet. Beyond that line of spruce is a grove of holly. We'll start there."

Together the three of them cut and gathered the holly, then boxwood and other greenery until the back of their wagon was full.

"What about the mis'toe, Papa?" Lady Anne asked as Tarkington once more boosted her on to the wagon seat.

"We have to go farther for that," he said, picking up the wagon reins.

"I know what mis'toe is for," Lady Anne confided to Jocelyn.

"Oh, you do?" Jocelyn said to the dimpling child.

Lady Anne nodded, then giggled behind her gloved hand. "It's for kissing!"

"My goodness! Are you sure?"

"Don't stand under the mis'toe or you'll get kissed!"

"Well, I shall certainly take your advice. Imagine, being kissed!" she said. Then her eye caught the marquess's tense gaze. All humor left her lips. Unconsciously she licked them. The marquess's eyes narrowed briefly. In confusion Jocelyn blushed and looked away. She was attracted to this man. Dangerously attracted. How foolish! A tingling rose in her chest, catching in her throat and zinging throughout her body in a form of panic she'd never felt before. She was about to be betrothed to his cousin—though perhaps not. Mrs. Bayne would likely do her best to squelch the match. She considered that consequence and knew it wasn't the cause of her panic. She knew the worst last night, though only now would she put the feeling to thought. If she married Charles Bayne, her life would continue in the fashion she'd grown up with. Unfortunately she was beginning to realize she did not want that life for herself: an endless round of parties, of late nights and late risings, of maintaining appearances, of being somewhere just to be seen there, of listening to gossip, of laughing at some ridiculous joke, or clucking one's tongue at another's misfortune. That was her parents' world, and they thrived in it. She now knew that as a child when she'd observed them—from a distance, the way children were meant to—she had enjoyed that distance, that vicarious participation, far more than she'd ever enjoyed its actuality for herself.

This she enjoyed, she thought, looking around her at the pearl-gray skies and the shades of green and brown in the landscape. She enjoyed the slow sway of the wagon as it rumbled down the dirt lane and the birds that flew before them, disgruntled at the intrusion into their feeding grounds. She enjoyed the time to play the harpsichord and the time to merely sit by a fire or a window to think. She realized she even enjoyed the silence of the night without the calls of the night watchman or the rattle of carriages along the pavement, or the drunken bawdy songs of the town bucks as they made their way home after a night carousing on the town.

She was not made as her parents were, and that identification of the uncomfortable itch on her soul eased some of the turmoil in her heart. She smiled.

"Miss Maybrey?"

"I beg your pardon, my lord. I was woolgathering, I'm afraid."

"From a very odd lot of sheep."

"Pardon?"

"Your face, Miss Maybrey. It has run a gamut of emotions. Every time I glanced your way, a different emotion was there. I was so fascinated by the changes I could scarcely keep my attention on driving the cart.''

Jocelyn blinked and blushed. She opened her mouth and closed it several times in succession as she thought of, then quickly discarded, one answer after another. Ultimately she realized there was no direct answer to be given.

''Is something troubling you, Miss Maybrey? Aside from my Aunt Bayne, and I beg you not to let her trouble you. I believe she would try the patience of a saint,'' he said with a soft laugh. ''But leaving that unfortunate situation aside, is there anything wrong? I know this is being forward, but I am concerned.''

She shook her head. ''What troubles me would not halt an ant. It is nothing, my lord. Merely my own silliness. Mother tells me I can be a goose at times.''

''That I do not believe. I think you are far wiser than most. . . . There, Anne, do you see that bunch of green high in the oak tree ahead? That's your mistletoe.''

''Up there? But how do we get it, Papa? It's too high!''

Tarkington laughed. ''I haven't done so in years, but I believe I still can climb a tree.''

''My lord!'' exclaimed Jocelyn.

''Don't you believe I can, Miss Maybrey?''

''Yes, yes, of course you can,'' Jocelyn stammered, ''But what of your clothes?''

He glanced down at his immaculate fawn-colored great-coat. ''Yes, I see your point. Greatcoats are not conducive to climbing.'' He jumped down from the wagon seat, took off his coat, and slung it over the edge of the seat.

''My lord! You'll catch a chill!''

''Devil a'bit, Miss Maybrey. You fuss more than my mother,'' he teased. He reached for Lady Anne. ''Come on, poppet, down you go. . . . I need you to help catch the mistletoe when it falls.'' He set his daughter down and wordlessly held out his hand for Jocelyn.

Jocelyn, flustered by his teasing, tripped over the end of

the lap robe that had fallen to the floorboard. Tarkington caught her by the waist as she stumbled forward. As her color soared higher, the marquess's grin grew broader. Never did he look less like the serious man of Lady Mary's description.

The intimate feel of his hands around her waist ricocheted tingling heat throughout her body. In shock she raised questioning eyes to meet his only to have their gazes lock. Slowly he set her on the ground, but his hands remained at her waist. The air grew thick between them. Jocelyn saw a pulse beat in his neck and knew he was as strangely affected as she. That knowledge calmed her fears, and the tingling heat grew, spreading throughout her body. Her lips parted in wonder at the sensations she felt, at the warmth of the expression in his gray eyes like sunlight reflecting on a still pond. The tips of his fingers pressed against her back to pull her closer while his muscles tensed, his head dipped, and the pulse in his neck quickened.

''Papa, can I climb the tree, too?''

Tarkington's hands dropped from Jocelyn's waist. He crossed to his daughter's side and swung her up in his arms, his expression shuttered and rigid. ''No, poppet,'' he said in a strangled voice. He cleared his throat. ''It's too high a climb for you.''

Jocelyn gasped at the realization that he'd intended to kiss her! Red surged into her cheeks, and she turned away from Tarkington and Lady Anne—ostensibly to look out over the countryside, in reality to hide the myriad emotions she knew to be chasing across her face. Vaguely she was aware of the marquess setting his daughter back down and instructing her where to stand.

The sound of boots scraping against bark as he climbed the tree matched the emotions inside her. *He'd been about to kiss her!* And she'd wanted him to! Never had Mr. Bayne attempted more than to kiss her hand. Nor would she have allowed him further liberties. But she would have allowed Tarkington—would have welcomed them!

She brought a cold gloved hand up against her flaming cheeks. What could have possessed her? She was acting the flirt. Was it because he was a marquess? Was she enamored with his title? She hoped not, for that would not allow her to think well of herself. Was it his widower circumstances? Was it his country lifestyle? She acknowledged she did enjoy the different pace, the truth in nature, and the estate. Was it just some reaction of her disquiet, that curious dissatisfaction she'd felt with London and her season?

Why?

She glanced over her shoulder toward the tall oaks. Tarkington was on a high branch stretching to reach a clump of mistletoe. Jocelyn's heart constricted with fear. She closed her eyes tightly, afraid to see him fall.

"Good, Papa!" cheered Lady Anne, clapping gloved hands together.

Jocelyn opened her eyes to see Lady Anne jumping up and down. She looked up into the tree to see the marquess edging back toward the trunk, a large clump of mistletoe in one hand.

"Miss Maybrey!" he called out as he worked his way down the tree from branch to branch. "Can you come catch this, please? There is a spot here where I shall need both hands."

"Certainly, my lord." She caught the bunch easily with only the loss of a few of its berries. She hurried to place it in the wagon, then clamor onto the seat before he could assist her. She didn't want him to touch her again. She was afraid if he touched her, she'd go up in flames.

Tarkington looked at her, a wry grin kicking up one corner of his lips, but he refrained from comment. He merely shrugged his greatcoat back on and swung Lady Anne up beside Jocelyn.

She didn't know what was wrong with her or how to

control it. She came to Bayneville to celebrate Lady Mary's betrothal and possibly hear a proposal from Charles Bayne. She didn't come to Bayneville to fall in love with the marquess!

A small cry rose up in her throat before she could stop it. *In love!* Where had that come from?

"Is something the matter, Miss Maybrey?"

"What? Oh, no, no, my lord. I just . . . I just had a small twitch in my leg. Reaction to the cold, I'm sure," she babbled against the tight breath in her chest.

"Wrap the lap robe securely around you and Lady Anne. We've gathered enough greenery for this jaunt. If Mother wishes more, she can send the grooms out. Time for some hot chocolate, I should think. What do you say, poppet?"

"Yes, Papa. And can I help dec'rate?"

"What of your nap?"

Lady Anne pouted. "I'm not sleepy. I'm too big for naps."

"Too big? And here I was thinking of napping this afternoon. Am I too big, too?" Jocelyn teased, though her voice was tight with strain and the awareness of the marquess's closeness. She laughed, and there was a touch of hysteria in her tone.

Tarkington frowned, a pensive light in his eyes. "We shall see," he told his daughter.

When they neared the bridge, the marquess stopped the wagon and jumped down. He walked around the wagon to Jocelyn's side and reached for her. "Come here, Miss Maybrey."

"My lord, what . . . ?"

He reached up to pull her out of the wagon. Her startled, feeble resistance only caused her to fall heavily against his chest. Her gasp and protest were cut short when he stooped down to pick her up and hold her high against his chest.

A searing anger burned away embarrassment and fear. She struggled against the strength of his arms around her.

"My lord! Put me down at once! How dare you! Put me down, I say!"

"In a moment, Miss Maybrey."

"What are you doing? What gives you the right? Who do you think you are? You go beyond yourself, my lord."

"Do I?" he asked in a calm, almost laughing tone that sent the heat of her anger burning brighter. "My only wish is to see you across the bridge without that terror."

"Noble sentiments, my lord, that to another might be an excuse but not to me. It will not work. I told you. Bridges make me nervous, but it is something I deal with. I do not ask others to do so, nor do I accept anyone's effrontery that they know more than I. You, my lord, are too full of a sense of self."

"Am I?"

"Yes. Now put me down at once!"

"Certainly, Miss Maybrey." He set her down and turned to walk toward the wagon. *Which was on the other side of the bridge!*

"What? . . . But . . ." Jocelyn floundered. Then as suddenly as her anger grew bright, it dimmed. She began to laugh. She laughed until she could no longer stand. She sank down onto the cold, hard-packed earth.

Tarkington had used her anger, her preoccupation with his effrontery, to carry her across the bridge. She'd had no opportunity for fear to tie her mind and heart into coiled knots. Not only had her anger burned away, but also her fear of him! What a predictable fool she'd been! She buried her head in her arms. At least she now understood his actions when they stopped to gather the mistletoe. He'd said he would make her crossing less traumatic. She supposed emotions like anger were less traumatic. He'd set it up very nicely. He should have been in the military. He'd shown his political acumen to be as good as always.

She sighed wearily and looked up as she heard the jangle of the wagon reins.

"Miss Maybrey?"

"Coming my lord," she said, her voice and face bland. She climbed up into the wagon, pulled a corner of the lap robe across her legs, and sat stiffly staring straight ahead.

"My apologies, Miss Maybrey."

"Nonsense, my lord. Come, Lady Anne, cuddle up against me. It is turning colder. I fear the wind has picked up."

The rest of the trip back to the manor was made in silence. Not even Lady Anne made a sound, burrowed as she was up against Jocelyn. By the time they reached the manor, Lady Anne was sound asleep. A footman would have taken the child, but the marquess waved him away and came around the wagon to take her from Jocelyn's arms. As they passed the precious burden between them, their arms touched. Jocelyn's eyes flew to the marquess. He met her glance, but she could not read what she saw there. Quickly she looked down at Lady Anne, and when she was certain he had her full weight, she pulled away.

She entered the house after the marquess and was surprised to discover he had not immediately taken Lady Anne to the nursery. Instead he stood in the hall talking to someone in whispers lest they wake the child. Curious, she stepped to the side to see past the marquess.

"Father!" she exclaimed, then clamped a hand over her mouth. "Father," she said again, this time on a whisper, "you're early! I did not expect to see you and Mr. Bayne until tomorrow! Mr. Bayne did come with you, didn't he?"

"Aye. The meeting was canceled. Too many complained of its proximity to Christmas. It's been rescheduled for after Twelfth Night, if you can imagine that long a delay. Bah! Charles has gone on to see his mother." He scratched his head. "Some dust up, or another bit of nonsense, I gather from the garbled message he received from her addlepated maid."

Jocelyn blushed, last evening's impassioned defense of the marquess on her mind. She looked up to find the marquess watching her, an expression of sympathy in his eyes. For some reason that look of sympathy distressed her. She did not want him to feel sympathy for her. She wasn't certain sympathy was needed anywhere! If she had to do it again, she would, and if Mrs. Bayne dissuaded Charles from proposing, well, that was to the better, for she knew now she could never marry him. Not now, not when she'd fallen in love with his cousin, whether that regard was returned or not. She could not bear being related to him, seeing him at family functions, and keeping her secret safe and her heart from breaking again and again. But neither did she wish the marquess to think her a flirt! Oh, was there never such a coil? Best at least to warn her father.

"Mrs. Bayne and I had a slight disagreement last night."

"Disagreement?" her father asked.

A strangled sound, like a cut-off laugh, came from the marquess.

She lifted her head high. "Hadn't you best take Lady Anne upstairs?" She linked her arm in her father's and led him toward one of the parlors. "Yes, I'm afraid I took exception to a few things she said." She was gratified to hear the sound of Tarkington's boots on the marble staircase. She relaxed and even allowed herself a small, wry laugh. "All your precepts on political negotiations were wasted, Father. When the moment came to disagree, I found myself blurting it out."

Sir Jasper Maybrey chuckled and patted her hand. "Mustn't refine too much, my dear. Charles will set things to right. Fine chap. Go far in government if he chooses."

"The thing is, Father, I'm not so certain I do wish him to set things right."

"What? What's this?" He cupped her chin in one broad hand.

She shrugged and pulled her head away. "I don't know, Father. I'm not like you and Mother, you know."

"Course you're not. Silly thing if you were. You're your own person. What you're feeling is just nerves, puss."

"But—"

"Trust your father. Everything will be fine once you see Charles again. Mark my words. Now, if you'll excuse me, I'll just peek in on Tarkington's library. Said I might when I met him in the hall. I hear the library here at Bayneville is a veritable archive of world political history." He rubbed his hands together. "If one must be immured in the country, a good political library is just the tick to take the edge off boredom."

"Yes, Father," Jocelyn said on a soft sigh as she watched him walk away.

Perhaps she really should take that nap she'd mentioned to Lady Anne. She felt exhausted, wrung out like an old kitchen mop. Slowly she made her way upstairs, but when she got to the top she stopped and stood thinking for a moment. Then with a smile she turned—not toward her own room, but toward Lady Mary's. Maybe she could help her sort out her troubled thoughts.

"Jocelyn! Come in! Come in! So tell me, what have you been up to while I've been confined here? I so chafe at staying in bed. But I am getting better, and Edward will be here tomorrow!"

"And you must be at your best for Lord Killingham!" Jocelyn sat on the edge of her friend's bed. "While you have been recovering, I've spent time antagonizing Mrs. Bayne, gathering Christmas greenery with Tarkington and Lady Anne, and generally confusing myself."

"This sounds like quite a story."

"I don't know about that. If it is a story, it is one without end, and boring at that. Last evening Mrs. Bayne said some dreadful things to Tarkington."

"I assure you, Jocelyn, it wasn't the first time."

"Perhaps not, but I could not sit quietly and listen to her malign him in the manner she did."

"What do you mean?"

"She doesn't believe he is worthy of his title. She believes he shirks his responsibilities. She doesn't see that, far from shirking his duties to his family and his title, he is fulfilling them beyond what many of his peers do."

"To be blunt, Jocelyn, my aunt wishes the title for her son. She has always chafed at being one step away from the dignities."

"I know, but I don't know why she believes an endless social round of parties and political speeches would make Tarkington a marquess. The land and his people do. It does not matter if he is socially seen. It matters if he is seen by his daughter."

A frown creased Lady Mary's pale brow. "I had not thought of it in that way. . . ."

Jocelyn nodded, eager now to communicate her ideas. "Everyone comments on how he's changed since his wife's death, and they all say it as if the change has been for the worse."

"But he's *not* the same, Jocelyn."

"So, is that necessarily bad? What, precisely, is bad? I'd like to know. I'd like to understand. I *need* to understand! What I've seen is a man who is attentive to his estate and its people, a man who is also loving and attentive to his motherless daughter. Where is the bad in that? Is he mistaken? Is he supposed to place society before those things?"

Lady Mary blinked at her friend, then a wide smile lit her face, chasing away any image of illness. "Jocelyn, you're in love with my brother!"

Jocelyn bit her lip and looked down at her hands clasped tightly in her lap, a painful blush creeping up her neck and staining her cheeks. "For my sins, yes," she said softly.

Then she looked up with a fierce, determined light in her eyes. "But do not say that to anyone. *And I mean anyone!*"

"But why? Why not?" Lady Mary leaned forward to lay her hands over Jocelyn's. "I think it's wonderful. What do you mean?"

"Charles Bayne."

"Oh. Yes, a bit awkward, that." She sighed and leaned back against her pillows. "Are you still going to marry Charles?"

"No. I don't know that I ever would have." Jocelyn rose from the bed and began to pace the room. "When I came to Bayneville, I was feeling uncomfortable about the entire matter. Nothing terribly wrong, just an odd itch. I first attributed it to a desire to leave London just for a spell. But it was more than that." She shrugged. "I have discovered I do not want to live the same life my parents have. I don't enjoy the endless rounds of parties. They pall after a time."

"And that's the life Charles leads and will continue, for it is in that arena he has chosen to make his fortune."

"Yes. I believe in Mr. Bayne my parents see a kindred spirit and because of that first encouraged me to Mr. Bayne. I admit I like him, and now that I've time to consider, I realize I've felt comfortable with him because he reminded me of my parents. It was a safe, comfortable feeling. But I don't wish to be married to that feeling."

"No, I can see that. What are you going to do?"

"I don't know." She stopped pacing and turned to look at Lady Mary. A rueful smile touched her lips. "Strange, I never considered that one of the Christmas gifts I would receive this year was the knowledge of love. It's a beautiful gift, but I'm not certain what to do with it."

"Perhaps it would be best if you stopped thinking and just let it be. Enjoy the feeling."

"Live for today, for tomorrow it may rain?" Jocelyn asked cynically.

"Something of that nature."

"I don't know. . . ."

"Jocelyn, I promise I will not say anything to Tarkington if you promise not to avoid him. You mentioned yesterday you'd like to help with his rocking horse. Why don't you do so? He doesn't have much longer to finish it, you know."

"But I do not wish to throw myself at him."

"Helping him is not the same as throwing yourself at him," Lady Mary said with a laugh. "Honestly, Jocelyn, I've never heard you so tentative before. Explore your feelings, your thoughts, and let the spirit of Christmas guide you."

Let the spirit of Christmas guide you. . . . Jocelyn turned that phrase over in her mind half an hour later as she stood before the carpenter's workshop. Today there was not the odd sound of the lathe. It was quiet. She pushed the door open. In the center of the room, on a low bench spotlighted by the afternoon sun, stood an assembled rocking horse. Behind the horse, with a tan, paint-laden brush in hand, stood the marquess. He looked up at her entrance, and it seemed his eyes burned through her.

"Miss Maybrey?"

She hated that remote expression on his face and almost turned to leave. "I—I wanted to know if I could do anything to help."

He was silent a moment. "You really can paint something more than a watercolor?" he asked coolly.

"Yes."

He was silent a moment, studying her. Then he smiled, and it was one of his smiles that reached his eyes. "Do you think you could do his head, Miss Maybrey? Every time I even contemplate painting his eyes, my hand trembles."

She laughed then, knowing her apology for her earlier cold behavior was accepted, and she was forgiven. Maybe there was something to the notion of Christmas spirit.

* * *

"Excellent, Miss Maybrey," Tarkington said two hours later as she put the last touches on the horse's head. "And those touches you have added to your own face are quite adorable as well."

"What? I have paint on my face? Where?"

Tarkington laughed. "Hold still, and I'll remove them." He clasped her chin in his hand to hold her head steady.

Jocelyn froze. His very touch made her knees weak. She could have wept at the silence she must keep!

Tarkington's glance caught hers as he raised the rag to her cheek, and as easily as that Jocelyn knew that the awareness they'd both felt was back. It crowded in upon her senses, threatening to overwhelm her. Her eyes flared. Panicked, she twisted away from him, afraid of what might happen next, afraid of making a fool of herself. Afraid of revealing what was in her heart.

With her eyes she pleaded with him to understand, to let her be. His face turned to stone. He handed the rag to her. She turned away, willing tears not to fall as she scrubbed at the paint smeared across her cheek.

The gust of cold air coming into the room warned them both, as it had Tarkington the day before, that someone had come in.

Jocelyn looked around. "Mr. Bayne!"

"Hello, Charles. Be a good chap and close the door, please," Tarkington said easily.

Jocelyn glanced from him to Mr. Bayne, her cheeks flaming with the thought of what Mr. Bayne might have seen if she had not pulled away from Tarkington when she did.

"Miss Maybrey, I have been searching all over the estate for you!" Charles Bayne declared. From his tone Jocelyn knew what would follow would not be a pleasant interview.

She sighed. "And you have found me."

"What are you doing here?"

"I have been helping Tarkington. See, I painted the

face,'' she said, pointing to the rocking horse. ''What do you think?''

He blinked and stared at the rocking horse. Patches of wet paint still glistened. A dull red crept up his neck.

''You didn't think that Tarkington and I were . . . ?'' Jocelyn trailed off, afraid to finish her thought.

''Well, dash it, Miss Maybrey, Mother said—''

''I'd stop right there, Bayne, before you make a fool of yourself.''

''Damn it, Tarkington! You've been alone with her for hours!''

Tarkington leaned up against a post and crossed one ankle over the other. ''Are you implying that Miss Maybrey has been compromised?'' he asked as casually as if he were asking after the weather.

''Yes . . . I mean, no!'' Charles ran a hand through his hair. ''It's just, well, what would society think?''

''What would society think? Is that all you're concerned with?'' Jocelyn asked, barely contained anger raising her voice higher.

Both men looked at her with surprise at her outburst. Mr. Bayne frowned; Tarkington grinned.

''I, for one, do not care what society thinks,'' Jocelyn continued, her tone now coldly modulated. ''I am tired of being forever lectured on what society would like or wouldn't like. I am tired of bowing before that god, and I refuse to do so anymore!''

''Miss Maybrey, only consider—I didn't mean—''

''Well, I know what I mean!''

''And she is, if you have noticed, cousin, an honest woman. She cannot help but be honest. All her thoughts and feelings are reflected in her face,'' Tarkington interjected.

Jocelyn glared at him. Had he seen her love reflected in his eyes? She swore he was laughing behind that rigid expression he held. She saw it in his eyes, for they were not a cold, metal gray. Mortification chilled her soul.

"Tarkington, I do wish you would leave," Bayne said.

"So you could do what I haven't? No, no, dear cousin. Now that you have pointed out the situation to me, I can see that it would not be seemly. I suggest we all leave. Let some fresh air clear our heads and cool this anger you have developed." He took down Jocelyn's cloak from a peg on the wall and handed it out to her. Jocelyn slipped into it, settled her bonnet on her dark curls, and walked past the two gentlemen. She was angry with both of them, and with herself. She had been very close to making Mr. Bayne's imaginings real. But what right did he have to imagine anything of her? And to believe that what society thought was of so high importance! And Tarkington! His laughter and denying that they'd been tempted—even for a moment—toward further intimacy was hurtful. So much for a Christmas spirit.

"This is ridiculous!" Lady Mary exclaimed the next morning when Jocelyn arrived at her room before the breakfast tray. "You cannot hide here. All the guests are arriving today, and my ball is tonight!"

"I'm not hiding. I'm keeping you company until your fiancé arrives."

"You are hiding. You hid in here last evening, and I understood, after what you told me of Charles's and Tarkington's behavior. But this is not the answer, Jocelyn. Nor is it like you."

Jocelyn nodded. "That's the problem," she said sadly. She sank down into a chair by the window and looked out over the Bayneville park. "I don't know what is like me anymore. Every day I've been here I've grown more and more confused. How ironic, for I saw coming to Bayneville as an opportunity to sort things in my mind. I never expected to get them more jumbled."

"That's because you never expected to find love," Lady Mary said softly.

Jocelyn laughed weakly. "I didn't even know what that emotion was beyond what I'd read. And I'd always thought those descriptions to be exaggerations. I was wrong. They pale by comparison."

"So what are you going to do about it?"

"Do?" Jocelyn asked, turning her head to look at Lady Mary.

"Yes. What are you going to do?"

"Nothing. What is there to do? I have received a great gift in discovering what love is, my Christmas gift, and I shall treasure it."

Lady Mary made a rude, exasperated noise. "Jocelyn, you have barely discovered anything about love and nothing about Christmas gifts! A solitary love is no true love. It needs its mirror reflection or it shrivels and dies, leaving bitter emptiness behind—"

"The memory is a treasure."

"Worse, you are forgetting what is the special magic of Christmas gifts. Their magic lies in the giving, not in the receiving. Give, Jocelyn. Don't be the lonely dragon guarding its hoard, for it shall turn to dust long before you will."

Their magic lies in the giving.

Jocelyn returned to her own room to think about Lady Mary's words once again. The phrase spun in her mind, echoing. How could she take her heart in her hands and give it to Tarkington? How could she let him know?

Then she remembered the gift line. One practical gift, one fanciful. Could she do it?

She had a practical gift. A token really. Meant to be a simple thank-you for the visit: monogrammed handkerchiefs. And for her fanciful gift . . .

Smiling, she went to the nursery to borrow paper, paints, and glue.

* * *

"Lawks, miss, you're already half dressed!" exclaimed Miss Barnes when she came later that afternoon to get Jocelyn ready for the Christmas ball.

"I don't want to miss the gift line prior to the ball."

"But, miss, that's an affair for the family and their people. And belowstairs they're all looking forward to it."

"I know. Now hush and help me."

With Miss Barnes's help she was ready quickly, and for once without complaint from her abigail. Her gown was made of layers upon layers of white muslin gauze delicately embroidered with red, green, and gold thread. Through her dark hair Miss Barnes wove a gold cord knotted with red and green ribbons. Finally she draped a gold-spangled shawl over Jocelyn's arms and declared her finished.

To the woman's surprise, Jocelyn kissed her cheek in thanks. She'd scarce recovered when her mistress pressed two packages into her hands.

"One practical, one fanciful. It is up to you to decide which is which," Jocelyn said, smiling warmly.

"Oh, miss!" exclaimed her astonished maid. Quickly, as if she were afraid they would disappear, Miss Barnes opened her first gift. It was a new reticule, a most practical gift. The second proved to be one of Jocelyn's best Chinese silk fans painted with exotic Far-Eastern flowers.

"Oh, but, miss, I couldn't!" Miss Barnes said, her eyes shining, her expression half fearful that Jocelyn would agree and take it away.

"Hush. Yes, you can. And I want you to use it to good advantage at the servants' ball tomorrow night."

"Oh, miss!"

"Enough. I must go." She twitched her shawl higher up on her shoulders, then picked up two wrapped packages from a table near the door.

The gift-giving was to be in the Great Hall at the base of the stairs. As Jocelyn didn't want to call immediate attention to herself by descending the main staircase, she went down

the back stairs and made her way through a small antecham-
ber to the family gathering.

There was Lady Mary leaning on Lord Edward Killingham's arm. Lady Anne was dressed in red velvet and
perched halfway up the stairs so she could see all that went
on. The dowager marchioness sat regally in an Elizabethan
chair pulled up before the base of the stairs, presents stacked
all around her. Lord Tarkington was passing out the gifts
one at a time. Everyone watched as each servant in turn
opened his or her gifts.

The practical gifts were opened first, and they were, as
Lady Mary had said, items like coats and boots and shawls.
But the fanciful gifts sent everyone laughing, master and
servant together like family. Lady Mary's abigail received
paper dolls to dress and undress. A footman, receiving a pair
of gloves covered with some sticky substance, was told
maybe now he wouldn't drop so many things. Mrs. Penneybacker, the housekeeper, received an oversize chatelaine
that the marquess dared her to try to lose.

Laughter rang throughout the Great Hall as each servant
in turn received some silly or fanciful gift. Jocelyn laughed
with them. Soon she was caught up in the fun and slowly
moved closer and closer, the better to see.

Tarkington was expounding on the story behind the last
present when he saw her. Without halting his humorous tale
he walked toward her. In confusion, Jocelyn stepped backward and collided with a wall of servants who were now
behind her. Before she could decide what to do, he snagged
her arm and drew her to his side in the center of the Great
Hall. When he finished the story, with his free hand he
handed the unfortunate subject his present and laughed with
everyone else when it was opened. Still he did not look at
Jocelyn, though he kept her anchored at his side.

"Papa! Papa!" came Lady Anne's high-pitched voice
over the general laughter. They all turned to look at her. She

stood on a step pointing one chubby finger at something above his head. "Mis'toe, Papa!"

Jocelyn glanced up, stricken to see a large clump of mistletoe hanging from a kissing bough. As she looked down, her uncertain brown eyes locked with Tarkington's very certain gray eyes.

"A kiss! A kiss!" shouted the crowd.

In embarrassed confusion Jocelyn tried to pull away, but the marquess held her fast. "No, you don't. Mustn't break with tradition. I claim a kiss." Tarkington lowered his head, then murmured softly for her ears only: "I've wanted this kiss for the past two days." Then his lips were on hers, hard and brief, but with a burning afterfire that left Jocelyn's knees weak and her color high.

Behind them Lady Anne giggled and clapped her hands.

Tarkington let her go, then addressed his people, wishing them all a merry Christmas and thanking them for another year of fine service. The servants cheered the family and moved off clutching their presents, talking and laughing in small clumps of friends as they returned to their stations throughout Bayneville. The nurse told Lady Anne it was time for bed, Lady Tarkington walked off with the butler going over last-minute details for the ball, and Lady Mary and Lord Killingham drifted into the shadows.

Tarkington tucked Jocelyn's arm in his and led her into his library.

"Lady Mary told me of your gift-giving tradition with the servants," Jocelyn said too brightly. "I had to see it. And it was all she said. You are very good, my lord."

"It's not goodness, Miss Maybrey. Good sense. And I am merely continuing what was begun long before I inherited the responsibility."

She held out the two presents she'd wrapped for him. "Here. I thought it was time you received two presents as you give to your servants."

He raised a quizzical eyebrow. "One practical and one silly?"

"One more fanciful than silly, I'd say." She bit her lip. "Maybe more a fantasy than a reality," she said on a little self-deprecating laugh.

He looked at her steadily for a moment, then down at the packages he held.

She watched nervously as he unwrapped the first gift, and the squares of white linen spilled out over his hands. "Ah, my practical gift," he said with a smile in his eyes that caught Jocelyn's breath.

She walked a few paces away from him to curl her fingers around the back of a chair and stare into the fire. Would he understand? Had she been too obscure? She waited, listening to the tissue unfold, waited for him to say something, but all she heard was silence.

She squeezed her eyes tightly shut against tears, and a great roaring sound rose in her head with a thousand voices calling her a fool. She swayed slightly.

Hands gripped her shoulders and turned her around. Questioning gray eyes searched her face. He lifted a hand to cup her cheek in his palm.

"I love you, too," he said honestly. He cleared his throat. A watery sheen danced in his eyes. "You can't imagine how jealous I've been of Charles." He pulled her head against his chest and laughed brokenly. "I don't know how it happened, or even when. It was certainly not something I anticipated. I scarcely hoped that what I saw in your beautiful expressive eyes was the answer to my heart's desire."

She raised her head and looked up at him, letting her heart and soul rest in her eyes.

He smiled, and his smile was more brilliant, more beautiful than any fireworks at Vauxhall Gardens.

He lowered his head to kiss her, and this time she stood on tiptoe to meet him. When their lips met, Jocelyn was

caught in a maelstrom of sensations. Tarkington pulled her
tightly against him, molding her to his lean frame. She
melted into him.

Behind them on a small table was her second gift to him,
as much a symbol of her love for him as was his gift for his
daughter. Lit by a pool of bright candlelight stood a
miniature rocking horse crafted out of paper, yarn, paint,
and love.

A
Memorable
Christmas

Sheila Rabe

*T*HE snow falling outside the carriage window was symbolic of what was happening in the life of the new Countess of Chesterfield. How cold, she reflected. And all those little flakes remind me of my heart, shattered into so many pieces.

She pulled the rug up farther on her lap, trying to comfort herself with the warm cocoon. Don't be such a baby, she scolded herself. You are wealthy, you are warm, and you are headed to the Colby family manor for a Christmas filled with rich foods, expensive presents, and good company. But I'm headed there alone, she finished, and sadness again settled over her.

In the past, Maxim had accompanied her to the family estate the week before Christmas. During their journey home they would talk about the family and try to guess what each had bought the other for Christmas. But this year Maxim had sent her on ahead, pleading pressing matters.

She knew those pressing matters were simply a matter of pressing a certain dark-eyed ballerina to his heart. The beast! "I'll be along no more than two days later, Diana," he had said, and it had been all she could do to keep herself from kicking him.

Diana sighed. She knew most wives had to put up with this sort of thing. It was fashionable for members of the upper class to amuse themselves by keeping a mistress. But somehow, Maxim had seemed different. She'd supposed it was because he wasn't the sort of dashingly handsome man women swooned for. Of course, he wasn't repulsive-looking, either. It was just that he was rather lanky, and his face was a little too long. Compared to men with finely chiseled features and well-muscled torsos, he wasn't much.

But he was fun-loving and kind, more like an overgrown boy than a man. Which was exactly why she had never dreamed women would throw themselves at him. He had never been the hand-kissing, flattering sort of ladies' man who attracted an abundance of female attention. But Diana had not minded that. He was sweet and he was all hers.

At least he had been until he had come into the title after his great uncle's demise the previous year. Now it seemed every demirep and dancer in London was discovering that Maxim Colby, the new Lord Chesterfield, was a witty and amusing man.

She supposed it was only natural all the attention and fussing should turn his head. And a graceful little dancer was bound to seem much more exciting than a young lady he had known since she was in the schoolroom. Theirs had been a marriage based more on friendship than any grand passion. Their families had known each other for years. And when Maxim saw that with the red curls put up and the childish garb exchanged for a ball gown Diana looked rather pretty, he must have figured she would do quite as well as any other young lady for a wife and mother to his children.

His proposal had been anything but romantic. "How would you like to be married, Di? I think we should suit. And just think of the fun we would have: parties and theatricals with all our family and friends."

At the time Maxim's proposal had sounded wonderfully charming and romantic. It was only later, when Diana began to hear of the empassioned declarations some of her friends were receiving, that she began to feel discontented with what she had gotten. Of course, Maxim had given her a fine necklace of emeralds and earrings to match, but still she had felt cheated. Her husband did not share her thrill over the match. He enjoyed her adoration. She simply had his regard.

Their married life had produced no great sparks, either. For the last two years they had gotten along splendidly, enjoying a warm friendliness that even seeped into their lovemaking. But there had been no jealous quarrels, no possessive demands. In short, Maxim had taken her very much for granted. And now, more so than ever. At the rate she was going, she would soon be no more noticeable to him than one of the ancestral portraits that hung on the upstairs walls at the manor.

She wondered how he talked to his dancer. Did he smile at her with the same easy friendliness he did his wife? Or did he look at her with hungry eyes, jealous of any other man she spoke to? And did he come to her bed with a good-natured grin as he did his wife? Or did he take her in his arms like a ravenous animal?

Diana blushed at her unladylike thoughts and stole a glance to see if her abigail, Peale, was observing her. Fortunately, Peale's attention was occupied with the winter scene outside the carriage windows.

Diana bit her lip and returned to grappling with her painful thoughts. What was the use of being jealous? Best resign herself to things as they were.

She thought of Lady Colby, her mother-in-law, who was awaiting them. Had the woman she now called "mother" borne such treatment from her husband when he was alive? Diana thought not. She remembered the comfortable famili- arity that Lady Colby and her husband had enjoyed. Surely they couldn't have been such good friends had Sir John been carrying on with some Cyprian.

And then there was Louisa, her sister-in-law, also ex- pected at the manor with her family. Did she have to contend with such things? Louisa had borne her husband, the honorable Mr. Dashwood, two children, but Diana couldn't remember ever having heard any rumors about James.

And one did hear. For a subject considered unsuitable for discussion by well-bred females, it was amazing how often it came up in conversation. She was sure the subject of her husband's new mistress had come up often enough among her friends.

Friends, indeed! Diana was convinced that horrid Lady Elizabeth Palmer had enjoyed being the one to let the news drop that morning two weeks ago, like so much poison into a teacup. Of course, the others had offered her such small comfort as they had to give: "My dear, you must not let it distress you. Why, there is not a lord in London who doesn't have his mistress. It is the way of things. And only think. If your husband is occupied elsewhere, you will have time and opportunity to entertain someone more to your tastes."

More to her tastes? There was no one more to her tastes than Maxim. A tear slipped from one large brown eye, and Diana wiped it furtively away.

Such a fuss her relatives had made at her come-out. "So beautiful," they'd said. "She'll make a fine match."

And she had. And now she was miserable.

Another hour's sad reflection brought her to the manor. The drive was lined by trees sparkling with their diamond coat of snow. Normally the sight would have thrilled Diana with the joy of homecoming. But this late afternoon her eyes glistened like the snow-whitened branches.

The carriage steps were let down, the front door was opened, and Diana was ushered into her husband's ancestral home.

Her mother-in-law rushed to greet her. "Diana, my love!" she cried. "You look chilled to the bone. Come and drink a dish of tea." Lady Colby looked past her daughter-in-law. "But where is Maxim?" she asked.

Diana felt the warmth of a deep blush spreading across

her face. "He was delayed in London. He sent me on ahead."

A momentary frown crossed Lady Colby's face, but she replaced it with a warm smile. "How fortunate for us! We shall enjoy a comfortable time together without my rascally son underfoot to annoy us. Andrews, we shall require a fresh pot of tea, I think." Leaving the matter of tea as well as dealing with Diana's bags and her abigail in the butler's capable hands, Mrs. Colby linked her arm through Diana's and drew her into the drawing room. "I expect Louisa and James and the children day after tomorrow. And Bernard, I believe, will make his usual appearance before joining his family."

Diana was settled before a roaring fire and plied with hot tea, which took the chill from her flesh. But neither the fire nor the kind attentions of her mother-in-law could take the chill from her heart.

Lady Colby scrutinized her daughter-in-law as she sipped from a thin china cup. "My dear, are you feeling quite the thing?" she asked.

Diana dredged up a smile. "I am a little tired. I do apologize for being such poor company."

"Make no apologies, child," said Lady Colby. "Drink your tea and we'll send you to your room for a nap before dinner. I am sure you'll feel much better after you have rested."

Diana was sure she would never feel better, but she kept her opinion to herself and after twenty minutes let the older woman shoo her off to her bedroom, where Peale waited, a look of worry on her face.

"Oh, dear," fretted Peale at the sight of her mistress. "I had hoped some tea would make you feel better, but you look every bit as peaked as you did when we arrived." She bustled over to help her mistress out of her gown.

"I am afraid my head hurts something fierce," said

Diana. This was certainly no lie, for all her miserable stewing had produced a painful throbbing at her temples.

Peale produced a wrapper and helped Diana into it. "Well, you just lay down and we'll bathe your forehead in lavender water. That and a nice nap should surely help."

Diana sighed. "Nothing will help," she said.

Diana struggled through the evening and the next morning as well, trying to pretend to be what she once was: a carefree bride. She was sure she wasn't fooling her mother-in-law. Once, at breakfast, Lady Colby looked about to say something, but she apparently thought the better of it, asking Diana instead if she would care to help with the holiday decorations.

Ordinarily Lady Colby had no more enthusiastic helper than Diana. She had always loved arranging greenery and candles on the mantelpiece and the pianoforte, and she had taken great pride in helping to make the kissing bough as elaborately beribboned as possible.

"Oh, yes," declared Diana with what she hoped was a good imitation of enthusiasm. "The children will be very disappointed if they arrive and the house does not look like Christmas."

The two women set to work early that afternoon, and soon the downstairs was filled with an earthy scent, and green boughs threaded with ivy and holly decorated the drawing room and parlor.

They were hanging the kissing bough over the doorway between the dining room and drawing room, Diana teetering precariously on a ladder, when a new arrival made his appearance at the other end of the room. Although Andrews was following him in an attempt to take it, he still wore his driving coat, which was dusted with new snow. He looked amazingly cheerful for a man whose conscience should be bothering him. "Well, it looks like Christmas," he observed.

Lady Colby broke into a wide smile. "Maxim!" she cried. "'Tis well past time you got here."

Her son strode across the room to kiss his mother, who offered him her cheek. His gaze moved to his wife, who was making her way down the ladder, and his smile broadened. "And who have we here, the spirit of Christmas?" He bounded over to her and plucked her from the ladder, swinging her to the ground.

In a happier time Diana would have laughed and her face would have glowed. Now she found it hard even to smile at her husband.

He gave her a great smacking kiss and smiled at her. Only when he saw what a tiny one he received in return did his Christmas cheer diminish. "'Tis good to be with you again, Di," he murmured.

"Welcome home," she said dully and turned from him to busy herself with a piece of ribbon. The wounded look on his face gave her a little thrill of satisfaction. Good! He should suffer. He deserved to suffer, if only a little, for the pain he had caused her.

"Perhaps Your Lordship would care to remove your coat?" suggested the long-suffering Andrews.

Maxim was still regarding his wife. "What? Oh." He shrugged out of his greatcoat and handed it over to be added to the collection of hat, gloves, and scarf. "I hope you both mean to pause from your labors long enough to eat a bite of luncheon, for I must confess I am starved."

"Oh, Maxim. When are you not?" retorted his mother. But she left the room immediately to give orders for a cold collation to be laid out for them all.

Maxim turned once more to his wife. "Your decorations look quite nice," he ventured.

"Thank you," she replied stiffly.

He stood for a moment, thinking, then tried again. "I know what you are getting for Christmas," he teased.

Diana still did not turn to face him. How dare he try to

pretend things were the same between them! She forced her voice to be light. "Is it something I deserve?" she asked.

"Have you been a very good girl?" he asked.

"Oh, yes," she replied. "In fact, I have been better than most," she added, her words heavy with hidden meaning.

"Then in truth I must tell you that you are getting something very nice," he said.

All I want is my husband to be once more mine alone, she thought. But that was rather a hopeless wish. Well, if she couldn't have things the way they once were, then she wished for a present of pointed ballet slippers. She would don them for the express purpose of kicking her heartless husband. She said nothing, and once more silence lay between them like a blanket of snow.

"Do you know what I am getting for Christmas?" Maxim prompted, still trying to breathe life into their conversation.

Diana's anger finally bubbled over. Her wicked husband had his mistress to welcome him with open arms in London, and now that he had arrived at his country estate he expected his wife to do the same thing. She didn't care if every other woman in the *ton* put up with such cavalier treatment. She would not! "I hope you are getting what you deserve," she replied. "A lump of coal." And with that she sailed past him into the dining room, leaving him gaping after her in astonishment.

There was no more opportunity for private discussion. Luncheon was served, and afterward Diana followed her mother-in-law to the drawing room to resume decorating with not a word for Maxim. Frowning, he changed his clothes and retired to the library for the rest of the afternoon to consider his wife's mysterious behavior.

Finally, after dressing for dinner, he knocked on her door, determined to find out why she was behaving so strangely. Peale had just finished arranging Diana's hair and was clasping the diamond necklace he'd given her the previous

Christmas around her neck. She was wearing a simply cut green gown of some sort of thin material. A silk shawl was draped on a nearby chair, ready to lay across her shoulders. The earl signaled Peale away, then picked up the shawl and did the honors himself. "I don't know how you expect to keep from freezing," he said, smiling at her reflection.

She smiled at him as one would a stranger and rose from her seat. "I shall be fine. But thank you for your concern."

The corners of Maxim's mouth turned down. "Perhaps it is I who should be worried about freezing," he said. "For I cannot remember when I have been treated so coldly."

Diana was halfway to the door. She turned and her face betrayed her hurt. "Nor can I remember when I have been treated so cruelly. Thrown aside like an old glove for some cheap little—" She clamped her lips firmly shut and made for the door.

"What? What's this?" In three long strides he was beside her, grasping her arm.

"Let me go, you beast!" she cried and shook her arm as if an adder clung to it.

"Diana, what is this? I don't understand," he pleaded.

"What exactly is it you don't understand? Do you not understand how your simple little wife could find out about your simple little dancer?" Maxim's mouth dropped as Diana continued her diatribe. "Or are you having difficulty understanding how hurt, how betrayed . . . Oh, let me go!" Again she shook her arm, this time escaping his grasp.

She fled the room and headed for the stairs with her husband in pursuit. "Di, wait!" he called. "Let me explain." Again, he reached for her arm to detain her.

She jerked away from him and, losing her balance, tumbled headlong down the stairs to the first landing, where she lay still at last.

Maxim stared in shocked disbelief. "Di," he whispered. The whisper grew into a cry. "Diana!" He thundered down the stairs and landed on his knees next to her. Scooping his

hands under her shoulders, he lifted her face close to his and
called her name again. She moaned. "You are alive. Thank
God," he said.

By now Peale had rushed to the top of the stairs. With a
cry she ran to her mistress, nearly falling herself in her
haste.

"Find Andrews," commanded Maxim. "Tell him to
send for the doctor immediately." He lifted Diana in his
arms and made his way back up to her bedroom, where he
tucked her tenderly beneath the covers.

Mrs. Colby rushed into the room. "Maxim! What has
happened?"

"She fell down the stairs," said Maxim, trying for a level
voice. "I thought at first—" His voice broke and he
clenched his jaw tight.

Diana's eyes fluttered open. She squinted at her husband
as though he were someone she couldn't remember.

Maxim's eyes widened in alarm. "Diana!" he said
sharply.

It was all too much. Diana let her eyelids drop, shutting
out the torturous throbbing in her head and various other
parts of her body. As she slid back into blackness, she heard
Maxim's astonished cry, "Mother! She doesn't recognize
me."

The doctor arrived and pronounced Lady Chesterfield
free of any broken bones. "It would appear she has suffered
a nasty bump on the head, and she is badly bruised. But I
think you may safely plan on seeing her in fine fettle by
Christmas Eve. Of course, tomorrow she will be in great
pain, make no mistake. Keep her abed and dose her with
laudanum."

The doctor left them, and Maxim repaired to the library
and poured himself a brandy.

"Maxim, dear," said a gentle voice behind him.

He didn't turn to face his mother. Instead, he busied
himself with refilling his glass.

She reached out and laid a comforting hand on his shoulder. "Diana will be fine," she reminded him.

He nodded mutely.

His mother hesitated, studying her son's back. "Whatever is causing you both such pain can surely be mended," she said at last.

Her son did not insult her intelligence by pretending not to understand her. "I don't know, Mother," he said, sighing.

"'Tis Christmas," she said. "Miracles are in the air. Perhaps you can reach out and grab one for yourself."

Diana opened her eyes. The gentle sunbeams filtering into her bedroom felt like so many daggers piercing through them, bringing pain to her whole head. Better to keep her eyes shut.

As she closed them she heard a deep voice pleading with her to look at him, give him some sign she knew him. Her head hurt. She didn't wish to talk. The voice finally was silent, leaving her alone with her thoughts behind closed eyelids.

Why did Maxim think she would not know him?

Ah, yes. Now she remembered. The ballerina, the argument, the painful, crashing fall to unconsciousness.

And now, here she was stretched out in bed with her husband beside her, pleading with her to recognize him. An idea was dancing at the edge of her mind. But it was causing too much pain. *Be still. I shall consider you later.* Diana slept.

Afternoon shadows were creeping along the edge of her bedroom floor when she again opened her eyes. Thankfully, she realized the pain in her head had lessened.

Maxim no longer kept vigil next to her bed. Instead, his mother's smiling face greeted her return to the conscious world. "'Tis time you finally woke, sleepyhead," she teased.

Diana smiled but said nothing.

"Could you do with some tea and toast?" asked Lady Colby.

Diana's stomach rumbled appreciatively at the mention of food. "Yes," she said and smiled. "That would be nice."

"You've had us quite worried," continued Lady Colby. "Maxim, especially."

The idea at the edge of Diana's mind fairly leapt to the fore. Here is your chance! it cried. Remember your cousin Cornelia after she was kicked by the horse? It was some time before she could remember her own name let alone anyone else's. If you wish to bring your errant husband to heel, this may be your only chance. You must act now, while he's vulnerable!

She certainly had nothing to lose. Why not pretend to have forgotten who Maxim was? He had certainly forgotten her this past month. Why, she was surprised he had even remembered her name, so caught up had he been with his precious little dancer! Perhaps she would show him just how it felt. And if she did, he might see what a treasure he had so foolishly thrown aside. Yes! She would do it. Her eyebrows knit as she feigned concentration. "Maxim?"

Lady Colby's eyes flew open and her head snapped back as if someone had slapped her. "Your husband," she prompted.

"I have a husband?" asked Diana.

"You most certainly do. A fine husband to whom you have been married these past two years."

Diana pretended to consider this. "You look familiar," she said at last. "Are you my mother?"

"I should like to think so," replied Lady Colby. "I am your mother-in-law."

"Do we like each other?" asked Diana.

Lady Colby smiled at her and patted her hand. "Very much," she said.

And I hope we still will when this farce I have just begun is at an end, thought Diana with a tinge of conscience.

"Rest now, my dear. I shall have something sent up to you. Then, perhaps another nap. You have had a nasty fall, but the doctor says you will be fine. I am sure before many more days are out you will be able to remember things much more clearly."

Diana watched her go, feeling guilty for playing such a trick on the woman who had been like a second mother to her. She was sure her own mama would be shocked if she knew about her daughter's scheme. Diana hoped her parents never found out. She hoped *no one* would guess what she was up to. She would only carry on her little act for two or three days, making sure she was "well" by Christmas Eve. That way, no one's Christmas would be spoiled—except hers, if her plan didn't work.

While she ate her toast she planned her strategy. After her nap she would let Peale brush her hair and help her wash and change before seeing Maxim again. Although her body still ached miserably, her head no longer felt as if someone were plunging an ax into it. After a little more rest it would be working well enough for her to pull off her little deception. Smiling, she drifted off to sleep again.

She awoke to see Maxim perched on a chair next to her bed, staring out the window into the dark. So, the play was to begin sooner than she had planned. Very well, she thought. Pull the curtain.

She moaned and stirred, sure this would draw her husband's attention from his self-pitying thoughts. Slowly she opened her eyes to meet his. At the sight of him she screamed and tried to pull the covers up over her nose.

Maxim jumped in his seat and looked nearly as frightened as she. "Diana!"

"Who are you?" Diana demanded.

"Who am I? Do you not recognize me?"

Diana shook her head. "Leave my room at once," she ordered.

"'Tis I, your husband, Maxim."

"Husband?" said Diana suspiciously. "You cannot be my husband. You have the eyes of a villain, and I am sure I would not marry a wicked person."

A red flush spread up Maxim's neck and covered his face. "I am certainly not a villain," he said, trying for dignity." I am sorry you are not feeling quite yourself yet. I will leave you to dress for dinner."

Diana watched him go and grinned triumphantly. Ah, Maxim. How does it feel to be the one scorned?

Peale made a timid appearance a few minutes later. "Would you care to get dressed, my lady?" she asked.

"Thank you, Peale, I would."

Joy and wonder spread over Peale's face. "It's a miracle," she breathed. "Oh, my lady. You've come back to us. And here your poor husband was worried to death!"

Too late Diana realized her mistake. She should have never used her abigail's name. Now she would either have to take Peale into her confidence or abandon her scheme. Could Peale keep a secret? What possible reason could she give for wishing to play such a trick on her husband? She certainly had no desire to share the tale of Maxim's perfidy with a servant. Peale was studying her, obviously puzzled by her mistress's thoughtful silence.

"Peale, no one must know that my memory has returned." Peale stared at her, now thoroughly confused. Diana bit her lip, then continued. "I am afraid His Lordship has been taking me rather for granted lately." Understanding dawned on Peale's face, and Diana felt herself blushing. Their servants all knew about Maxim's dallying, most like. There were few secrets the upper class could keep from those who served them.

Peale was a quick study. "And this is to teach him a

lesson,'' she said. Diana nodded and Peale smiled at her conspiratorially. ''I can keep a secret,'' she said.

Diana smiled back. ''Good! 'Tis a mild deception, and only for a short while. My memory will return in plenty of time for Christmas.''

Peale giggled. ''What a wonderful idea,'' she said.

''Remember, not a word to anyone,'' said Diana.

Peale looked insulted. ''I hope you wouldn't think I would be gossiping about such a thing with the servants,'' she said.

While Diana had slept, new arrivals had descended on the household. The Dashwoods had arrived and shortly after them, Maxim's cousin, the honorable Mr. Bernard Caldwell—Bozzy to his relatives. Now they sat in the drawing room, discussing poor Diana's terrible condition.

''But what did the doctor say?'' asked Louisa.

''He said she would be fine,'' Maxim answered bitterly.

''Well, obviously she is not,'' said Louisa in disgust. ''Why have you not called him back?''

''Because he is a quack and there is nothing he can do,'' snapped Maxim. ''How can you make someone remember who they are, anyway? What magic powder would you expect him to produce?''

His sister bit her lip and fell silent.

''Perhaps she just needs another day or two to mend,'' said Bozzy encouragingly.

Maxim frowned into the fire.

''Yes, I am sure Bozzy is right,'' agreed Lady Colby. ''After all, it hasn't been so very long since the fall.''

''How did you say she fell?'' asked Louisa's husband.

''What has that to do with anything?'' demanded Maxim, turning to glare at him.

James clenched his jaw, obviously biting back a retort. He continued to regard his brother-in-law, waiting for civilized manners to override raw emotion.

"She lost her balance," Maxim muttered. He turned again to stare into the fire, his shoulders stooped. "We were quarreling, and she lost her balance and fell. It is my fault she is as she is. I can hardly blame her for not wishing to remember me."

"Here now, old fellow," protested Bozzy. "Mustn't be too hard on yourself."

"Of course not," agreed James. "If a husband blamed himself for every quarrel he had with his wife, there wouldn't be a sane man in all of England."

Maxim merely shook his head.

It was at this point Diana made her entrance and surveyed the room. Louisa sat on the sofa, lovely as usual, her light brown curls arranged in ringlets around her face. She had her brother's brown eyes. But there the resemblance ended, for Louisa was a fine-looking woman. Her face was not so long as Maxim's, and her features were regular and pleasing. Unlike her brother's lanky frame, her body was small and delicately curved. She had probably never had to worry about her husband straying, thought Diana bitterly.

James rose to greet her, as handsome as his wife, with golden locks, a strong chin, and finely planed cheekbones.

Bozzy had been lounging in a nearby chair and now struggled up. She smiled timidly at him. She had always liked Bozzy. A hint of little boy still clung to him, with his upturned nose and freckles and curly hair. But there was nothing childish about the well-developed torso beneath the cloth of the finely cut coat and evening breeches. It was that boyish charm coupled with the handsome masculine physique that made Bozzy a general favorite with the ladies as well as the gentlemen.

As she studied him from under her lashes, Diana wondered if Bozzy wouldn't be a very useful tool in teaching her husband a lesson.

Maxim came to her and took her hand. "Di! I am so glad

you could join us," he said with forced heartiness. "Er, would you care for me to introduce you?"

"Please," said Diana.

Maxim performed the introductions, finishing with Bozzy.

Diana dimpled up at him. "It is nice to meet you," she said.

Bozzy blushed and bowed over her hand, and Maxim frowned.

Andrews appeared to summon the party to dinner, and Maxim led his wife into the drawing room, followed by Bozzy, escorting Lady Colby, and Louisa and James.

"The house looks especially lovely this year," Louisa said to Diana after they had taken their seats. "The children were completely awestruck by such a grand sight. I think you and mother have outdone yourselves."

"I am afraid I must own it was Diana who did most of the work," said Lady Colby. "She has a gift for these things."

Diana smiled her thanks at both women. Almost, she said, "I enjoyed decorating the house," then realized such a statement would betray her. She settled for a murmured "thank you."

The two women smiled encouragingly at her. How very hard they are trying to make me feel at home, she thought, and felt a sudden twinge of guilt. Both Louisa and Lady Colby had shown nothing but kindness to her since the day she had become betrothed to Maxim. She hated deceiving them. But there was no help for it. Her scheme would hardly work if half the house knew of it.

After dinner the company returned to the drawing room and settled into an awkward silence. "How about a little music, Louisa?" suggested James, nodding in the direction of the pianoforte. "Perhaps a Christmas carol."

"There's an excellent idea," agreed Bozzy, jumping up. He turned to Diana. "You always liked to sing carols."

"Did I?" asked Diana.

"Oh, yes," said Bozzy. Louisa had already seated herself at the instrument, and he led Diana over to it, and handed her some music.

Diana noticed that Maxim made no move to join them, remaining sprawled in a wing chair. But he was observing her carefully. Good. Then she would give him a show. She regarded Bozzy from under her lashes and smiled at him. "I must have liked singing carols because of the company in which I sang," she said.

Bozzy's face showed a mixture of embarrassment and pleasure. "I am afraid my voice ain't true, but my enthusiasm is unequaled."

Out of the corner of her eye Diana saw Maxim frown, and she giggled. She was beginning to have quite a merry Christmas.

Louisa played a short introduction, and Bozzy began to sing in a rich tenor voice, Diana humming along as though she were relearning the songs. She made sure to smile at her companion in a way she knew would infuriate her husband, and before the first song had ended, Maxim had joined them, standing possessively in back of her. A thrill of triumph ran through her. Perhaps she would get what she really wanted for Christmas yet.

The singers finally exhausted their repertoire, and the company settled into a comfortable conversation about Louisa's children as they awaited the arrival of the supper cart. "Of course, Matthew is too young to understand anything except that his sister is excited," Louisa was saying. "But he knows something important must be about to happen, so he is excited, too."

Diana listened to her talk and smiled. Louisa was a doting mother. And why shouldn't she be? Her children were beautiful, possessing James's fair hair and lovely blue eyes. China dolls, both. Diana wondered if she and Maxim would ever have children. Two years seemed such a long time to wait. Perhaps he blamed her. Perhaps that was why he'd strayed.

Don't be a goose, she scolded herself. Maxim had not been in the least worried that she hadn't produced an heir. "There's plenty of time," he'd said. No, it hadn't been because she had failed to produce an heir that his attentions had wandered. It had been becoming an earl and having people make such a fuss over him. Her kind and humble Maxim had become conceited and selfish.

She looked in his direction. He smiled at her. It was a tentative smile, the smile of a man suddenly unsure of himself, and because it pleased her to see him discomfited, it drew a much larger one from her in return than she had intended. Obviously thinking her expression one of encouragement, Maxim's smile broadened.

The conceited beast! thought Diana angrily. Her lips fell back into a straight line, and she turned her face from him, once more pinning her attention on Louisa.

Maxim's face flushed and he busied himself with making selections from the newly arrived supper cart. Having filled a plate he dutifully presented it to his wife, who took it and rewarded him for his efforts with a merely polite smile.

Soon after supper Diana pleaded fatigue and excused herself.

"Allow me to escort you," said Maxim, following her through the doorway.

Diana found her heart thumping nervously but allowed him to accompany her up the stairs to the second floor, where the family had their rooms. "Did you enjoy yourself this evening?" he asked.

Diana nodded. "Very much."

"Did . . . anything come back to you? Any memories?"

She shook her head. "I am afraid not. But I must say I like your family very much."

"Our family," corrected Maxim gently.

"Our family," she amended.

"And what of your husband?" he asked.

She paused at her bedroom door and regarded him with a steady gaze. "He seems to be a kind man. Were we happy?"

Maxim sighed. "For the most part, yes."

"There were times when we were not?"

"I believe for most couples there are times when one or the other is not happy. We were no different than most."

"Which one of us was not happy?" persisted Diana. If he would confess his perfidy, she would forgive all, regain her memory that very night, that very moment.

Maxim bit his lip, considering her question. "Perhaps," he said, taking her hand, "we should let the past remain forgotten." He kissed her palm, looking up at her with his most endearing little boy look.

His answer did nothing to endear him to her. Let the past remain forgotten, eh? Leave Maxim's sins unatoned for? Leave him free to do as he pleased in the future? Never! Diana seethed inside, but she forced her voice to be light. "Perhaps we should," she agreed and removed her hand from his. She stepped inside her room and turned to shut the door.

"Diana," said Maxim, laying a hand against the door.

She looked at him questioningly.

"Wouldn't you like me to come in with you?"

Diana raised an eyebrow. "Whatever for?" she asked.

Maxim gave her a look that said, you know.

Diana widened her eyes in a good imitation of astonishment. "My dear Maxim," she said. "If we are to leave our past problems forgotten, I think it wise to leave the entire past equally forgotten. It would be best if we were to start completely over."

"Oh, I agree," said Maxim heartily, ready to follow her inside.

Diana's hand against his chest stopped him. "Completely," she said firmly.

His mouth dropped. "What!" he exclaimed. "You mean you expect me to start all over? Court you?"

"I certainly do not intend to allow a complete stranger in my bedroom," said Diana. "Good night, Maxim." She closed the door on his startled face and grinned. Well, my dear husband, she thought. This will be a Christmas you shall not soon forget.

The world outside Diana's window the following morning was white and gleaming, the tree branches glistening like fairy wings. At breakfast Louisa was looking for volunteers to play in the snow with the children. "Elizabeth wants Daddy and Uncle Max and Auntie Di to help her make a snowman."

"And what about Cousin Bozzy?" demanded Bozzy.

"Oh, especially Cousin Bozzy," teased Louisa. "Elizabeth still remembers a certain highly entertaining tumble you took last year."

"Almost broke my neck," muttered Bozzy.

"How well we all remember," said Louisa. "But Elizabeth is sure you did so purely for her entertainment."

"I hope she don't expect me to slip and fall again simply to amuse her," said Bozzy.

"I am sure she will be equally pleased if you roll her a snowman," Louisa assured him.

After consuming a hearty meal, the company donned coats, warm knitted caps, gloves, and scarves and met on the whitened lawn in front of the manor.

Two small figures encased in bright wool peeked out at Diana from over their scarves as she came down the steps. The taller figure gave a muffled cry and ran to her, the smaller one following as fast as he could on chubby legs. "Hello," she crooned, scooping them into her arms. "My, what a big girl you are!" she exclaimed to Elizabeth.

"I am four years old now," announced Elizabeth.

"Then 'tis no wonder you are so big," said Diana. "Four is very grown up for a little girl."

"Matthew is only two," said Elizabeth in superior tones.

"Ah, but he will soon be four," said Diana. "In the meantime you can show him how to build a snowman."

"Will you help?" asked Elizabeth.

"Of course. We all will."

Elizabeth took her aunt's hand and led her to where the others were already rolling snowballs along the ground.

Bozzy formed one and casually tossed it at Maxim, who felt obliged to return it, and soon snowballs were flying in all directions. Diana felt one thud against her rump as she bent to form her own weapon. Instinctively she knew who had thrown it, but she chose to single out Bozzy. "You bully!" she cried and flung her snowball at him. Quite by accident it hit him, and swearing revenge, he quickly formed a ball to retaliate. With a yelp, Diana took off, Bozzy in hot pursuit.

He narrowed the distance between them quickly, catching her by the arm and attempting to stuff his snowball beneath the scarf around her neck. Squealing in mock terror, she tried to break free and toppled them both into the snow.

Bozzy scrambled up and held out a hand to help her up. A snowball splatted against his head. His eyes crossed, and he let out a cry. He glared at his approaching cousin. "I say, Max. You needn't take my head off. We're only playing, don't ye know."

Max smiled innocently at his cousin. "Sorry, old fellow. I didn't mean to hit you in the brainbox." He reached down and pulled Diana from the snow. "You look like a snow angel," he said, brushing her cloak.

"I feel more like a snowman," Diana said and shivered.

"Perhaps we had best get you inside," he said.

At that moment Elizabeth ran up to him and grabbed his

arm. "Uncle Max, come watch me put on the snowman's face." She tugged on her uncle's arm.

"Go on," said Bozzy agreeably. "I'll see Diana gets warm."

Maxim frowned, displaying an obvious ingratitude for his cousin's kindness. "I'll be along in a few moments," he promised Diana.

"Oh, do not rush on my account," she said airily, turning her back on him. She smiled up at Bozzy and took his arm. "I am sure your cousin will keep me very well entertained."

Maxim plowed off through the snow, scowling, and Diana and her escort went inside, where they sat by the drawing room fire drinking tea and visiting with Lady Colby.

The others followed them in soon afterward. The children were divested of their coats and scarves and led off to the nursery with promises of hot chocolate and biscuits. The other adults joined the party in the drawing room. "Well," announced James. "Now that I have done my parental duty, I think, perhaps, if no one cares, I shall settle down with a good book for an hour or two."

"I am sure you have my permission," said his wife. "I intend to do some stitching on my altar cloth."

"How does that progress?" asked her mother, looking up from her own stitching.

With his mother and sister absorbed in talk of threads and colors, Maxim turned to Diana. "And what would you like to do?" he asked.

"Oh, I don't know that I wish to do anything other than idle the time away in pleasant conversation," she said, smiling coyly at Bozzy.

"Oh, no," put in Louisa, who had been keeping up with her brother's conversation as well as her own. "One must do something. Else what will you have to talk of at dinner?"

Diana was thoughtful for a moment. "I know!" she cried. "I shall sketch you," she said to Bozzy.

"How did you know you could draw?" asked Maxim sharply.

Diana felt a warm tingling on her cheeks and knew a blush threatened to betray her nearly as much as her rash proposal. "I don't know," she said. "I simply thought it would be an enjoyable pastime. Can I not draw?"

"Oh, yes," said Maxim. "You draw beautifully. I have a portrait you made of me hanging in the library. I suppose you don't remember doing it, however," he finished sadly.

"I am afraid I don't," said Diana politely. She turned again to Bozzy, once more all life and charm. "Shall I draw you, then?"

Bozzy squirmed uncomfortably under his cousin's glare. "Perhaps you would prefer to draw old Max, here."

"Oh, I have probably drawn him several times," said Diana dismissively.

The smile that had begun to grow on Maxim's face died.

Diana turned to him. "Perhaps you would care to watch," she suggested.

"I think I shall read," he announced. And with that he took himself off to the library to join his brother-in-law.

Diana collected her drawing materials and placed her subject in a chair by the window. Much time was spent in arriving at a suitable pose, Louisa and Lady Colby each adding their suggestions as Diana twisted Bozzy this way and that. At last the three women decided to pose him standing contemplatively in front of the window. "Bozzy is really not the contemplative type," said Louisa, "but he has such a fine leg, 'tis a shame to have him sitting down."

Bozzy looked a little embarrassed by his cousin's teasing, but he obliged the ladies and stood, trying his best to look contemplative.

Maxim returned to the drawing room and was greeted by the others with surprise. "The light in the library is terrible,'' he announced and took a seat in the corner near his wife.

She ignored him, concentrating on her sketch pad. ''You have a very nice profile,'' she informed her subject.

Maxim shut his book with a snap, and Diana bit back a smile. He came to her side and peered down at her handiwork. ''It's very good,'' he said.

''Thank you,'' she murmured. And then, as if her husband had never spoken, she continued her conversation with her cousin.

''Why do we call you Bozzy?'' she asked.

Bozzy shrugged. ''Can't really remember. Everyone's called me Bozzy since we were little.''

''How very peculiar,'' said Diana.

'' 'Tis just a nickname,'' said Bozzy.

''Nicknames can be a term of endearment,'' put in Maxim. ''I always called you Di.''

''And was it a term of endearment?'' asked Diana.

Maxim looked insulted. ''Of course it was, er . . . is. Why shouldn't it be?''

''Oh, I don't know,'' said Diana. ''Perhaps such a pet name begins as a term of endearment and ends as merely a habit.''

''I don't know about that,'' said Bozzy. ''But if after all these years someone in the family were to start calling me by my Christian name, I'd feel as if I were in their black books. Besides, I don't particularly like my Christian name.''

''Bernard is a nice name,'' said Diana.

''Bernard!'' exclaimed Maxim. ''You called him Bernard.''

Another slip! Maxim hadn't used his cousin's Christian name when he introduced him to her the other night. Diana felt her heart race. ''Did no one tell me his name was Bernard?'' she asked.

"No," replied Maxim. "Di, don't you see what that means? It means your memory is starting to come back."

"Perhaps it is," said Diana. "I wonder what I shall remember about you." She looked at him as one might a curious bug, and he flushed under her gaze.

"I hope you will remember that I am human," he said softly and returned to his chair and his book.

An uncomfortable silence fell over the room, and Diana sighed inwardly. She was ruining everyone's Christmas. And for what? Simply to punish her husband for succumbing to the same temptation as nearly every other male in the upper ten thousand? Was she making too much of this?

Her jaw set stubbornly. No, she was not! She had given Maxim her heart and soul. And she had never denied him her body. She had always welcomed him to her bed with open arms. And this was how he rewarded her, by running to the bed of a cheap little ballet dancer. Let him suffer. It was nothing compared to the suffering he had inflicted on her.

She made her last stroke with a flourish. "'Tis done," she announced.

Bozzy hurried over to have a look. "This is quite good. Why, I really am a handsome fellow," he proclaimed.

Louisa laughed. "And so very modest," she added.

"Now sketch old Max," suggested Bozzy. "His nose will be quite out of joint if you don't."

"Very well," said Diana graciously.

"I had rather not," said Maxim stiffly.

"Now, Maxim," chided his mother. "Don't be churlish."

"I am not being churlish," said Maxim. "I simply don't wish to be sketched." He turned to his cousin. "Piquet?"

Bozzy looked embarrassed by Maxim's rudeness, but he agreed and the two men settled at a small table with a deck of cards.

Diana smiled. She knew she had slipped a little sliver into

Maxim's heart, and it was irritating him greatly. And it will irritate you a great deal more before I am done with you, my not-so-fine husband, she thought gleefully.

"'Tis almost Christmas Eve," said Peale as she helped her mistress dress for dinner. "When will you recover your memory?"

"Not for another day or two," said Diana. "Does anyone belowstairs suspect a trick?"

Peale shook her head. "Mrs. Jameston is very unhappy. This will be the first year since you and the master were engaged that you have not come to stir the Christmas pudding and make a wish."

Diana frowned. How very many people were being upset by her deception. Even the kindhearted servants. Well, soon it would be over. Maxim would either be a changed man, or she would be sentenced to live the remainder of her life as every other highborn woman in London, turning a blind eye to her husband's succession of ladybirds, burying a broken heart under a mountain of social engagements. "Tell Mrs. Jameston I shall be down tomorrow morning to stir the pudding. Heaven knows I need a wish come true. And I may as well do everything possible to get it."

On her way to the drawing room she determined to do more than simply stir the Christmas pudding to get her wish. She entered the drawing room to find Bozzy and James already there and waiting, James lounging in a chair and Bozzy warming himself in front of the fire. Maxim, she was sure, would be along any moment.

She bid the gentlemen good evening and strolled over to the kissing bough to admire it.

"You'd best be careful where you stand," cautioned James. "You are liable to find yourself most embarrassingly put upon."

Diana grinned coyly at Bozzy. "Am I?" she asked.

He smiled in return and joined her under the mistletoe.

"I am told I did this," she said. "It is quite lovely."

"You remember what it is for, don't you?" asked Bozzy.

Diana peeped up at him from her lashes. "I was told," she said.

Bozzy smiled down at her. He took her hand and placed a kiss on her palm. "Happy Christmas, Cousin," he said.

Diana pouted. "I think someone who has worked so hard on a kissing bough should be more properly rewarded," she said.

"You mean improperly, don't you?" teased Bozzy.

"I agree with you both," came a voice from the door. Diana turned to see Maxim, resplendent in his evening dress. His eyes flashed and she felt her heart give a nervous skip. He strode purposefully across the room to her and pulled her fiercely to him, bestowing on her a kiss that sent molten fire through her body.

He finally released her, and she opened her eyes to see him regarding her in a way he never had. It was a hawklike, possessive gaze, and it both frightened and thrilled her.

He turned and smiled triumphantly at his cousin. "You weren't planning on taking advantage of the kissing bough and my wife's lack of memory, were you?" he asked.

"Course not!" Bozzy exclaimed.

Maxim smiled down at Diana, and it was not an altogether gentle smile. "I see your memory has returned enough to know what the kissing bough is for," he said.

She was spared answering him by the entrance of his mother and sister.

For only a moment Louisa's brows knit at the sight of the trio under the kissing bough, looking the picture of brewing trouble. But her forehead quickly smoothed, and she smiled warmly at the company. "I must confess I am absolutely famished," she said. "There is something about the country air that gives one quite an appetite."

Lady Colby came to Diana and took her hand. "How are you feeling tonight, my dear?"

"I feel quite well, thank you," said Diana politely. "I think I am remembering more things all the time."

"She is even remembering some things she didn't know," muttered Maxim.

Andrews appeared to announce dinner, ending the conversation, and by the time they were all seated at table the subject had been changed. Diana tried to relax and enjoy her soup, but the memory of Maxim's disturbing kiss hung on her lips, and his mysterious remark teased her brain, making the simple task of eating difficult. What had he meant? Dared she hope her wild scheme was working?

She found out when he escorted her to her bedroom later. "Is something bothering you, Maxim?" she ventured as they made their way down the hallway.

Maxim's jaw was working, a sure sign something was, indeed, bothering him. "What makes you think that?" he hedged.

"You seem to be rather quiet. And then there is that odd comment you made before dinner."

"My comment was not half so odd as your behavior," said Maxim stiffly. "Really, Diana. You never used to be such a shocking flirt. I think that fall you took has unhinged something in your brain."

"I beg your pardon?" replied Diana between clenched lips.

"You are forgiven," said Maxim, deliberately misunderstanding her. "But I wish you would be more careful in the future. Making such sheep's eyes at Bozzy—it doesn't look right."

"I suppose it would look better if I were to make sheep's eyes at you," said Diana.

"I am your husband. It would certainly be more appropriate," said Maxim in pompous tones.

"Was ours a love match?" asked Diana suddenly.

"A what? What are you talking about?"

"I think that is a simple enough question. Was our marriage a love match? Do we love each other?"

"Of course we do!" exclaimed Maxim, shocked by such crass honesty.

"Do we really?" asked Diana coyly.

Maxim scowled impatiently. "Why on earth do you ask such a question?"

"Oh, because I am just wondering why I continue to feel such a strong desire to . . ."

"Yes," prompted Maxim, his voice softening. He put an arm around her waist. "What do you have a strong desire to do?"

"This," she replied.

The ringing sound of her hand slapping his face startled him nearly as much as the unexpected pain, and he stared at her, stupefied. "What was that for?" he demanded.

"You must tell me," she replied haughtily. "After all, you are the one who can remember."

She turned and walked the rest of the way down the hall to her bedroom alone. Maxim stood frowning after her for some time. Absently he rubbed his cheek.

Diana rose early the following morning. At breakfast her only other companion was Lady Colby, a habitual early riser. "How are you this morning, my dear?" asked the older woman.

"Very well, thank you."

"I trust you rested well."

Diana nodded.

Lady Colby took a casual sip from her cup. "And are you finding yourself remembering anything more?"

"A little here and there," said Diana noncommittally.

Lady Colby set down her cup and smiled at Diana. It was a smile at once reproachful and full of empathy. "Some things are best forgotten," she said.

She rose and left a guilty Diana to consider her words. She knows, thought Diana. She knows what I am up to. And she knows what her son has been up to. Or at least suspects. Some things are best forgotten? Was a certain dark-haired ballet dancer one of those things?

Diana left the dining room and made her way back to the kitchen. Mrs. Jameston, the cook, a rotund, gray-haired woman, was already damp and red-faced from her many morning projects, but she beamed at Diana, pleased to have her visit her domain. "Peale said you'd be coming in this morning to stir the Christmas pudding, Your Ladyship." She produced a large bowl and a big wooden spoon. "Do you remember how to get your wish?"

Diana remembered. But she shook her head.

"You have to stir the pudding seven times without speaking to anyone or your wish won't come true," instructed the cook.

Seven times. Diana had tried for the last two years to get her wish, but Maxim had always come into the kitchen and said something silly and tricked her into speaking. The last time she'd been wishing for a baby. This Christmas that wish would have to wait. This time she must wish for her husband.

Diana took the bowl and began to stir, counting under her breath. ". . . three, four, five . . ."

"Eight, nine, ten," whispered a voice at her elbow.

"Six, seven!" she cried. "You did not trick me out of my wish," she teased her husband.

"What makes you think I would do such a thing?" he said, the picture of wounded innocence.

"Wouldn't you?" she asked suspiciously.

He smiled. So did she. "Have you forgiven me for last night?" he asked softly.

Diana set the bowl down. "Perhaps," she said.

"Will you come for a sleigh ride with me?" he asked.

"Why do you ask me?"

"Because I would like to win your love again. I wish to court you."

Diana pretended to consider.

"If it were spring and we were in London, I should take you for a ride in my curricle. Alas, this is not curricle weather. So I must take you for a ride in my sleigh instead."

"Very well," said Diana. "I shall fetch my cloak and muff."

Within the hour Diana found herself snuggled under warm rugs next to her husband and gliding through a snow-muffled world, silent except for the *swoosh* of the sleigh runners and the jingling of the tiny bells on the horses' harness. He smiled down at her. "Are you enjoying yourself?" he asked.

Diana nodded.

"Not cold?"

She wriggled her nose. "Only my nose," she said.

Maxim leaned over and kissed it. "I promise I will take you back before it gets frostbitten," he said.

Maxim was trying. He was really trying. He must love her. Yet the specter of a dark-haired beauty sat between them. If her hair had been dark . . . "Do you like red hair?" asked Diana.

Maxim pretended to consider this. "Oh, yes," he said. "No, that is not quite right. Normally, I am not all that fond of red hair. I only like it on one particular woman."

"How did I come to fall?" she asked suddenly.

Maxim bit his lip. At last he spoke, looking straight ahead at the horses' backs. "We were quareling. You were very angry. I am afraid in the heat of the moment you lost your balance and fell."

"Why was I angry?" she persisted.

Maxim hesitated, obviously considering his answer. "I am afraid I have not been the best of husbands," he said at last.

"Oh?" prompted Diana.

Maxim shrugged despondently. "Perhaps it is best left in the past."

"Was I the best of wives?" she asked.

Maxim pulled on the reins and the sleigh stopped. The wind, which had been whipping at her bonnet and blowing on her cheeks as they *whooshed* along, seemed to stop, too, and Diana felt as if they suddenly hung suspended in time. Her husband turned to her, and she saw a new passion in his eyes—a longing she couldn't remember having ever seen before. "You were, indeed, the best of wives," he said. "And if you could remember anything, I wish you could remember that. And remember how happy we were when we were first wed."

"I wish I could," she said. And she meant it. But it seemed that Maxim's perfidy was lodged in her memory, like some gigantic burr.

He put an arm around her. "Do you, Diana? Do you really wish such a thing?" For a moment his eyes searched her face, as if seeking the answer to some deep, anguish-laden question. Then, before she could speak, he pressed his lips to hers with a fierceness that startled her. In spite of all her resolve she leaned against him, treasuring the closeness of his body. The kiss deepened and softed, and Diana gave herself up to the luxury of enjoying the sensual oneness of it. At last he pulled back and once more searched her face. "Diana, how I wish I could destroy the past, remove all my mistakes. But I cannot. I—" His voice broke, and he struggled to regain control of his emotions.

Diana knew if she would but put a hand to his cheek, if she would but meet him halfway . . . She hesitated, wondering if such a gesture would end her problems or simply end the farce she had begun.

The moment was lost. Maxim removed his arm from around her. "We had best go back," he said with a slap of the reins.

Maxim was unusually quiet that evening at dinner,

obviously in mourning for his past sins. Mourning was all well and good, thought Diana, but it would never do to leave him in such a state. Much as she'd have loved to wrap things up that afternoon like a neat little Christmas present, she knew now it would have been premature. Maxim had to be brought to repentence. He had to admit the error of his ways and vow to change. And soon, for she couldn't allow him to remain sulking with Christmas so close at hand.

After dinner Louisa played the pianoforte so they could sing Christmas carols. "Am I fond of dancing?" Diana asked Maxim suddenly.

"Yes, you are," he said.

"Will you dance with me?" she asked.

"I should be honored," he said. "Louisa, play us a country dance."

"Here now, this is most unfair," protested James. "My wife is playing the pianoforte, and I have no pretty lady with whom to dance."

Bozzy snatched a shawl from a nearby chair, draped it over his head, and tied it under his chin. "I should be delighted, sir," he said in a high falsetto.

Diana giggled as James grinned tolerantly and bowed over Bozzy's extended hand.

Louisa launched into a spirited if slightly flawed rendition of a favorite piece, and the four hopped and twirled around the drawing room floor, dodging occasional tables and chairs as Lady Colby clapped encouragingly.

After allowing them several turns around the room, Louisa slowed the tempo for the panting four and switched to a waltz.

"Are you fond of dancing?" Diana asked her husband.

"As fond as any man," replied Maxim. "I have other pastimes that I prefer. But dancing is a necessary social skill, and I admire any man who can master it."

"And do you admire women who dance well?" Diana asked innocently.

A guilty flush stained Maxim's cheeks.

Diana ignored her husband's flushed face and his clenched jaw. "I am definitely fond of dancing," she declared. "I am sure I danced with any number of charming men when we attended balls."

Maxim's expression changed from one of embarrassment to one of shock. "Diana! What an improper thing to say."

Diana looked at her husband in surprise. "Did I not dance with other men?"

"Well, of course you did," said her husband. "But—"

"But they were all boors. How sad for me."

"Of course they were not all boors. You are being ridiculous."

"If they were not boors, they must have been charming."

"Oh, I suppose," said Maxim shortly.

"Well, then. What I said a moment ago was perfectly true. Whyever did you get so cross?" Diana wondered.

"Because the way you said it sounded most improper. It sounded very much as if you enjoyed the attentions of other men as much as those of your own husband."

"I see," said Diana slowly. "How very curious. Men and women only enjoy the attentions of the one to whom they are married. Is that what you are telling me?"

"Well, yes, in a way that is so."

"And you have never enjoyed the attentions of other women?"

Fortunately for Maxim, Louisa chose that moment to end the music.

"You beast!" exclaimed Bozzy and playfully slapped James. "Of course I won't go out in the garden with you. Not unless you mean to propose marriage."

"Heavens!" exclaimed James in mock horror. "You're much too whey-faced for my tastes."

"Well!" exclaimed Bozzy with a toss of the head.

Everyone was laughing. Except Maxim.

*   *   *

The following day found Bozzy and Maxim playing at billiards. "Does any more of Diana's memory appear to be coming back?" asked Bozzy casually as he aimed his cue stick.

Maxim's jaw set, a sure sign he was not pleased with the turn the conversation had taken. "I don't know," he said shortly.

Bozzy took his shot and had the satisfaction of seeing his ball plop into a leather pocket. He took aim again. "She seems rather different ever since she got that bump on the nob."

"If I didn't know better, I'd swear she's behaving the way she is simply to drive me mad," said Maxim.

This statement was enough to draw Bozzy's attention from the balls on the table. "What, pretending she don't remember?"

Maxim shook his head. "You're right. It sounds preposterous."

"Why would she want to do such a thing?"

"Revenge?" guessed Maxim.

"Revenge! What the devil for?"

"She knew about Estelle."

Bozzy gestured impatiently. "A lightskirt? Your wife would want revenge simply because of a lightskirt? That's the craziest thing I ever heard. Why, if every female took after her husband because he had a ladybird on the side, every household in London would be turned upside-down."

Maxim sighed. "I know that. So do you. But I don't think Diana does. We were having a terrible quarrel about it when she fell." Maxim looked sadly at his cousin. "This whole tangle is my fault."

Bozzy looked disgusted. "You'll spend the rest of your life under the cat's paw if you say such a thing to Diana."

Maxim shook his head. "I really do love the chit, Bozzy."

Bozzy returned his attention to the game with a shake of

the head. "I still think you'd be making a big mistake if you were to talk so wildly."

Maxim was too preoccupied with his own thoughts to hear his cousin's advice. "The pity of it is I'd broken with Estelle. Sent Di on ahead and had the business done in a day. I was going to tell Di. But she fell before I could. And now I can't tell her anything." He sighed. "I can't seem to have any sort of conversation with her without her tying me in knots or getting my hackles up."

Bozzy chuckled. "She's leading you a merry dance."

"I don't find it merry in the least," said Maxim. "Which reminds me. I'll thank you not to encourage her."

"I haven't been encouraging her!" protested Bozzy. "Just been my normal friendly self."

"Well, you can stop being so curst friendly," snapped Maxim.

Diana wasn't finding the dance she was leading her husband any more merry than he. Oh, she was taking a sort of grim pleasure in it. But really, living like this was little improvement. Perhaps it would have been better to continue to pretend she knew nothing of her husband's light of love, she thought miserably. No. She had tried that and it had made her stomach sick, making meals a horror and turning Maxim's company to torture. This was somewhat better. At least she had the perverse satisfaction of seeing him squirm.

Diana set down the enameled snuffbox at which she had been absently staring and took up scissors and paper. It was the last present she had to wrap. Normally she would do so with great pleasure, but this afternoon she took no joy in wrapping it, no more than she would in giving it. Gifts were a token of love and esteem. Gifts were something exchanged between friends, loved ones. What a hollow ritual it would be when she and her husband exchanged their presents. Diana sighed.

A tiny knock at her door brought her back from her melancholy future. "Come in," she called.

Elizabeth ventured shyly into her room, the picture of guilt trying to look innocent.

Diana smiled. "Elizabeth! What a pleasant surprise." She studied her niece. "Aren't you supposed to be taking a nap right now?"

"I am too big for naps," Elizabeth informed her. "I couldn't sleep." She walked to the bed and examined the small pile of presents clothed in bright paper and ribbons. "Tomorrow is Christmas Eve," she announced. "We will have dinner with the grown-ups."

"Yes, you shall," said Diana. "Then we will all go to church."

"Is one of those for me?" asked Elizabeth, eyeing the presents.

Diana picked up a long, doll-size package. "This one is yours," she said and handed the box to the child.

Elizabeth's eyes grew big. "Oooh." She bit her lip in anticipation. "What is it?"

Diana smiled at her. "You shall have to wait till Christmas to see," she said.

"Elizabeth!"

The child jumped, nearly dropping the box, and turned to see her mother in the doorway.

"Aren't you supposed to be napping?"

"I was visiting Auntie Di," said Elizabeth.

"And I am sure you had a very nice visit," said Louisa, "but now it is time to have a nap." She held out her hand.

Elizabeth reluctantly put down the mysterious box and went to take her mother's hand. At that moment the nurse appeared, and after several exclamations of surprise that Elizabeth would be so naughty as to sneak from her bed and a gentle reprimand, the child was led back to the nursery.

Louisa watched her go, then turned, still smiling, to her sister-in-law. "May I come in?"

"Of course," said Diana.

Louisa glided into the room and surveyed the pile of presents. She tapped the one Elizabeth had just been holding. ''A doll?''

Diana nodded. ''I hope she will like it.''

''She will love it, I am sure. She has discovered dollies this last year and thinks they are wonderful.'' Louisa picked up the snuffbox. ''This is quite lovely,'' she said.

''Max does have a fondness for snuff . . .''

The betraying slip hung half finished between the two women. Louisa regarded Diana with concern. ''Diana, what has happened between you and Maxim to bring things to this pass? Why are you pretending not to know him?''

''You knew before this, didn't you?''

Louisa nodded. ''Those tiny slips you made—mentioning Bozzy's Christian name, offering to draw him.''

If Louisa had guessed her secret, who else knew? Diana wondered.

''I am sure no one other than Mama suspects,'' said Louisa, as if reading her sister-in-law's mind. She studied Diana's face. ''There is only one thing I can guess that would drive a woman to such desperate measures.''

Sudden tears sprang to Diana's eyes. She blinked hard in an effort to hold them back, but the betraying drops escaped and slid down her cheek. ''Oh, Louisa,'' she sobbed.

Louisa gathered her sister-in-law into her arms, and the two women stood entwined for some time, Diana's sobs telling her story more eloquently than words.

''I know it is silly,'' Diana said at last. ''I know other men have their ladybirds. But somehow I never thought Maxim would do such a thing. I thought he loved me. Oh, I knew it wasn't some wildly romantic love. But I thought he was happy.''

''And so he is,'' said Louisa. ''Maxim cares deeply for you.''

Diana shook her head. ''He changed after he came into the title. I suppose all the fuss people made over him would have turned the head of a lesser man, so perhaps I should have been more patient with him. But he became so very conceited. Things were fine when he was simply a baronet, but once he became an earl it was as if I were no longer good enough for him.''

"I am sure Maxim never felt that," said Louisa, springing to her brother's defense.

"Perhaps not. But something definitely came between us. We had been so close. Such good friends. I suppose that is why it hurt so very much when I heard he had taken up with this . . . person. I am afraid I was jealous. I love Maxim so very much, you see. And we were such good friends. I suppose I felt he had betrayed our friendship more than he had betrayed our marriage. Oh, Louisa, can you understand at all?'' she ended desperately.

"Of course I can," said Louisa. "I remember when I was expecting Elizabeth.''

"Oh, not James!" protested Diana. "You are so very beautiful, Louisa.''

"I must admit I was not very beautiful when I was increasing. At least, I did not feel beautiful. And I felt so ill all the time. I am afraid I was not very good company.''

"You make it sound as if it were your fault," accused Diana.

Louisa looked at her sister-in-law with world-weary eyes.

"'Tis no one's fault when these things happen. It is the way men are. And there is nothing a female can do about it, except turn a blind eye to her husband's faults and make her life the best she can.''

"I don't believe that," declared Diana. "I think if more wives did something, less men would behave in such a callous manner toward them.''

Louisa shook her head and looked at her sister-in-law as if she were simple-minded. "This is a man's world, my dear. How many marriages do you think are really love matches? How many men would really care if their wives treated them the way you are treating Maxim? They would simply stay at their clubs that much more. No, a woman's best strategy is to feign ignorance and take her happiness where she can."

"My happiness is with Maxim," said Diana. "And I cannot be happy sharing him with a string of other women."

"You wage an impossible battle," said Louisa.

"Perhaps. But I must fight it to the end. You won't give me away?"

Louisa smiled. "Of course not. I must admit, although I find your thinking quite radical, I do admire the spirit behind it. So, I will not only keep your secret, I will do all I can to help you."

"Oh, thank you," breathed Diana.

"We women must stick together," said Louisa.

They had barely finished speaking when a maid tapped timidly at Diana's door, holding a scroll tied up with a bright red ribbon. "I was told to give you this," she said.

"Who is it from?" asked Diana.

The girl giggled excitedly. "He said not to tell you. Yer supposed to read it and guess."

Diana smiled at her sister-in-law. "How exciting!" The maid skipped off, and Diana untied the ribbon and read.

"Well," prompted Louisa, "what does it say?"

Diana blinked back tears. "Oh, Louisa. 'Tis beautiful." She read: " 'This Christmastide my heart doth yearn, not for goodwill of men. But for one woman's precious gift—to love me once again.' "

"Heavens," breathed Louisa. "I begin to believe you might succeed in your scheme."

A look of determination settled on Diana's face. "He must do more than court me, Louisa. I must know he is not just behaving like a little boy who wants a toy he has been deprived of. I must know I really have his heart, for I'll not share so much as a corner of it with that dancer."

"We shall make sure of it," said Louisa with equal determination.

Maxim knocked on Diana's door just as she was about to go downstairs for dinner. His eyes sparkled at the sight of her. She was wearing a low-cut satin gown of her favorite color, a deep green. On her throat and at her ears glittered the emeralds Maxim had given her for a wedding present. "You look incomparable," he murmured. He caught her hand and planted a kiss on it that bordered on reverent. "May I escort you down?" he asked.

"You may," she said graciously, linking her arm through his. They walked along in silence. She was sure Maxim was waiting for her to mention the poem he had sent earlier. Play your hand wisely, she cautioned herself. Do not succumb too quickly, else you will find yourself taken for granted all over again. She waited till they were on the stairs. "I received a lovely poem this afternoon," she said.

"Did you like it?" asked Maxim eagerly.

"It was most beautiful," she replied calmly. She wished to cry out, "Oh, Maxim! Did you mean it?" and throw herself into his arms. But she restrained herself. She had been cheated of her passion and sparks when she became a bride. This time she would have them. And it must be Maxim who struck the flint. He had made a fine beginning, but it was still not enough, not enough to repair the damage he'd done to her heart, not enough to sustain her for a lifetime.

The others were already in the drawing room, waiting for the butler to announce dinner. Bozzy smiled appreciatively at Diana, and she smiled back. Would the sparks begin to fly tonight? She sincerely hoped so.

At dinner Diana was in rare form. She sparkled like fine crystal in candlelight. One moment she was listening raptly to her husband's every word. The next she was ignoring him completely for Bozzy.

As his wife became increasingly more gay, Maxim's mood became more and more sour. Louisa's laughing comment on the merriness of the company brought a prudish frown to his face. He turned to his brother-in-law and observed, "Does it seem to you that the woman of today often displays a levity of mind which betrays a certain lack of . . ." He stopped momentarily, searching for the appropriate word. "Modesty," he finished with pedantic heaviness.

"Maxim!" exclaimed his sister. "I have never in my life heard you say such a pompous, silly thing."

"I think Maxim makes a very good point," said James. "If frivolity goes beyond certain bounds, it is most unpleasing."

Louisa made a face. "You only agree with him because you are both males," she said. "I think Maxim is merely pouting because he feels ignored," she continued. "The one who is left out of the laughter always deems it ridiculous." She looked pointedly at his empty wineglass. "And if you continue as you have started, you will not only miss the laughter, you will miss the entire evening."

Lady Colby cleared her throat nervously. "I think, perhaps, it is time the ladies left the gentlemen to their port," she said and, rising, led the way to the drawing room.

"Really!" exclaimed Louisa in disgust after the three women had settled themselves. "Men are all alike. And they certainly will go to great lengths to defend another member of their sex, no matter what ridiculous thing he may say."

"I suppose I was having a little too much fun," said Diana guiltily.

"Nonsense," scoffed Louisa. "If you had been some demirep or diamond of the first water out to make a match, the gentlemen would all have pronounced you a splendid creature. But because you are now merely a wife, too much vivacity is no longer allowed, especially if it is directed at someone other than your husband. But, oh, if a man should choose to flirt or laugh with a woman not his wife, does anyone reprimand *him?*''

"Louisa! What has come over you?" demanded her mother.

"Nothing mother," replied Louisa. She looked at Diana. "It is only that I have been doing a great deal of thinking of late. That is all."

The gentlemen finally joined the ladies in the drawing room, and it was soon apparent that Maxim had fulfilled his sister's prophecy.

Louisa gave her husband a look that said, "See, what did I tell you?" Then, ignoring her bosky brother, she rose, announcing, "I think some music would be in order. Perhaps Diana would care to dance," she suggested as she made her way to the pianoforte.

"Oh, yes," agreed Diana merrily. Maxim made an effort to rise from his chair. "Not with you, Maxim," she said, gently pushing him back. "You have had entirely too much to drink, and you would merely tread on my toes." She turned to Bozzy with an arch smile. "I am sure your cousin would much prefer waltzing as a man instead of a lady."

Bozzy looked to his cousin.

Maxim waved his permission. "It is obvious my wife prefers your company to mine," he slurred. "I should hate to deprive her of her entertainment."

Bozzy smiled nervously at Diana. "Let's have a go at it, then," he said.

The two began to twirl about the room, Diana's face enraptured, Bozzy's merely pleasant.

Bozzy was an easygoing man, always good company at a party, and a family favorite. And normally, he would be most comfortable dancing with his cousin, but there was something about this night, this dance, that spelled trouble. And while Bozzy was not above a little dalliance with a willing demirep, he did draw the line at carrying on with his cousin's wife, especially under that cousin's very nose. Feeling Maxim's eyes on him, not to mention the gaze of his aunt, he tried to keep a respectable distance between himself and his partner, but she fought him, edging provocatively closer every chance she got. By the end of the dance he was sweating profusely, and not from physical exertion.

"Ah, that was delightful," said Diana, lifting a curl from her neck and fanning herself.

Lady Colby looked from her glowering son to his wife and suggested they sing some carols. "After all, we can only enjoy them once a year."

"Excellent idea," agreed James, moving to join his wife at the pianoforte.

The others followed, and Diana was careful to place herself next to Bozzy as they gathered around Louisa. Out of the corner of her eye she saw Maxim frowning as he came to stand at her elbow, and she couldn't help grinning. She would win this battle. She would show Louisa it could be done. It was a man's world, but a woman had the power to spin it.

And Maxim's world was, indeed, spinning dizzily. One moment his wife was looking at him adoringly, the next she was fawning over his cousin. His head was beginning to hurt, and he was not at all sure he cared for that pest Bozzy. Why didn't he go harrass his own family? His father was still alive, along with that old aunt of his. Why didn't he go take his Christmas dinner with them? Why the devil did he have to hang round the manor till Christmas morning, making a nuisance of himself? And why was the fellow encouraging his wife to make a fool of herself? Did he have designs on Diana?

Maxim took in his wife's auburn curls and creamy white skin. His eyes ran appreciatively down her body. It had been a long time since he'd visited her bed. Too long.

Did Bozzy have hopes of visiting her bed? Maxim looked

at his cousin through blurry eyes and thought he looked every inch the satyr. That was why he was hanging about instead of going home where he belonged. He had designs on Diana! Well, Maxim would see him dead before he'd let Bozzy get his greedy paws on her!

The evening bumped awkwardly along, Maxim's sulking and Diana's flirting making most of the others uncomfortable. Lady Colby greeted Andrews's arrival at ten-thirty with the supper cart with the kind of joy one reserved for long lost friends.

"Ah, oysters!" declared Diana. "They look delicious. I hope you are going to have some," she said innocently to Bozzy.

Maxim had become a man of the world in the past few months. He knew of the purported power of oysters. Why would Diana wish Bozzy to indulge himself unless she had plans for him later that night? He glared at his cousin. "You had best not eat any," he growled.

Bozzy looked at Maxim as if he'd gone mad. "Are they spoiled?" he asked.

"Maxim, don't be ridiculous," snapped his mother. "Of course Bozzy may have some oysters if he wishes."

"He may not!" roared Maxim.

Bozzy's chin jutted out. "I will have oysters if I please," he said.

"You shall have oysters over my dead body," Maxim informed him.

"Curse it all, Max! What the devil's gotten into you?" demanded Bozzy.

"Here now," said James firmly. "This is no way to be acting in front of the ladies."

"You keep out of it," snarled Maxim. He turned again to Bozzy. "I tell you if you eat any oysters, I will find my gun and shoot you."

"Maxim!" cried Diana.

"And you keep out of this. I will deal with you later."

"I think, perhaps, we had best retire," suggested Lady Colby, rising.

Louisa, biting back a smile, followed her mother's example, and taking Diana by the arm, led her from the room. "I do declare," she whispered once they were out of earshot, "I cannot remember when I have enjoyed myself more."

"You don't think he will really shoot Bozzy, do you?" asked Diana nervously.

"In his condition? Maxim would most likely shoot himself in the foot instead."

"Oh, dear!" cried Diana and turned to go back.

Louisa drew her away. "He will be fine. James will see to it that neither man comes to any harm."

"What is all this about?" demanded Lady Colby suspiciously.

"Come up to my bedroom," said Louisa. "We shall tell you all about it."

"I suspected as much," said Lady Colby once the entire story had been told, "but I thought it too fantastic to credit. I am so sorry, my dear," she said, taking Diana's hand.

"No. It is I who should be sorry," said Diana. "I thought, perhaps, you guessed what I was about."

"I knew right away something was terribly wrong between you and Maxim," said the older woman. "And I can hardly blame you for feeling hurt, for you must know, I never have approved of infidelity." She bit her lip. "I suppose had I been in your slippers and a similar opportunity presented itself, I should have been strongly tempted to take it. But this current situation threatens to get out of hand."

"Oh, Mother, don't be such a killsport," said Louisa. "I must admit I had my doubts about all this when Diana first told me. But the more I think on it, the more I begin to see her point. Why should we allow our husbands to treat us so cavalierly, to take us for granted as if we were dolls to be picked up and played with or cast aside at will? I think Maxim should be taught a lesson. And, perhaps, so should a few other men of our acquaintance.'' From the look on her face it wasn't hard to guess which particular man she had in mind.

''Oh, dear'' was all Lady Colby could say.

Christmas Eve day dawned gray and cold. And it was well past noon when Maxim woke with a splitting head and the memory of a very strange dream. He had been pursuing Bozzy around the drawing room, throwing oysters at him. Maxim shook his head. It had been a dream. Hadn't it? Gingerly he felt his jaw. The last thing he remembered was James's fist hitting it. He moaned and grabbed his aching head.

It took his valet a good hour to get the earl in any sort of condition where he could even think of going downstairs. He walked past the dining room and shuddered. The door to the drawing room was slightly ajar, and his mother's voice drifted out to him. ''I do think Maxim has paid enough for his sins.''

Maxim stopped.

''I think Diana should continue to punish him until he confesses all and begs her forgiveness and promises never to do such a thing again,'' came Louisa's voice.

Maxim frowned.

''Of course,'' she continued, ''how can a woman expect a man to keep such a promise? We all know what men are.''

Maxim's eyes widened, and his frown deepened.

Diana's voice drifted out softly to him. ''I am afraid I was foolish to think I could shame Maxim into being as he was when we were first married. In fact, I wanted him to be more than he was, and that was most unfair. He never cared passionately to begin with. This was a ridiculous plan, and it has done nothing but upset everyone's holiday. I shall have to recover my memory and resign myself to having lost my husband.''

Maxim backed away, his poor, befuddled brain a jumble of thoughts. He made his way back upstairs in search of his room, where he could think in peace. This memory loss had been nothing more than a ruse to punish him for Estelle. To punish him for doing what every other man in London did! How dare she? The vixen! And what the devil did she mean by talking of losing her husband? Did she think that because he merely chose to amuse himself with a pretty girl he no longer cared for her? Of all the totty-headed females! He knew she had been upset, but this was just too much. How could she have allowed herself to be hurt by something that meant so little to him?

But that was just it. She had been hurt. Obviously deeply hurt. And what was he to do to bring them back to the comfortable relationship they had previously enjoyed?

With sudden insight he realized they might not get back to that comfortable relationship for some time. For, after watching her flirt so outrageously with Bozzy, he had discovered he was much more fond of the chit than he had ever realized. If she decided to kick the traces come spring and amuse herself in London with some other man, he would not like it one little bit. And if she thought he no longer loved her, that might be exactly what she'd do. Unthinkable!

On the way back to his room he encountered Bozzy, dressed for travel, followed by his valet and a footman, burdened with three large traveling cases. ''Where the devil are you going?'' demanded Maxim.

''Home,'' snapped Bozzy.

''Home? You never go home till Christmas Day.''

''Well, this year I am going home Christmas Eve day,'' said Bozzy, continuing on his way.

''What the devil is the matter with you?'' demanded Maxim. ''Has everyone in this house gone mad?''

"Perhaps," said his cousin stiffly. "And if that's the case, it must be catching. I'm going home before I wind up in Bedlam. Or before I get any more oysters thrown at me."

"So I really did that," muttered Maxim. His cousin was nearly to the stairs now, and Maxim shook himself out of his reverie and gave chase. "Wait! Bozzy, old fellow. You surely can't hold against a man something he did when he was in his cups! Stop, I tell you." Maxim grabbed ahold of his cousin's arm, halting him at the top of the stairs.

"Let go!" commanded Bozzy between gritted teeth, jerking his arm away.

His action put Maxim off-balance, and he tipped backward. With lightning speed Bozzy grabbed his cousin and yanked him upright, glaring at him. "Have a care, man. All we'd need is for you to fall down the stairs to completely ruin everyone's Christmas."

His cousin suddenly looked at him as if he'd just said something very brilliant.

The three ladies sat glumly in the drawing room. "I still say you shouldn't give in," said Louisa. "Think of the service you are doing other women."

"If I thought there was any hope in succeeding, I should continue," said Diana. "But Maxim has showed no sign of changing. He has only been selfishly irritated because I have not given him the attention he thinks his due. That is not the behavior of a changed man."

"Maxim does love you, dearest," put in Lady Colby. "I know he does."

"Oh, I am sure he does in an offhand sort of way"— Diana sighed—"rather like one would love a lap dog."

Her mother-in-law looked shocked.

"'Tis true," said Diana. "He has always taken me so very much for granted. I never realized it until I began to really observe other couples. Oh, the fireworks, the jealous rages!"

"Very much of that is most uncomfortable," said Lady Colby dampingly.

Louisa giggled. "And besides, you had your jealous rages last night."

"Throwing oysters is not very romantic," said Diana.

"It is better than watching the cousins run each other through with swords," retorted Louisa.

The conversation was interrupted by a sudden loud cry and much thumping, as if someone were falling downstairs. With fear in their eyes the three women jumped from their chairs and dashed out into the hallway and up the stairs.

Bozzy was kneeling on the first landing. Next to him lay Maxim, silent and still.

"Maxim!" cried Diana and fell on her knees next to him. "Oh, Maxim, dearest—speak to me!"

Maxim's eyes fluttered open, and he squinted at his wife as if trying to recall the name of an old acquaintance.

"We must send for the doctor," said his mother sharply. She looked around for some sign of a servant, but none was in sight. Both Bozzy's valet and the footman, who had been present no more than five minutes before, had vanished, along with Bozzy's coat and luggage.

"Wait," said Bozzy, holding up a hand. "I think the fall just stunned him." He gently slapped his cousin's face. "Max, old fellow. Wake up."

Again, Maxim opened his eyes and squinted up at his cousin. "What happened?" he asked, trying to sit up on one elbow.

"You tripped and fell down the stairs," Bozzy informed him. "Can you stand?"

"I think so," said Maxim.

Bozzy took one side, Diana the other, and together they helped the fallen man to his feet.

"Does it hurt to put weight on either leg?" asked Bozzy.

Maxim shook his head. "No, not too much."

"Good," said the self-proclaimed doctor. "That means no bones broken. A little afternoon rest and he'll be good as new."

"Oh, thank God," breathed Diana. "You scared us half to death."

Maxim smiled down at her. "I believe we haven't been introduced," he said.

Diana's mouth hung open. "Maxim! I am your wife, Diana."

Maxim shook his head. "No. If I had such a pretty woman for a wife, I surely would have remembered. I . . ." Before he could complete his sentence, Maxim's eyes rolled backward and he fell against his cousin in a swoon.

"Don't worry," said Bozzy, struggling to throw the limp body over his shoulder. "I'll just cart him upstairs and tuck him into his bed. I'm sure when he wakes up, he'll be right as rain."

The three women exchanged worried glances. "I am sending for the doctor," said Lady Colby grimly and went to dispatch a footman.

"I shall have Mrs. Jameston brew him a posset," put in Louisa and hurried off after her.

Diana followed Bozzy back upstairs and down the hall to the room her husband had been occupying. She tried to bite back the tears as Bozzy tenderly laid the fallen Maxim on his bed, boots and all, and covered him. "He'll be fine in no time," Bozzy whispered and tiptoed out of the room.

Diana took a seat at the side of the bed. "Oh, Maxim," she sobbed. She leaned over and stroked his forehead. "I would give anything to have you wake up and remember me."

Maxim's eyes remained closed, but he smiled. He caught her wrist in one hand and wrapped an arm around her back, drawing her onto the bed with him. "Would you, really?"

he murmured. "Would you even give me another chance to be the kind of husband you deserve?"

Diana's eyes narrowed. "You weren't hurt at all!" she accused. "This was all a ruse."

Maxim opened his eyes. The look he gave his wife sent a pleasant pain shooting to various parts of her body. "You must play fair, Diana, and answer my question. Would you give me another chance?"

Diana's lip began to tremble. "Oh, Maxim."

"That is all I wanted to know," he said and kissed her fiercely. "I've been a fool," he said at last. "I never meant to hurt you. I suppose I thought you'd never find out about the dancer. And even if you did, I felt sure you'd know it was nothing more than amusement."

"What is amusement to a man is serious to a woman," said Diana, hurt anew by such a callous statement.

"I begin to see that. And I must admit, after giving it some thought, I should hate to find you in the arms of another man and have you tell me you were only amusing yourself." He regarded her for a moment, as if trying to relearn every line and curve of her face. "I ended it with Estelle. Before I came."

"Will there be others?" asked Diana.

"Only one. You."

Belowstairs Bozzy was still hard at it trying to convince his aunt that Maxim really didn't need the services of a doctor. "His memory was already returning when I left him, and I think right now Diana is all the medicine he needs."

"Maxim is tough," put in James, who had been lured from the library by all the commotion.

Louisa looked at her cousin suspiciously. "He is mending rather quickly for someone who just had a bad fall."

Bozzy studied his nails. "Yes. Rather remarkable, ain't it?"

"And funny he should experience a memory loss just as Diana did," continued Louisa, staring hard at her cousin.

Bozzy shrugged. "Life is full of strange coincidences."

"Isn't it, though?" agreed Louisa sarcastically.

Later that evening the family enjoyed their traditional Christmas goose more than they had in many years. For there was much to celebrate. The memories of both Diana and Maxim had returned, and along with their memory each had regained the easy and kind dispositions to which everyone was so accustomed. There were no scenes at dinner, and while Diana was friendly with Bozzy, she had eyes only for Maxim, a circumstance that Bozzy found himself oddly regretting. There was much toasting and many expressions of thanks for the returned health of the happy couple.

After dinner carolers appeared at the door. And as the family stood listening to them singing their joyous Christmas song, Diana offered up a little prayer of thanks. She felt her husband's loving arm around her waist and thought that of all her nineteen Christmases, this one was, and would always be, the most memorable.

The
Baby
Shoppe

Ellen Rawlings

Miss Penelope Archer rose abruptly from the Egyptian-style pink sofa and began to pace about Willowtree's elegant drawing room. The skirts of her black mourning costume made a rustling sound as they moved. Otherwise, the room was depressingly silent.

After a few minutes she stopped pacing to look with large, pleading eyes at the only other person in the room. This was a gentleman named Mr. Hippe, solicitor to the Archer family since before Penelope was born.

"Truly, I've tried," she said to him in her rich, musical voice, "but I'm afraid I still cannot take it in. Are you certain that Papa ran through *all* of his fortune—and mine? There must be something left for me and for the servants."

Reluctantly Mr. Hippe shook his head. He had come to Willowtree from London to attend Mr. Archer's funeral and to read his client's will. However, he might as well have stayed at home and kept the will in his desk drawer. There was nothing with which to meet the bequests it listed.

Indeed, everything Mr. Archer had owned would have to go to pay his extensive debts, not just the diamonds and emeralds, locked away in the vault for safekeeping, but even the Turkey carpet upon the drawing room floor and the Egyptian-style sofa which was Penelope's favorite. Worst of all, Willowtree would have to be sold.

With distracted fingers Penelope pushed back a strand of pale blond hair. "Then what shall I do?" she asked, more to herself than to him.

Mr. Hippe coughed diffidently. "If I may suggest it, you must marry your young man—Lord Randolphe, is it not?" He paused. "He wasn't at the funeral."

Penelope gave him a cool look. "He couldn't be."

Although he knew nothing of the matter, Mr. Hippe nodded his head knowingly.

"Besides," she continued, "I cannot marry in propriety before the mourning period is over. What shall I do until then?"

"I . . . uh . . . I believe that is something for you and Lord Randolphe to discuss. But do not lose heart, Miss Archer. You are not beggared, you know."

Penelope's face brightened. "Am I not? Have I means of which you haven't informed me?"

"Why, certainly. You still have your personal possessions, your clothing, and your books. Also, you have your little trinkets, and, of course, you have your babies."

Penelope stared at him.

"You do still have your wonderful collection of babies, do you not?" he asked, referring to the enormous doll collection she had, some of it inherited and a great deal of it which she had amassed herself.

"My babies? Yes, I have them, but what does that have to say to anything? Do you think I can pay for lodgings with them or . . . or . . . eat them?"

Mr. Hippe closed his eyes for a moment, as though to blot out the expression of anguish on Miss Archer's vulnerable face. "I don't know," he mumbled. "Lord Randolphe is the one with whom you must speak. I'm sorry, my dear."

A short while later, as soon as he could decently contrive it, Mr. Hippe decamped. Penelope was left alone in the house that would soon belong to someone else, with just the servants for company.

She cried for a while, for her father, for herself, for all of the people who depended on them. Unlike many other establishments, the Willowtree estate had always treated its dependents well. Perhaps too well?

In any case, after a time she went to her one confidant in the household, her old nurse, Nanny Minster. Nanny took Penelope in her arms and rubbed her back as though she were three years old again and needed comforting for a badly skinned knee.

Finally she stopped and put Penelope from her. "It's a pity," she said in a doom-laden voice, "and just a few months before Christmas, too. That always makes it worse. Tell me, have you decided what you will do?"

Penelope shrugged. "I haven't had time; this was so unexpected. What will you do, Nanny? There will be no more pension for you. You're as destitute as I."

"If that means *poor*, I don't think I am!" she said stoutly. "I've put by a wee bit every quarter day since I can remember. I've never counted on men to see me through." She looked at Penelope shrewdly. "That reminds me, child. What about Lord Randolphe?"

Penelope's expression was not nearly so guarded as it had been when Mr. Hippe had mentioned him. She bit at her soft lower lip before saying, "What about him, Nanny?"

"He'll take care of you, won't he, until you and he can wed?"

Penelope flushed. "I'm sure he would, if I permitted him to do so. I won't, however. I mean to release him from his promise."

Nanny Minster frowned. "Now, why would you do that?"

"I think it's the only honorable thing to do. He became affianced to Miss Archer, heiress to Willowtree. Now I'm plain Miss Archer, pauper."

"And why should he care about that? He's swimming in lard, that one," Nanny said with all the brash familiarity of a long-time retainer.

For the first time that day Penelope smiled, revealing her

lovely white teeth. In truth, everything about her was lovely, from her oval face with its beautiful sculpted features to her kind and even nature. "Don't be vulgar, Nanny," she said mildly.

Nanny ignored the admonition. "And where is he, Lord Swimming in Lard?"

"Lord Randolphe is with the Prince Regent in London and probably could not get away," Penelope said, choosing to ignore his apparent disconcern. "Besides, with the snow and other bad weather we've been having, he probably couldn't have got here in time for the funeral even if he'd tried."

"Mr. Hippe got here," Nanny muttered, as she spoke giving her white cap a violent pull as expressive as any words. "I hate to say it, Miss Penelope, but sometimes I wonder if your fine lord loves anyone but himself."

If he didn't, it would be understandable, Penelope thought. He was a paragon, a nonpareil. He was what every woman dreamed of: charming, amiable, and as fair to look upon as Narcissus, that beautiful boy in Greek mythology who fell in love with his own image.

Penelope wondered what he would say when she told him she meant to release him. She was not altogether sure.

She was given her opportunity to find out that evening. At about half after nine Lord Randolphe arrived at Willowtree, full of apologies and excuses.

He looked as beautiful as ever, she thought as a lump lodged in her throat. His hair gleamed guinea gold in the candlelight; his perfect features suggested both manly strength and an exquisite sensibility.

People said that she and Lord Randolphe were an astonishingly well-matched couple, both of them being so good to look upon; in truth, however, she thought that of the two of them, he was the prettier.

"It doesn't matter that you missed the funeral, Charles," she said gently, interrupting his fifth effort at an excuse for his absence. "Come into the book room. I need to talk with you."

Lord Randolphe seemed about to refuse. He had very high standards when it came to the behavior of the female members of his family; since Penelope was his affianced bride, those standards applied to her, also. "Very well, darling," he said after some hesitation, "but just for a few minutes."

She supposed that would be enough time to tell him. Despite his protests, she closed the book room door, then insisted that he sit next to her on the deep brocade sofa. "Charles," she said, taking his resistant hands in hers, "there is something about which we must speak. I learned today from our solicitor that my papa left me penniless. Even Willowtree will have to be sold. Therefore, in light of my changed circumstances, I am releasing you from our engagement."

Lord Randolphe's thick lashes came down over his sky-blue eyes. His mouth tightened. Finally he said, "I cannot talk about this with you tonight. You have had too much to contend with, and I am exhausted from my service to Prinny and my trip back here. I will come to see you tomorrow."

The next morning Penelope dressed very carefully in a trained black wool gown; Charles was such a stickler for the proper attire. Then she went downstairs to the drawing room to wait for him. She waited and waited. He did not come.

"It's too bad that you can't be a governess or a companion like others in your circumstances," Nanny said.

Although Penelope had never entertained the slightest desire to be either one of those, she said indignantly, "And why can't I?"

"Because you can't. Don't get your head swelled, but you're too pretty-like. Either the ladies wouldn't want to have you—or the gentleman would."

Penelope looked shocked. Then her face relaxed, and she giggled. "Very well," she said in a more cheerful tone, "I shall be something else. There is an idea I considered last night, before I fell asleep." She did not mention that it had been many hours after she retired before she finally was able to fall asleep. "I shall be a shopkeeper in London."

Now it was Nanny Minster's turn to be shocked. "No, you won't. Nobody will talk to you if you become a shopkeeper, let alone want to marry you. Least it wouldn't be no one you'd feel right with. You'll see. You're going to ruin yourself forever."

Penelope knew as well as Nanny that turning herself into a shopkeeper would deny her her place in the *ton* forever. But, it seemed to her that she had already lost her place, at least in Lord Randolphe's estimation. If nothing else, owning a shop would give her independence. "I don't have any other choice," she said.

"Of course you do, Miss Penelope. You can come with me."

"With you?"

It was Nanny's turn to look indignant. "And why not? I told you afore I have some savings. We could retire to a small cottage in the country, you and me. Not here, but someplace new. We could raise chickens and grow cabbages. We could manage."

Before Penelope could object, Nanny added, "Course it's a shame to hide a fine young lady like you in the country, but at least we'd eat."

"Chicken and cabbage—somehow I'm not tempted. No, we shall set up shop in London and sell . . . uh . . . we'll sell babies."

"Babies? Your father will turn over in his grave!"

"No, he won't," Penelope said firmly. "This is the best plan of all. Indeed, it's the only plan."

"I don't call that a plan," Nanny derided. "It's barmy,

Miss Penelope. Asides, I don't want to go to London. It's a sinkhole of iniquity."

Penelope gently touched her old nurse's brown-spotted hand. "You will accompany me, though, won't you, even to London?"

"Of course I will. I'm loyal, even if some aren't, and even if I do think your idea is foolish and a disgrace. Opening a shop—you!"

Penelope smiled at her former nurse. "If I were anything other than a shopkeeper, I couldn't have you with me. I want you to be with me, Nanny, if you want it, too."

Nanny Minster drew the back of her rough hand across her eyes. "Oh, all right. But don't think I still don't believe you can do it."

"You'll see," Penelope said with as much conviction as she could summon up. "A baby shop would go well in Mayfair, especially one stocked with my collection."

"Maybe it would, and maybe it wouldn't. But the point is, Miss Penelope, you don't have a shop, not in Mayfair nor anywhere else. And I don't see how you're going to get one."

"I will get one," her mistress said, thrusting out her softly rounded chin. "I will."

And so she did, from Mr. Brigham, a former, though unacknowledged, business partner of her father who would soon be living at Willowtree in her stead. He owed her some help, she thought, and, apparently, he agreed. When she finished talking with him, she had the promise of a lease on a shop in Mayfair.

A week later Penelope and Nanny Minster moved out of Willowtree. Only Nanny looked back at the elegant four-story brick house before it was lost to view. They were on their way to London, to set up a business in Half Moon Street. It would also be their home from that time on.

As they neared their destination, Penelope said to her

companion, "I've been thinking, Nanny. Would it be a good idea for me to put off mourning?"

Nanny choked. "Blessed God, child, your papa is hardly cold yet. How can you even think of doing a thing like that?"

"I don't want to look gloomy," Penelope explained, "especially near Christmas, when everyone wants to feel happy. If black makes me and the shop look gloomy, I won't wear it. I'm determined to be successful in this venture, Nanny, so that I'll never have to depend on anyone else again."

Nanny might not have thought much of Penelope's plan, but she did approve of the young woman's sentiment. "Keep the mourning," she said mildly now. "It makes you look like a shopgirl."

In fact, Nanny was telling an untruth. Penelope's black bombazine day dress made her white skin seem whiter, her blond hair blonder, her beautiful face more compellingly beautiful. Nanny hoped Penelope's lovely appearance would draw people to the shop and induce them to buy her wares.

With high hopes she and Penelope put up the sign the estate carpenter had made: THE BABY SHOPPE, it read in large gold letters. Then they set out the goods Penelope had collected.

Penelope also used this period to put the finishing touches on her shop and living quarters. Because the kitchen was directly behind the store, separated only by a pink and white flowered curtain, she needed to ensure that no odors of mutton, cheese, or other strong-smelling foods seeped through. Therefore, she set Chinese *Famille Rose* bowls about in which she put dried orange and lemon peels. Others she filled with potpourri.

She also added rose and orange blossom oils to the pools of melted wax that had collected around the wicks of partially burned candles. When the candles were reused, they would give off a delicious odor.

The last thing she did was to put out a few holly boughs, although Christmas was still almost two months away and the thought of it without her father brought her pain. Nevertheless, after she'd put up the boughs, the glossy green leaves and red berries still evoked some of the joy of the coming holidays.

When she finished her little tasks, the shop smelled like a garden.

Then it was time to open for business. Penelope couldn't believe it: not five minutes after she'd put back the shutters and unlatched the front door, a customer entered. He was in evening dress and had a curious, crooked walk.

"Good afternoon," he said, although it was but ten o'clock in the morning. "What have you got in here?"

Penelope realized that the gentleman was well-to-go. He belonged at home, asleep in his bed, until he was sober again.

"Babies," she said gently. "They aren't anything you'd want to purchase."

The gentleman looked as though he might cry. "But I do. I've wanted a baby every Christmas since I was a small boy, but no one ever got me one. Will you deny me one now, madam?"

What was she to do with him? Being the sheltered only child of a country gentleman was hardly preparation for dealing with the world at large, and inebriated gentlemen in particular. "No, no," she said hastily. "Please do choose one."

He lurched over to a shelf, hesitated as though he could not decide among such riches, then took down a pretty flaxen-haired baby with a papier-mâché face and a smooth kid body. It was one of Penelope's favorites.

"I'll take this one. How much?"

As she began to wrap his choice, it looked up at her with

reproachful blue eyes, or so it seemed to Penelope. Her own blue eyes filled. She felt as though she were selling a member of her family, and to a drunkard, no less. Being in trade was going to be more difficult than she'd anticipated.

She sold another baby the following day, a red-haired boy baby with a wax face. However, since it was not an especial favorite, or, perhaps, because she'd become used to the idea, she was less troubled to see this one leave.

By the time the next customer came through the door, she was feeling almost comfortable in her new role. She gave the gentleman her lovely smile.

He did not respond to it. She was not even certain that he saw it, or her. He seemed intent upon looking about the shop, to the exclusion of everything else. If it weren't such a foolish idea, she would think that he was measuring the spaces with his eyes.

As she waited for him to finish his inspection, she studied him. He had hair as black as a raven's feathers and eyes that were a cool, unimpressible gray. He looked to her to be but a year or so away from his thirtieth birthday, the same as Lord Randolphe. Unlike Lord Randolphe, however, he conveyed the impression of being someone who not only knew exactly what he wanted but also had total confidence that he would—and should—get it. If Lord Randolphe was Narcissus, this man was Zeus.

Perhaps it was his height that made him appear so confident, she thought, for it was much above the average. Or it might have been his square, stubborn chin or haughty nose. Whatever the cause, Penelope did not admire his aspect, or the fact that his many-caped greatcoat was left unbuttoned, as though the elements were beneath his notice. She decided she did not like the masculine odors of starched linen, bay rum, and expensive cigars that he brought into the shop, either. They warred with the lovely fragrances she had created for her pretty world.

Suddenly she felt ridiculous. She did not have to like or

dislike this person. He was a customer. After this little while, she'd probably never see him again.

Her mood inexplicably gone flat, she said quietly, "How do you do?"

For the first time he directed his attention to her. Indeed, those cool eyes went from the top of her blond head, down her trim figure, to her small, black-slippered feet. A little shiver of excitement ran down her spine. She did not like that, either. She frowned, then said quickly, "May I be of some assistance?"

The gray eyes looked into hers. "I am the Earl of Treymaine. Are you Miss Archer?"

His question startled her, as well it might. She could not imagine how he could have come by her name. Tight-lipped, she nodded.

"You are much younger than I expected," he said, quirking a dark, thick brow. "How old are you?"

Of all the effrontery! She would not answer.

"I said . . ."

Penelope's expression became frosty. "I heard you, my lord. I was just rather surprised by your question—as well as by your knowledge of my name. How did you come to know it?"

He smiled. The smile lightened his face, making it seem less formidable and more attractive. To Penelope, somehow it also made him seem more of a threat to her well-being.

"I always find out what I have to know," he said. "I asked your name of someone. I did not learn your age, however. Will you tell it to me? You need not be shy."

Her age was none of his concern. She shook her head.

"I must guess, then. You are sixteen."

She knew he was baiting her, but she could not bear it. "Sixteen! I am nineteen, my lord, and soon will be twenty." This last was not precisely true, but it made her feel more secure to say it.

He laughed. "Thank you."

As Penelope glared at him, he said, "You are young to be a shopkeeper. Tell me, is your business prospering?"

Another question. She could make no sense of their direction and began to wonder if he were not some sort of Bedlamite. Even tall, arrogant men with calm gray eyes could be lunatics. Perhaps she should humor him until he decided to go away.

"It's doing well," she lied. "May I show you our wares? We have all sorts of babies in stock. Some of them are quite interesting."

He shrugged, making her wonder if only the physical aspects of the shop, not its contents, meant anything to him. However, he did trail after her and even appeared to listen with some interest to the histories she gave him of several of her older and rarer babies. The only time he seemed genuinely enthusiastic, however, was when she showed him a book of paper dolls. Each figure, accompanied by a story in rhyme, had a removable head which slipped into a paper pocket located on its back. She had bought several of the books, hoping that they would be popular. Thus far, of course, she hadn't sold any of them.

As though he could read her thoughts, Lord Treymaine said, "Exactly how many of these things have you sold?"

"What, the paper dolls?"

"No, I mean all of these things, these toys."

"Why are we back to that, my lord?"

"You haven't answered my question."

"Many," she snapped. "Many, many. And I expect to sell many more now that Christmas is approaching."

He shook his head. "I don't think you've sold many, and I don't believe you will sell many more, either. London is always thin of people—people who are willing to buy things they don't need—in November. Those sort don't come back until January, if they come back even then."

She supposed he was speaking the truth. Nevertheless, since she did not like what he said, she did not want to hear any more about it. "Lord Treymaine," she said, "I am very busy now, despite what you believe, and I do not have time for someone obviously uninterested in purchasing a baby. You must excuse me."

"I doubt you are busy," he replied with a firmness that made her want to kick him. "Still, I will get to the point, Miss Archer. I would like to take over the lease of your shop, which I am convinced is not doing well at all. Naturally, I am prepared to compensate you for your expenses thus far and, in addition, give you a generous sum with which to obtain another place and buy much more stock—or go home to your family, which is where a young female like you should be. What do you say to that?" He smiled at her as though the matter were settled.

How casual he was about her life. That rankled. Furthermore, she didn't have a family. "I don't want a place somewhere else," she said. "I want to stay here, and I will."

His lips narrowed. "Don't be ridiculous, Miss Archer. Why should it matter to you where you are?"

"I could ask you the same thing: Why should it matter to you? Indeed, why do you want a shop at all? You don't mean to be a shopkeeper, do you?"

He looked annoyed. "Miss Archer, I want this shop."

"Lord Treymaine, you cannot have it."

"I could get it from whomever rents it to you, you know; or I could make it so unprofitable for you by telling my friends not to patronize you that you'd be happy to give it up."

Penelope was tired of having difficulties in her life. Indeed, she was angry: angry with her father for leaving her, angry with Mr. Hippe for bringing her bad news, and very angry with Lord Randolphe. And now, this . . . this detestable person had cut up what little peace she had garnered over the past few weeks. Her full, rosy lower lip quivered with rage. "Would you do that?"

"I might," he said, grinning once more. "You can't be sure I won't."

Her rage evaporated, to be replaced by a feeling of helplessness. Her eyes filled with tears.

Lord Treymaine said hastily, "However, I'd rather make you change your mind."

The tears dried up. "I won't, and you can't. I mean to stay here forever."

"We shall see." His gray eyes were cool now. "This is not over, Miss Archer. I want and shall have this shop. I will be back soon again."

"Must you? Please, don't hurry."

She saw his neatly manicured fingers clench, as though they'd enjoy curling around her slender throat. Her breath quickened. Then his fingers straightened, and he stomped to the door. Penelope heard it slam shut. She was alone again.

How glad she was that he had gone, she thought as she began to return to her usual calm. She hated having her emotions churned. But then, why did the morning suddenly seem so uninteresting, so very dull?

The following week she looked up in nervous anticipation every time the shop door opened. However, the dreadful Lord Treymaine did not come.

Indeed, almost no one did, and the few customers she had bought very little. Only one purchased a baby. The others bought odds and ends, such as some jewelry she had made for girl babies and a set of tiny toilet articles purchased from someone else's collection. By Saturday she would have been delighted to dispose of even her most favorite baby, a rare German glazed porcelain with exquisite lace-edged clothes that Penelope had made herself, stitch by tiny stitch. No one as much as picked it up to examine it, however.

Lord Treymaine must be correct, she thought: People who bought expensive toys were at their country homes. On the other hand, she began to suspect that, partially at least, she was at fault. She'd noticed that several of the women who'd come into the shop did not seem to take to her, even appeared to enjoy refusing to buy from her. She didn't know if they disapproved of an obviously upper-class female in trade or if they disapproved of her good looks. She'd had difficulties in that direction before.

Nanny tried to cheer her. "Probably everyone will buy your babies just before Christmas," she said. "It's not like they don't have time to shop. Besides, some people can't bear to spend money till the last minute. But you don't need to worry. As I told you afore, I have enough saved that we can eat and pay the rent for a long while."

Penelope still looked despondent.

"Christmas will be here sooner than you know," Nanny continued. "Trade will be sure to pick up somewhat, probably by next week."

"Do you really think so?"

"With all my heart, child."

Even though she knew her faith in her old nurse's statement was unfounded, Penelope chose to believe her. Now all she had to worry about was Lord Treymaine barging into her shop to make her change her mind and do as he wished—but she wouldn't.

Monday she opened the shop at ten o'clock, wondering if he would arrive. She waited and waited, but he did not put in an appearance. He was just like Lord Randolphe, she thought with contempt.

Unfortunately, she was mistaken in that. When she unlocked the front door on Tuesday and folded back the shutters, she saw him standing outside. Her heart jumped. An excess of sensibility, she told herself, ignoring the fact that she felt anticipation and excitement as well.

Lord Treymaine entered on a rush of chilly air. She noted with displeasure that once again his greatcoat was unbuttoned as though he were impervious to the harsh winter weather that made lesser mortals shiver.

"Oh, it's you," Penelope said in as good an imitation of ennui as she could manage.

"Yes, it is I, isn't it? He walked to the wall where she'd hung the Christmas holly boughs. "I like the way these look," he said cheerfully. "Well, have you changed your mind yet about turning over your lease to me?" When Penelope silently shook her head, he picked up a baby about nineteen inches high and shook it. Penelope bit her full underlip.

"Isn't it amazing," he said, his gray eyes filled with mischief, "that something seemingly beautiful and substantial has nothing inside of it, except, perhaps, a few loose bits of sawdust?"

He was baiting her again. She knew who he thought was empty on the inside. She flushed. "Give me that baby."

Lord Treymaine refused to release it to her. Unless she wished to wrestle him to the ground, she had no choice but to let him keep it. "This one looks like my niece," he said, holding the baby by the neck now. "Nelly's a silly chit."

Such family feeling! Penelope deeply resented his remark about his niece, even though she did not know her. "Tell me, Lord Treymaine, is there anyone of whom you approve?"

The gray eyes looked over her figure. They gleamed for a moment. Then he said casually, "Actually, I approve of this baby. I'll buy it. How much does it cost?"

"One hundred million pounds."

"I'll give you three pounds." Carelessly he threw some money on the counter. "Now, where can I put my coat?"

"Where? You can keep it on your back, of course. Then you can walk it outside." She set the baby in a sack. "Here is your purchase, Lord Treymaine. Goodbye."

He placed his package on the floor, behind the counter—as though the shop were already in his possession, she thought resentfully. Then he strolled to where the curtain separated the baby shop from the kitchen.

"Don't go back there!"

He ignored her. Thrusting the curtain aside, he entered the kitchen.

Penelope heard a scream.

"What are you doing, you beast?" she called. Shoving the flowered material out of the way she rushed into the other room.

"Did he frighten you, Nanny?" She pushed Lord Treymaine out of the way and put her arms about her nurse.

"Nonsense," the tall man said dismissively. "If I know nurses, and I should, she's made of sterner stuff than that." He put a large, well-manicured hand on the elderly woman's arm. "Nanny, where can I hang my coat?"

"Don't you dare remove your greatcoat!" Penelope cried. "You aren't staying. And don't call her that. She's not your nurse."

Neither Lord Treymaine nor Nanny Minster heeded her. The former was too busy shedding his greatcoat, the latter patiently waiting to receive it.

Penelope pursed her mouth and walked back into the other room. As she drummed her fingers on the polished wooden counter, she heard laughter from the kitchen. Her thoughts swirled in her head. Why had he returned? Was it to undermine her servant's loyalty? Why had he bought a baby from her? That was hardly the way to put her out of business.

Lord Treymaine came back into the front room. He was carrying a cup of tea. Penelope's delicate nostrils flared at the delicious aroma. Then she frowned. Nanny hadn't prepared a cup of tea for her.

"For you," said Lord Treymaine.

"I don't want it."

"Very well." Before her outraged eyes, he drank the tea.

"Now that you've refreshed yourself," she said caustically, "I'd like to ask you a question. Do you still want my shop?"

Lord Treymaine nodded amiably.

"Well, then, what can I do—other than accede to your whims—to make you go away? I do so want you to go away."

Before he could respond, the door to the shop opened. In came a very pretty female of about one and twenty, followed by a dowdy woman of middle years who looked to be afraid of her own shadow.

Penelope guessed that the older woman was a companion. She shuddered. She could have been that person, condemned to follow some unheeding female about, helpless before every whim and folly. The thought made her more determined than ever to best Lord Treymaine.

"Your Lordship," the young female said, with an eager, sycophantic smile that set Penelope's teeth on edge. "I saw you from the street." She shook her large ermine muff playfully at him. "What are you doing in a place like this?"

Lord Treymaine bowed over her hand. "I came in to look for a gift for my niece."

"Oh, really." The young woman turned her head, her turquoise eyes cursorily examining the merchandise. "What a wonderful idea. I ought to purchase something, too, for my niece."

She picked up a carved applewood baby with painted eyes and a round face. Amazingly, it resembled her. "Do look at this baby," she said in a girlish voice, holding it close to her full, pouty lips. "Isn't it pretty?"

Lord Treymaine smiled at her. "Not as pretty as you, and not nearly so well made."

As the lady giggled, he took the baby from her hand. "Shoddy goods," he said. "You don't want that." He turned her toward the door. "You don't want anything here. Goodbye. I'll see you soon, at the Morningsides' soiree, perhaps."

Looking as though she didn't know how she'd got there, the young woman once more stood outside the shop.

Her companion, if that was what she was, gasped and then rushed after her. Lord Treymaine firmly closed the door behind them.

Penelope felt angry red color rush into her face. How could he have done that to her? Without a doubt, she could have sold that young woman the wooden baby.

"Why?" she asked between clenched teeth.

"I wanted to show you what I can do if you continue to disoblige me." He put his hand into one of his pockets. "Don't fret. I shall pay you for—"

Once again the shop door opened. Lord Treymaine stopped speaking and removed his hand from his pocket.

Two gentlemen came in. They seemed near Lord Treymaine's age and very well dressed. In their tight blue swallowtail coats and buff pantaloons, they seemed nearly as well dressed as he. Lord Treymaine looked at them, his gray eyes noncommittal.

His manner did not seem to affect the men at all. "Treymaine!" The taller of them reached out and slapped him on the shoulder. "I didn't know you had to resort to buying your ladies instead of merely renting them for a while."

Penelope thought he was talking about her. Her blue eyes ablaze with fury, she opened her mouth to give him a dressing down that would strip the skin from his handsome bones. He looked down at her, caught his breath at her beauty, and smiled with pleasure.

The smile was also polite. A little calmer now, Penelope realized that the bought "ladies" he was referring to were her babies.

She forced her hands to her sides, willing herself to serenity while she waited for Lord Treymaine to tell his friends what a dreadful establishment this was and that they must never come into it again. Still, her fingers twitched against her black gown.

Lord Treymaine retrieved his package from behind the

counter. "Early Christmas shopping," he said lazily as he held it up.

The second gentleman laughed. "You? Shopping for babies? I think what it is, you've lost your way. I'm sure you meant to spend the day at White's, playing cards, and somehow found yourself here."

A gamester, too. Penelope's short upper lip twitched with dislike.

Lord Treymaine's eyes went to her face. "You've given the lady a poor opinion of me," he said to the men without changing the direction of his glance. "Buy a baby, Nettlecreek, and leave. You, too, Mortimer."

"Buy a baby?" Nettlecreek repeated in a tone of astonishment. "What would I do with it?"

"Give it to a poor child. You might just wipe out some of your sins with such an act."

"So I might," said the gentleman, obviously much struck. "I'll do it. What is their cost?"

"Five pounds," Lord Treymaine replied before Penelope could speak.

"Five pounds for a toy for a poor child?"

"You can afford it. Both of you can. And think of the benefits. Take their money, Miss Archer."

Several minutes later Lord Treymaine hustled them, clutching their purchases, from the shop.

That made four babies she had sold that day—if Lord Treymaine remembered to pay her for the one his female friend hadn't bought. Even if he didn't, she still had far more money than she would have asked for or could have expected. In complete confusion, she stared at him. "What . . . ?"

"You've seen what I can do," Lord Treymaine said. "I can curtail your business with impressionable simpletons like the young lady, or I can bring you into fashion." His voice took on a coaxing note. "Wouldn't you like me to bring you into fashion? I've found another shop for you, you know; that's what I was doing last week. You'll like it.''

How dare he try to arrange her life! She'd had enough of men doing that. Sooner or later they always *disarranged* it. ''I don't want your help,'' she said. ''I want you to leave.'' She stamped her foot. ''I don't like you, Lord Treymaine. In fact, I dislike you excessively.''

''Temper! Temper!''

Penelope looked around, as though searching for something to hurl at him.

''For the sake of your shop,'' he said with a raised eyebrow that seemed to her to mock her feelings, ''I'll go.''

He passed into the kitchen, from where Penelope could hear him murmuring to Nanny Minster. Then he retraced his steps and left.

''Of all the horrible people—''

The opening of the shop door stopped her words. It was Lord Treymaine again. ''I forgot my baby,'' he said, coming back in. ''Excuse me. Oh, yes, and here is the money for the one the young lady did not purchase.'' His expression wicked, he took up his parcel. This time he did not return.

Penelope threw down the coins and stormed into the kitchen. ''What did that devil say to you?'' she demanded of Nanny Minster. ''What?''

Nanny methodically wiped her hands on her large white apron. ''No need to scream at me. He said he didn't know how I could work for someone as excitable as you. He said he felt sorry for me.''

''I? Excitable? I've never been excitable in my life!'' Penelope picked up a turnip Nanny had been cutting and flung it against the wall.

''That will fix everything, won't it?'' the old woman said, as though talking to a hysterical child.

Penelope turned her back on her and surged through the curtain.

"You're right, though," Nanny called after her. "You never was like this afore. I told you Lunnen was a sinkhole."

It snowed the next day, only flurries, but the wind was sharp. The weather made Penelope think of Christmas. In the past she and her papa would have been getting ready for the holiday by shopping for presents for the servants. She would have been sewing diligently on a new shirt for her papa, her stitches fine and even. He might be planning to go up to London, to Rundle and Bridges, to look for a special piece of jewelry for her. The Christmas before, he had given her a pair of small, beautiful pearl and diamond earrings. Penelope felt tears gather in her eyes.

Blankly she stared out the large window. The wind was making the white flakes dance. She would have thought it a pretty sight, except that she knew the snow would keep people away from the shop. At least she was warm, she thought, then fell to worrying about the price of wood and coal.

At any rate, the money she'd made had enabled her to buy some new stock. Her most exciting choices had been five Peddler babies: old women in print dresses and red flannel capes toting baskets or with trays about their necks. Although the old women's costumes were eye-catching, it was the miniature wares they carried that made them so wonderful. One of them had fifty little items in her tray; Penelope had counted them. They included combs, scissors, miniature graters and other kitchen items, and sewing notions.

She lifted two of the Peddlers from their wrappings and set them on the counter. Then she went about finishing a nightshirt for another of her new purchases.

After a half hour of steady sewing, she put down her work and stretched to relieve the ache in her back. She looked out the window. There was no one about in the worsening weather except for a thin, dark-haired little boy of about four or five, a veritable ragamuffin, who was standing outside the store. His nose was pressed against the glass, and he seemed enraptured.

She traced his gaze. He was staring avidly at the China-headed German doll, Penelope's favorite.

She smiled at him, but he did not smile back. She noticed that his little, pinched face was dirty and his cheeks carried burns in several places. He must be a chimney sweep, she thought with pity.

On an impulse she beckoned to him. At least he could warm himself in the shop for a few minutes. She would even let him look at the baby, although, unfortunately, because he was so dirty, she could not let him touch it.

For a moment the boy's green eyes lit with joy. Then the happy expression vanished, and he ran off.

"We should have had him in," Nanny said, standing in front of the curtain. "He looked as though he could do with some food."

"He looked as though he could do with everything, and I did try to get him to come in. As you saw, though, he ran away."

Nanny said sagely, "Probably, he's afraid of his master. Chimney sweeps have a hard life.

"That reminds me," Nanny continued. "Has that nice Lord Treymaine come into the shop again?"

Penelope looked down her delicately shaped nose at Nanny Minster. "Why a chimney sweep should remind you of Lord Treymaine is beyond my imagination."

Nanny shrugged.

"It also *astounds* me that you call him nice. He isn't nice; he's the most dreadful man I've ever met. The only thing I feel grateful for is that he has *not* come into the shop today." She looked heavenward. "Thank you, God."

If she'd had the second sight, she would have postponed her thanks, or used it for something else. Almost as soon as she got the words out, Lord Treymaine opened the door of the shop. He was accompanied by two finely dressed women, with hair as dark and eyes as gray as his. All three shook the snow from their garments, then turned toward her, the two women with smiles.

Penelope would have given her eyeteeth for the younger female's pelisse. It was of rose velvet, and its matching bonnet was a perfect foil for the young woman's hair and pretty complexion. She was so tired of unrelieved black, Penelope thought with a sigh. She truly mourned her father, but she wished her feelings could be more private. She was beginning to think black made her irritable. No wonder Lord Treymaine gave free rein to his nasty nature in her presence.

"Oh, look at the babies, Mama," the younger woman said in a gentle voice. "They are as wonderful as Tony said."

Now what was he up to? Penelope would not have been surprised to discover that he'd brought the women in to rob her. She was convinced he was capable of anything.

At the moment he looked pleased, as though the shop and its contents were his idea. "I told you that you would like this place," he said.

The pleased look abruptly disappeared. "What are those?" He swooped down on the Peddler babies. "I've never seen anything like them before."

The older woman laughed. "As though you would. I do not remember your having any interest in babies, even when you were one yourself. It was swords you liked, swords and guns and stones. Yes, and mud, too; you dearly loved mud."

This litany of mostly lethal objects didn't surprise Penelope. If the woman, whom Penelope surmised was Lord Treymaine's mother, had said he'd liked to stone kittens and cut off frogs' toes to bury in his beloved mud, she wouldn't have blinked.

Lord Treymaine ignored the speaker. "How many of these things do you have?"

"Five," Penelope murmured.

"I'll take them."

"All five of them? Why?"

He grinned at her. "What sort of question is that for a person in trade to ask? It's what I've been telling you, Miss Archer. You don't belong in a shop."

The two women looked at her with interest. "I beg your pardon," Lord Treymaine said. "Mama, Elizabeth, this is Miss Archer."

Although it was hardly *de rigueur* to introduce a shop-keeper to two ladies, they did not appear to mind. Indeed, how-do-you-dos were given all around, and then Penelope asked if they'd like some tea. The offer was gratefully accepted.

"This is such an attractive place," Lady Treymaine said, settling into a pretty green and white chair that Penelope had found discarded in a nearby mews and cleverly refurbished. "So interesting. It smells good, too, like flowers and a fruit seller's. Tony, I can understand why you want to wrest this shop from Miss Archer."

Penelope looked intently at her. "Can you? Would you mind telling me why he does? I've wondered and wondered."

"Ah, then I've been in your thoughts," Lord Treymaine said with a sardonic grin. "They were pleasant ones, I hope."

Penelope glared at him.

Lady Treymaine coughed. "I'm surprised my son didn't tell you. He wants the shop for his old nurse."

Lord Treymaine's light eyes were as cool as rain in autumn. "Miss Archer does not need to know why I want this shop, Mama."

"Certainly, she does. Otherwise, she might think you a monster for wanting to get it from her."

Penelope's lips turned up in a thin smile. "Never fear. Whether he has the best reason in the world, or no reason at all, my opinion of him won't change."

"Oh, good," said Lady Treymaine.

Lord Treymaine laughed.

"It's for Nurse Bertram, you see," Lady Treymaine said, ignoring her tall son's mirth. "She always said that when she retired, she wanted to have a shop on Half Moon Street and sell toys. My son promised her ever so long ago that he'd make her wish come true. Didn't you, Tony?"

"Miss Archer isn't interested in the subject," he said curtly.

Penelope ran a finger over the black grosgrain ribbons that she'd set into the front of her mourning gown to make it more attractive. "Oh, but I am. It explains certain things, you see."

Lord Treymaine gave her a forbidding look, as though he dared her to think well of him.

An idea struck her. "Is that why you are buying my wares, Your Lordship? To provide your nurse with stock?"

Lord Treymaine looked easier. "Is that what you think? Do you really believe I would purchase these goods at your prices if I meant to do that, Miss Archer?"

"At my prices?" she asked indignantly. "You are the one who is always quoting outrageous prices to people, as though you were selling carpets in a Turkish bazaar."

"Yes, and I've done very well for you, too. But I'm not purchasing these babies for Nurse Bertram to stock. That would be foolish, and I am never foolish."

Then what was he doing, buying so many of her babies and at such exorbitant prices? Could it be that he'd changed his mind about her and wanted to help? No, that was impossible.

Lady Treymaine looked up at her son. "I don't understand, Tony. Why do you quote prices and buy babies and those other things Miss Archer said? I never thought you were interested in trade.''

''Perhaps he's interested in Miss Archer,'' his sister murmured with a sly smile.

''No, darling. I'm sure he's not. I happen to know from Lady Sousa that he already has a . . . a friend.''

Never, not since she'd first had the idea of opening a shop, had Penelope truly grasped how her occupation affected her social position. Now she knew. She was only good enough to be a man's mistress. Unwanted tears sprang into her eyes.

Lord Treymaine noticed them. ''You must not speak so, Mama. Miss Archer is neither deaf nor unfeeling. Besides, she is not what you said. She is nothing more or less than a female whose shop I wish to acquire. I think you need to apologize to her, don't you?''

Lady Treymaine looked as though she might cry herself. ''I meant nothing by my words,'' she said. ''I do apologize.''

''And so do I,'' Lady Elizabeth offered.

''Good. Now each of you must buy a baby. Then you may leave.''

If he owned this shop, Penelope thought, he'd be as rich as Golden Ball Hughes in no time at all. He was unswerving, as stubborn as a donkey. Not a good person to defy.

But she meant to continue to defy him. Thus, she was somewhat on edge when the females departed, leaving him behind; she knew their battle would soon be joined again.

''Well?'' she asked. ''Have you stayed here to finish your mama's work?''

His eyes narrowed. ''I told her to apologize, didn't I? Not everyone would have done that.''

''Oh, no. Not for a shopgirl.''

He shrugged. ''I'm sorry. However, that is but the truth. Will you accord me nothing, Miss Archer?''

''No, nothing.'' She hesitated, her beautiful face pink

with some emotion she could not entirely suppress. "Well, I suppose it is nice of you to want to find a shop for your old nurse—but not at my expense. You know you only come here to distress me so that I will give up this place and go home." She did not mention that she had no other home.

"Is that what you think of me? Not that I care." Disdainfully Lord Treymaine threw down a generous number of coins, then snatched up his Peddler babies and departed.

"Perhaps I've finally got rid of him," Penelope said aloud. "I'm so happy." Once more her eyes filled with tears.

She was becoming a regular watering pot, she thought with shame. What was the matter with her? She blinked her eyes, then stared out the window.

The dark-haired urchin who had been there previously stared back. If anything, he looked even dirtier, colder, and more miserable than he had the last time.

Penelope's sadness dissipated. Here was someone she could help. "Hot chocolate," she mouthed. "Come in."

The chimney sweep hesitated, but apparently the temptation was too much for him. Slowly he opened the door—as though giving Penelope time to change her mind and slam it in his face, she thought.

"Did . . . did you say hot chocolate?" he stammered.

Penelope smiled her sweet smile. Thoughts of the horrible Lord Treymaine vanished, more or less. "Yes, I did. Come back into the kitchen with me, and I shall get some for you."

"My da can't see me in there," the child said in a light, high-pitched voice. "Yes, please, let us go."

She led him past the flowered curtain and into the kitchen. At once he ran to the hearth to warm his thin, dirty hands.

Penelope felt so sorry for him. Of what did she have to complain!

She put some milk into a pan. She had become rather good at cooking and serving herself, she thought with pride. ''I'll have your chocolate in just a minute,'' she told the boy gaily.

''Young man, you must take off your cap and scrub your hands. Your face, too.'' The speaker was Nanny Minster, who had just come down the stairs from the sitting room above. She sounded like the nurse she'd always been.

The boy flushed. ''Sorry.'' He went to the sink, after first turning to look at Penelope for permission. Then he scrubbed at his hands and face with a bar of the strong yellow soap that Nanny used for cleaning the pots, wincing when it touched the burns and scrapes on his skin. The soap didn't appear to do much good for the grime, either.

Nanny handed him a towel. ''Take off your cap,'' she repeated.

The boy clutched the towel, though water still dripped down his face. ''No, no, I won't take off my cap.''

''And why not?''

''I don't want no chocolate,'' he said. ''I got to go.''

Penelope said gently, ''You may keep your cap on.'' She studied the dark hair at the front of his face. It was really a curious color, streaked here and there with blond.

She was being silly. His hair color was of no moment. ''Sit down and have your chocolate, and there is bread and cheese for you as well.''

The child hesitated, his green eyes showing both longing and indecision. ''Thank you, missus,'' he said.

Penelope sat across from him. ''Are you a chimney sweep?''

His mouth too full for a reply, the boy nodded.

''What's your name, boy?'' Nanny Minster asked him.

The child was obviously struck by her authority. He gulped down his food. ''I'm Jem.''

''And how old are you?''

He hesitated. ''I disremember. No, I know. I'm eight.''

"Eight?" Penelope was horrified. He was such a little, frail thing.

She waited for him to take several more bites and swallows. "Do you like babies, Jem?"

Again, he hesitated, as though uncertain how to reply. Finally he said, "I like one of them. It . . . uh . . . it reminds me of my mam."

Penelope smiled. She doubted that very much. Because he was a boy, the child must be ashamed of appreciating babies. He was unlike Lord Treymaine, she thought, the smile disappearing. That one didn't seem to be ashamed of anything he did, or wanted.

Jem must have noticed her change of expression. "I'm sorry," he whispered.

The lovely smile returned. "Don't be sorry. Besides, if the one you like is the one I think it is, it's my favorite, too. Isn't it nice that we like the same things?"

Jem seemed a bit confused as to the value of her conclusion but ready to agree. "Could I see it up close?" he asked. "I promise I won't touch it."

"Of course, you may. If you've had enough to eat, come along."

She led him back through the curtain into the shop. The sky had darkened, so she turned up the lamps and lit some of the sweet-smelling candles.

"It's like heaven," the boy said, sniffing. "Can I see the baby now?"

Obviously, he had no expectation of heaven lasting for very long; for him, there was no time to waste. Penelope walked to a shelf and took down the baby she thought he wanted. It was the right one. With open delight the little boy put out his fingers to touch it. Then, apparently remembering who he was, he drew them back. He examined the baby avidly. As though he simply could not help himself anymore, he reached out a bony finger again and held it gently against one of the baby's blue glass eyes. "She's so beautiful,'' he breathed. "I never saw nothin' so beautiful.''

Penelope could well believe that. "Do you live with your parents?'' she asked gently.

"My da.'' The little face filled with fear. "I got to go, missus. Thank you. Thank you.'' He ran from the shop.

Quite a few customers came into the Baby Shoppe during the following week, although Lord Treymaine and his family were not among them. However, four of the customers said they'd been directed to the shop by Lord Treymaine or his mother or sister, all of whom had recommended its wares highly. Penelope took in so much money that she could look forward to paying the rent for several more months, and without using a penny of Nanny's savings. And it was only just the beginning of December. Surely, as Nanny had said, the closer to Christmas it came, the better she would do.

She should have been happy. In truth, however, she was not. It wasn't just that she'd lost her father or her home or her fiancé, either. It was also, she confessed to herself, that she missed the horrid Lord Treymaine.

Since he was horrid, she could not understand why she felt as she did. She thought about the matter, which meant she thought about him, a great deal. Finally she decided that, in a perverse sort of way, it was because he brought some excitement into her life. At least, when he was there, tormenting her, she felt stimulated and she was not lonely.

She must pull herself out of the doldrums, she scolded herself. To do so, she would go shopping for a new bonnet; even the purchase of a black bonnet must lift her spirits.

When she advised Nanny of her plans, the older woman was full of objections. "I got to stay here to mind the shop, which means you'll have to go out alone. Your papa wouldn't want you to do that, especially away from this neighborhood. This isn't safe, like the country, you know.''

Penelope saw her chance for a much-needed excursion

fast disappearing. "I will be safe," she said stubbornly. "Who would wish to accost me?"

Nanny clucked her tongue in exasperation. "You've never known how you really look," she said, "but I know. You're a prime article, and somewhere out there is a rake, or maybe more than one, waiting to ravish you and snatch your virtue. You listen to me; don't you go."

Penelope refused to listen, however. She knew that if she didn't get away from the shop, she'd be miserable.

Accordingly, she hailed a hackney coach and went off to Oxford Street to visit the warehouses. Like her shop, they were thin of members of the *haute ton.* Nevertheless, they had a festive, Christmas look, and the customers that were on the streets and in the warehouses appeared to be enjoying themselves.

Penelope, herself, wandered about happily for a while, until, finally, at Clark and Debenham's, she purchased a black crepe bonnet with two black feathers fixed by a bow. Then it was time to go home.

Her spirits as lifted as she'd predicted, she walked jauntily outside to the pavement to hail a hackney. Before she could do so, however, she was stopped by two young men.

"Don't I know you?" one of them asked, putting a hand on her arm. "I'm sure I've seen you before."

She was just as sure he hadn't. It seemed that Nanny's prediction also was coming true; Penelope had been foolish to venture out alone.

She pulled her arm away and looked about once more for a hackney. Once she found one, she knew she wouldn't have anything about which to worry.

A carriage stopped alongside her. Penelope looked up— and into the furious eyes of Lord Treymaine. In a trice he jumped down.

He did not bother to greet her. "Are you annoying this

young woman?'' he asked the men between his teeth. ''If you are, I shall call you out—and shoot you dead.''

That was plain speaking. Both men jumped back. ''Not I, sir,'' said the man who had touched her.

''Not I, either.''

Without waiting for Lord Treymaine's reaction, both of them walked hastily off.

Penelope wished she could do the same. Lord Treymaine was obviously not best pleased. She didn't want his anger directed at her.

''Where is your abigail?'' he demanded.

Penelope sighed. ''I'm a shopkeeper, Lord Treymaine. I don't have an abigail.''

He was not to be put off. ''Then where is Nanny Minster? Do not tell me that she let you go out alone?''

''Your Lordship, I am not in leading strings.''

His gray eyes glinted. ''Perhaps you should be. Come, I will take you home.

''You need someone to take care of you,'' he said after she'd settled herself against the squabs. He studied her lovely face a minute. ''Are you free to dine with me tonight?''

Penelope might be naive about some things, but she wasn't stupid. His Lordship's intent couldn't have been more obvious. He meant to be the one who would take care of her, by offering her a *carte blanche*. She felt sick.

''I'm not that hungry, '' she said disdainfully, then turned her face to the window. Not until the carriage stopped in front of the Baby Shoppe did she look at him again. ''Thank you for coming to my rescue, Your Lordship, and good-bye.''

He seemed about to say something but then, apparently, changed his mind. Penelope let the coachman help her down the steps. Without turning back, she walked into the shop.

''There you are. Did you have a good time?'' Nanny

asked as eagerly as though Penelope's jaunt had been her idea.

Penelope didn't answer.

"Was that Lord Treymaine who brought you home? If I'd knowed you was going to be with him, I wouldn't have worried."

Penelope opened her mouth to tell Nanny a thing or two about the gentleman. Then she closed it. What was the use? Once her old nurse decided she knew a person's character, she remained unshakable in her conviction.

Let Nanny continue not to worry. Penelope knew what she knew.

She should have been pleased to be correct in her assessment of Lord Treymaine's character, but she wasn't. Pleading a headache, she made her excuses to Nanny, then pushed her way through the flowered curtain to go up the back stairs and to bed.

Besides Nanny, the only other person Penelope knew whom she liked was Jem, the little chimney sweep. He had come into the store several times in the last few weeks. Penelope always made him welcome.

He was there when she came back from shopping at the butcher's and the greengrocer's on Saturday. She found him in the kitchen, talking diffidently to Nanny Minster, of whom he was still in awe.

"How nice to see you," said Penelope, laughing. "Here, let me put my parcels down."

She bent over the table, and as she did so, her string bag swung against Jem's head, knocking off his filthy cap. "Oh, dear," Penelope said, her face flushed. "I'm so clumsy. Did I hurt you, darling?"

Instead of answering, the boy hastily knelt to retrieve his cap. When he rose again, his hair had fallen down around his shoulders.

Penelope saw that not only was it long but also it was

very oddly colored. She had noticed the color before, of course, but couldn't have imagined his hair would look as it did now. Only the front was dark. The rest, which had always been covered by Jem's cap, was a pale blond. Openmouthed, Penelope stared at him.

"You're a girl!" Nanny Minster said roughly. "Here, what are you up to?"

The child began to blubber. "Nothin'. It's nothin'. It's my da. He makes me."

Penelope took the child on her lap, soot and all. "What does your da make you do, darling?"

"He makes me dress like this, like a boy, so I can be a chimney sweep. He said it wouldn't be good if people knew I was a girl." Tears fell down her face. "He'd beat me if he heard I told you."

"Just let him try," said Nanny as fiercely as though Jem—or whatever the girl had been christened—was her very own chick. "What's your *real* name, child?"

"Jessymyn Jones. He said I should be Jem 'cause it was like my name and I'd remember it."

Penelope suddenly felt herself about to burst with enthusiasm. Indeed, she looked the wondrous, happy creature she'd been before her tragedies had befallen her. "Jem . . . Jessymyn, why does your papa make you be a sweep?"

The girl looked at Penelope as though she were queer in the attic. "'Cause we need the money," she said, adding simply, "I have to work."

What an odd world it was, Penelope thought. Among her set—her former set—it was peculiar, indeed unacceptable, to work. This child would never understand that.

Penelope stroked the girl's dirty hair. "Tell me, if I gave your papa as much money as you make for him now, would he let you work for me? Of course, you'd have to live here so we could keep you clean and well dressed."

"Now, just a minute," Nanny said.

The girl looked up at her, the green eyes hurt and hopeless.

Nanny grumbled, "I suppose we could manage, if you'd promise to be very, very good and keep clean and say your prayers."

"I'll wash every single day," the child offered as though this was the most unusual and dramatic thing in the world she could provide as evidence of good faith. "And I'll pray every five minutes. Please, oh, please, won't you let me stay here?"

"Only if you promise not to pray every five minutes," said Penelope.

The deed was done. Although Jessymyn's father, a real brute, had proved difficult at first, finally, with a large enough bribe, he had agreed to the arrangement. Now Penelope had someone to take care of, someone to sew for and to teach, someone to stave off some of the loneliness she felt. Both Penelope and Jessymyn bloomed like sweet summer roses. Even Nanny seemed more agreeable and took to humming.

Penelope put her little helper to work setting out special dolls for Christmas. She had bought a number of Italian wax crèche figures, which she arranged in one half of the bowed front window. Now she and Jessymyn were putting out French *santons* in the other half. These were Christmas crib babies, so called, brightly colored clay figures representing the Christ child and the rest of the holy family. Penelope surrounded them with the figures that always accompanied them: rich folk and poor, villagers and craftsmen. How could anyone resist her shop with such an eye-catching display?

Jessymyn knocked over two of the figures, then peeked up at Penelope with a frightened expression. The child had still not recovered from her harsh former existence, but at least she was clean, well fed, and clothed now, and she'd only had one nightmare in the past week.

"Silly," Penelope said in her lovely voice. "It doesn't matter."

She stood up to ease the stiffness in her back, then looked out the window. Looking back at her, his gray eyes alight with some unreadable emotion, was Lord Treymaine. Why had she ever considered him an unappealing example of manhood? She caught her breath. He was exceedingly handsome, even if he was no better than he should be. She'd vow he was handsomer even than Lord Randolphe.

Well, perhaps not. However, she left the comparison uncorrected.

He came into the shop, letting the door bang behind him. Cold air rushed in, swirling around Penelope's feet and legs and stirring her blood.

Lord Treymaine tossed his curly brimmed beaver onto the green and white chair; his greatcoat followed. Penelope said caustically, "Please make yourself comfortable, although the answer is still *no*."

"Ah . . . *no* to what?"

With horror, she realized he might think she was referring to his implied offer to make her his mistress. That was one subject she did not even wish to allude to. "To whether you can have my shop," she replied swiftly.

"Oh, that," he said with a smile that confused her. "Are you still angry with me about it? Did you miss me last week?"

"Of course I'm not angry—nor did I miss you. In truth," she lied, "I do not feel any pronounced emotion regarding you, Lord Treymaine."

He did not appear pleased. His dark brows lowered over his eyes, making him look fierce. He took a few steps toward her.

Both of them had forgotten about Jessymyn. Indeed, Lord Treymaine seemed not even to have been aware of her presence. They noticed her now, however. Since she was swinging a large wooden baby in each thin hand, they could hardly fail to notice her.

"If you hurt my Miss Archer, I'll kill you," the child said, hitting Lord Treymaine on the thigh with one of the babies.

His Lordship winced. Instead of reacting with displeasure, however, he asked pleasantly, "And who is this?"

"She is my apprentice. Put down the babies, Jessymyn. His Lordship is a madman, but he is not physically dangerous."

"Oh, I could be," he murmured. "Indeed, I could be. Will you give me an opportunity to prove it to you?"

"Jessymyn, dear, please find Nanny Minster and ask her to come here at once."

A long arm reached out and snagged the child around the waist. "Jessymyn, don't do anything of the sort. Your mistress is just funning. Would you like to look at my pocket watch?"

The little girl seemed puzzled. "No, I don't think so."

"I forgot. It's boys who like to look at pocket watches. Here," he said, taking some coins from his coat. "Go down the street and buy us some cakes."

"We have cakes," Penelope said coldly, resenting his arrogance. "Nanny made them."

"Do as I say, Jessymyn. That's a good girl."

Jessymyn grabbed a heavy shawl and left.

Penelope stamped her foot. "How dare you order my apprentice about?"

"I had to. How else could I get her to leave so that we could be alone?"

"Alone?" Penelope swallowed hard.

How fortunate that she did not feel drawn to him, she thought in anger and confusion as he directed his attention not to her but to a holly wreath she'd purchased that morning from a street vender. When she'd chosen it, it had seemed the essence of Christmas with its beautiful green leaves and smooth, shiny berries. There was even a perky little robin attached to the red bow at the top.

"We'll be able to decorate the shop in peace," he said, his eyes so mischievous that she'd swear he knew exactly what effect he was having on her. "Do you want me to hang that for you?"

Penelope frowned but directed him to the mantelshelf, where she'd left a hammer and nails. "It's to go up there," she said, pointing to the bare wall above the fireplace.

"Certainly not," Lord Treymaine replied. "We must put it outside the shop, on the door. We must have other decorations, too, to make the shop a Christmas shop."

There he was, ordering her about again, as though the store were already his and she was his clerk. "I don't want it outside," she said stubbornly.

"Of course you do." Ignoring her continued protests, he opened the door and, in a trice, nailed up the wreath. Then he walked back inside. "That's done," he said briskly. "Now, where are the bay sprigs?"

"Bay sprigs?"

"Yes, little parrot. We can't decorate without them. Think how your nose would miss that wonderful, spicy Christmastime smell."

He was right; it would. "I shall purchase some tomorrow," she said defensively.

"Why wait? We can buy some on our way."

She almost said, "On our way?" but stopped herself. She didn't want to be called a parrot again. Instead, she said, "Where do you think we are going?"

He grinned. "Oh, I know where we are going. I am going to cut a yule log for your fireplace, and you are going to watch me do it." Before she could say yea or nay, he added, "Get your cloak; we shall leave now."

"Now? I do not wish to leave now. Besides, you sent

Jessymyn for cakes, and there is no one to stay in the shop, and—''

"Nanny," His Lordship bellowed, "come here."

Nanny Minster pushed back the flowered curtain as though she'd been waiting in the wings for her cue. "You sound like a bull, Your Lordship," she said reprovingly. "Now, what can I do for you?"

"You can't do anything," Penelope told her. "Don't listen to him. Go back to the kitchen, please."

"Stay here, Nanny. I want to take Miss Archer on an outing."

"Bless you, Your Lordship. It will do her so much good. She hasn't been out of the shop since she bought her new bonnet."

"It won't do me good. I won't go. I won't."

In a matter of minutes Penelope was wrapped in a warm black pelisse and found herself outside the door of her shop.

She glared at Lord Treymaine as he gave an order to his coachman and then pushed her into his carriage. Nevertheless, she had to admit, at least to herself, that she already felt relief leaving her shop.

London seemed so alive outside. The pavements, if not teeming with humanity, at least were dotted here and there with individuals too rugged or too intent upon their errands to heed the cold. They hurried along the pavement, heads down or held high in defiance of the wind, their curly brimmed beavers and bonnets, their greatcoats, shawls, and pelisses spots of color in the sullen weather.

Then there were the horses, their warm breaths turning to frost in the air, their harnesses making a jangling kind of music as the animals pulled coaches and carts along the cobblestoned streets. Some of the horses even wore Christmas decorations: green ribbons and red bows with long streamers—oh, it was all delightful. Penelope sat back against the swabs with a satisfied sigh. His Lordship smiled at her. "May I take it that you're glad you came out with me?"

She couldn't bear to concede a point to him. "No, you may not. You still haven't told me where we are going."

"Why, to Hampstead," he said, as though she should have realized it without asking. He captured one of her hands in his. "We're going to Hampstead Heath, to collect our yule log."

Penelope pulled her hand away. "Even you can't just cut down a tree at will, you know."

His gray eyes sparkled with laughter. "I do know. Actually, my brother-in-law has an estate bordering on the Heath. It is to his property that we will go."

Why was he being so pleasant to her? What was his game? Afraid to find out, Penelope sent most of the rest of their trip looking out of the window at the ascending road. After a while, His Lordship gave up trying to get a response from her.

At last they arrived at Hampstead. Lord Treymaine pulled the checkstring for the coachman to stop. "Let us get out here for a minute," he said to a surprised Penelope.

She did as he requested and was most glad for it. Down below them stretched all of London. It was a glorious sight.

"Thank you," she whispered before they got back in the carriage and went on again. His Lordship smiled at her.

As they continued on, Lord Treymaine pointed out places he thought might interest her, including Jack Straw's Castle and the Spaniard's Inn, reputedly a haunt of the infamous eighteenth-century outlaw Dick Turpin.

From the main road they turned into a private lane. At the end of it Penelope saw a large red brick house, four stories high. It reminded her of Willowtree. "I . . . I don't want to go up to the house," she informed him in a broken voice.

His Lordship gave her a curious look, then patted her hand and said soothingly, "Very well, we won't do that."

He gave directions to his coachman, and a little while later they stopped near a beautiful park thick with a variety of evergreen trees.

Lord Treymaine descended from the carriage. He looked magnificent, Penelope thought, his black hair as rich with shine and color in the winter light as a raven's feathers, the usually cool gray eyes exhilarated. She realized that he was having a good time. She'd give much to know whether it was because of her, the trip away from Mayfair, or the anticipated pleasures of physical exercise.

His hand closed firmly around hers to help her from the coach, and she stopped trying to determine what was in his mind—until he accepted an ax from his coachman. Unless he always traveled with such an accoutrement, he must have planned this trip, she thought. She could not decide how she felt about that.

They walked a little way into the park, before he said "May I?" and, without waiting for an answer, stripped off his greatcoat and tight blue coat. He handed them to Penelope, who almost staggered under their weight. His clothing was warm from his body and smelled of the bay rum he used. Unconsciously Penelope clutched the materials to herself.

Soon chips were flying as he felled a still upright dead tree that looked as though it had been struck by lightning. Staring at him, at his hard muscles bulging and straining against his shirt, Penelope felt as though she'd been struck as well. She averted her face from his; he noticed too much.

Finally the tree was down and a respectably proportioned yule log cut from it. It was time to go home.

Penelope helped His Lordship into his coat and greatcoat, then simply stood there, looking up at him with bemusement.

"What is it?" he asked, taking her chin into his hand and tilting her face toward his. "I'm hot and dirty," he said in a husky voice.

Slowly then, as though time were winding down, he took her into his arms. His fingers feathered over her closed eyes, her cheekbones, the contours of her mouth. Her lips softened beneath the touch. His mouth came down on hers.

His kiss was gentle and very beguiling. Penelope relaxed against him, forgetting that he was her adversary, that she did not understand him, that she did not trust him.

When he felt her surrender, his kiss grew more demanding. It no longer coaxed her to accept him. It insisted on a response—and respond she did.

Penelope felt a curious ache in her throat and an electric excitement in her stomach. Her mouth opened beneath his. She wanted—she didn't know what she wanted, just that it was something she lacked, something that he could give her. Her arms went to his shoulders, to cling to him.

His hands went under her pelisse, against her sides. Long fingers touched her breast. Penelope startled.

Lord Treymaine let her go. "I shouldn't have done that. I apologize," he told the stunned young woman. "I won't ask you to forgive me."

Penelope wanted to go back into his arms. Obviously however, he did not want her. She supposed her lack of experience had displeased him—or, perhaps, it was the unladylike passion he had aroused in her.

Yes, that was it; she'd convinced him, if he needed convincing, that she was not a lady. She felt ill.

"Damn you, Charles," she said.

If she had planned to revenge herself on him, she couldn't have done any better than she did inadvertently. He stepped back. Amazingly, there was a look of jealousy on his face. "My name is *Tony*," he said coldly. "Tony!"

"Oh, yes, I forgot."

His expression was forbidding. "Who is Charles?" he spat out.

"No one." She saw he didn't believe her. "I won't tell you."

"Oh, won't you? Then perhaps I must find out for myself."

"Don't be absurd!" she cried. "Why would you want to do that?"

He did not answer.

She forced her mouth into a sneer. "He's my fiancé. . . . He was my fiancé."

"Is that so? Why isn't he your fiancé any longer?"

"That's no concern of yours," she said, fighting down the tears. She turned her back to him. "Take me home, Lord Treymaine. Please."

"What is this concoction?" she asked Nanny Minster at breakfast a few mornings later. "It smells like a duck egg gone bad."

"Doesn't matter. It's a tonic and will cure what ails you."

Nothing could cure what ailed her. Even the fast approach of Christmas did not raise Penelope's spirits.

Nevertheless, she made a strong effort after that to seem as though she were enjoying the season. It was certainly a help that she and Nanny had Jessymyn about. If they lost her, Penelope didn't know what they'd do.

Thus, it was with real trepidation that she saw Mr. Jones, the child's father, enter the shop one morning. He brought with him not only the outdoor chill but also the smells of soot, perspiration, and long-unwashed skin. "What do you want?" she asked in a voice she kept cool only with great effort.

"I want to see my daughter, missus, just as any father would—especially at this season," the man intoned piously, tugging at his filthy tweed cap. "Where is the little darlin'?"

"She isn't here," Penelope lied. In fact, Jessymyn was upstairs, helping Nanny make the beds and tidy the rooms. She prayed the child would not come down.

"Doesn't matter. She has to come back sometime. I'll wait."

"But why?" Penelope cried, losing her battle to be calm. "You don't want her."

"I hear she cleaned up real nice," he said, apparently apropos of nothing. "That's what my friend said who saw her."

"So?"

Mr. Jones laughed. It was not a reassuring sound.

Penelope's beautiful face grew sharp with anger. "You can't see her unless I permit it," she said emphatically. "But I won't. We have an agreement, you and I. She's my apprentice."

"Now, missus, you're wrong about that. We didn't sign no contract, so if you think you can keep a man's own child from him, you'd better think some more. By law, she's mine. I'll give you back your money. Then I can do whatever I want with her."

Penelope felt her heart begin to pound. This man was frightening. "Just what is it that you want to do?"

"I told you. To get my sweet little daughter."

Penelope's lips thinned. "Well, I won't let you, so you might as well leave, Mr. Jones."

Mr. Jones wiped his hand across his mouth. "Look here, missus, you'll give me my daughter or I'll go to the Bow Street Runners. I'm acquainted with quite a few of them."

"How could one doubt that you would be?" a cool voice said from the doorway. Penelope quickly turned. The speaker was Lord Treymaine.

Penelope forgot that she had been angry with him. Her eyes lit with joy. "Your Lordship," she breathed. It was all she could do not to rush to his side.

Lord Treymaine did not take his gaze from the chimney sweep. "You have not satisfactorily answered the lady's question as to your intentions. Therefore, let me ask you:

Why are you attempting to take this child away from Miss Archer? Are you displeased with the arrangements?''

This time Mr. Jones did not sound quite so brash and bullying. ''That I am, milord,'' he said in a whining voice. ''I can get more money for the chit somewhere else. She's mine that I took care of from an infant, and I deserve that money.''

''How much is Miss Archer paying you?''

When the sweep told him, His Lordship said, ''She'll give you half again as much. Now be a good fellow and go away.''

''Just a moment,'' Penelope said. ''I can't give him half again as much, nor would I want to if I could. I appreciate your concern, Lord Treymaine, but you must let me handle this. I know what I can do.''

The gray eyes gazed into hers. ''Sit down, Miss Archer. You, fellow, remove your cap.''

Both did as they'd been told.

''It's like this, milord,'' Mr. Jones said, not quite looking at Lord Treymaine. ''You're a man of the world; you understand things. The chit is mine—by law and holy writ—and I've got someone who will give me much more for her than this lady here. I can't pass that by. What father could?''

Lord Treymaine looked at him with distaste. ''As you've heard more than once, she's apprenticed to Miss Archer.''

''Yes,'' said Penelope, unable to stay quiet, ''and she's happy here. Doesn't that mean anything to you?''

For a moment Mr. Jones seemed thunderstruck. Then he started to laugh. ''Of course it don't. Why should it?''

Penelope's hands went out in a helpless gesture. How could she communicate with such a person?

''This other work I got for her will do just fine,'' Mr. Jones said. ''Don't you give it another thought, missus.''

''Of course I'll give it another thought,'' Penelope

replied indignantly. "What sort of work is it? Are you going to apprentice her to someone else?"

"I guess you could say that, in a manner of speaking," Mr. Jones said with a smirk.

Lord Treymaine stared at him with undisguised dislike. "You mean to sell her into prostitution, don't you?"

Mr. Jones ignored Penelope's cry. "I ain't saying I am, and I ain't saying I ain't. But since I ain't saying I am, you got nothing to get worked up about now, do you?"

"I want you to come outside, Jones. We can continue this discussion there."

"Thank you, milord, but I can't. I come here to get my little darlin'. I can't leave this place without her. She's that important to me."

Lord Treymaine's face was grim. "How much will you get from her initiator, Jones?"

"What are you talking about?" Penelope asked. She turned ashen. "You can't mean it. She's just a little girl."

His Lordship looked full in her eyes. "I'm sorry, my dear, to speak thus in front of you." His voice gentled. "I had no choice, however. You needed to realize that there are men like that in this world you've chosen to take on by yourself."

"I don't know none of them," said Mr. Jones, scuffing one of his filthy boots against the floor.

"Jones, we've had enough of your lies. I insist you come outside with me now."

"What for?" the fellow asked suspiciously. "We've done all our talking."

Lord Treymaine opened the door and stood waiting. His face seemed without emotion, except for his eyes, which were cutting gray ice. The sweep shrugged, then silently followed him outside. They disappeared from view.

Penelope thought she would die if His Lordship did not come back soon. She wished she knew what he meant to do. And though it seemed frivolous under the circumstances, she wondered also if he had been planning to visit her or if he had come into her shop because he'd seen Mr. Jones through the window.

It was a half hour or more before he returned. To Penelope, it seemed like forever.

When he did return, the cold air he brought with him seemed to clean out the shop, to remove all traces of the griminess and dissolution that accompanied Mr. Jones like a threatening cloud.

"Well?" she asked breathlessly and clutched at his greatcoat. "Tell me what you said to him. Tell me what he said to you."

His Lordship gently loosed her fingers. "Come into the kitchen," he said, "and I'll tell you."

"The kitchen? Why? Are you hungry?"

"I always feel a hunger when I'm in your presence, Penelope. I can't seem to help myself."

She flushed.

"However," he continued, "since it is obvious that you don't wish to hear about that, I will let the subject lie. I want to go into the kitchen because there is a huge hearth in there, presumably with a fire in it, and I'm cold."

"Oh," she said lamely. "Let us go, then."

Once in the kitchen he walked to the fire and rubbed his hands together.

Penelope remained in the doorway, gazing at him. She wondered how she could ever have thought him other than an exceedingly handsome man. With his strong face, his wide shoulders, and tapering back fitted into a blue coat that sat upon him like a second skin, with his narrow hips and long, booted legs, he was, in her eyes, the epitome of masculinity. He stirred her senses, made her feel atingle with life-longing and sensuous yearnings. At the same time he made her feel safe.

But she wasn't safe with him. It wasn't just that his intentions were dishonorable. It was that she knew by now that she, herself, must be the guarantor of her safety. Except for Nanny, there was no one else on whom she could rely. She mustn't permit herself to forget that.

His Lordship turned to her, a quizzical look on his aristocratic features. "Don't you want to know what transpired between me and Mr. Jones?"

She blushed. "Of course I do," she said hastily.

"Then come over to me, Penelope." He pulled up a chair for her near the fire. "Come here, and I will tell you all."

With a little reluctance she did as she'd been bid.

He seated himself across from her and stretched out his legs in their shiny boots. "I walked with Jones to the end of the street," he said. "He was blustering and belching smoke and flames all the way."

Although Penelope could tell that His Lordship meant to lighten the atmosphere by his choice of words, it was not lightened for her. She wanted just the facts. "And then?"

"Then I repeated my offer to give him half again what he'd been getting from you."

"You shouldn't have made the offer," Penelope said with a frown. "I don't believe I can meet the terms."

He leaned over and lifted her hand. "I'm sure you can't, but I can. You must know I meant that."

Yes, and she knew what she would have to pay in return. She shook her head and withdrew her hand.

His grin was rueful. "You're an unyielding woman, Penelope. At any rate, it doesn't matter. He refused my offer. Therefore, I made him another."

"Oh, no, you shouldn't have." She plucked nervously at the black velvet cuff of her sleeve. "If I can't pay what you offered, I certainly can't afford to pay more."

"Since my 'offer' was to break him into pieces if he did not leave you alone—and that included not bothering Jessymyn—I don't think he expected any payment to come from you." He looked down at his knuckles, which, for the first time Penelope noticed, were red and split. "I gave him a foretaste of what I meant, and he agreed to the offer."

Penelope couldn't imagine Lord Randolphe doing anything like that. Lord Treymaine was wonderful. She felt the blood surge in her heart. "Thank you," she said with sincerity. "At least one problem is at an end."

His Lordship rose to his feet. "Damn it, woman. Nothing is at an end. First it was those two men outside the warehouse. Now it's Jones. Do you think a bit of pummeling can discourage a sewer rat like Jones? You're in as much danger as ever, maybe more. Jessymyn is a valuable commodity to the wrong sort."

"But . . . but what shall I do, then?"

He gave her a long look. "Well, you could sell the shop, take your precious Jessymyn and Nanny Minster, and return to the country."

"Can't you think of anything else?" she asked.

His face darkened. "I can," he said crisply. "However, you won't like it."

"And what is that?"

"To give Jessymyn up."

Penelope was stunned. How could he even mention such a possibility? "You'll do anything to get this shop, won't you?" she said with a feeble laugh.

"I hope you don't really mean that. I'm only talking sense to you."

"I won't do it. I can't. Don't you see, I . . . I need her as much as she needs me."

Reluctantly, it seemed to her, he said, "I can understand that."

"Really?"

"Yes, after what you went through before you moved to London, it must be very important to you to have someone you can trust on whom to lavish affection."

Instantly she was suspicious. "How do you know what I

went through? Did you go to my home to find out about me? Is that what you were doing last week?''

His look grim, he nodded.

''How dare you? Why did you do that?''

''I needed to know,'' he said simply. ''And now I do. I spoke with Mr. Brigham, with your clergyman, and some of your neighbors. I heard it all.''

''Oh, did you!''

''Why didn't you tell me *why* you had come here and rented this shop?''

Penelope raised her eyebrows haughtily, although they were so pale the gesture practically negated itself. ''Why should I have?''

''You cannot deny that it was a very odd thing for a female of your class to do.''

''Ah, but I had no choice. I doubt you understand that sort of thing, Your Lordship.''

''I understand matters when they are explained to me,'' he said stiffly. ''You could have told me.''

''My life was, and is, no one's concern but mine,'' she said defiantly.

''Is that what you think? Let me tell you, my girl, you are wrong.''

''I'm not your girl,'' Penelope snapped, although, in truth, she wished she were. ''And I don't want your pity, or understanding, or anything else; I didn't want it before, and I don't now.''

''As I just said, you're wrong. You know, I spoke with that Randolphe fellow, too. Charles. He's a pretty devil. Even prettier than you.''

''Yes, he is, isn't he?''

''He threw you over.''

Penelope blushed. ''Actually, I released him from the engagement. Go away, Lord Treymaine.''

''I wouldn't have done that.''

Humiliation and rage mingled in Penelope's breast. ''Is

that a fact? Tell me, Your Lordship, how many women have you been true to?''

Lord Treymaine flushed. "I never asked any of them to marry me."

And you won't ask me, either, Penelope thought. She turned her face away from him.

"Don't do that," he ordered. Unwillingly, Penelope turned toward him again.

"However," he went on as smoothly as though nothing had happened, "I didn't come here to argue with you. Willowtree is beautiful, isn't it, almost as beautiful as you. I wish I could have saved it for you."

"I'd rather sleep in the gutter."

"Or in rooms above your shop. Stop fighting me, Penelope. I want to help you, so that you will not need to do this anymore."

"I don't require that sort of help," she said with distaste, her lovely head held high. "I can manage for myself. Indeed, I prefer to do so."

The pale gray eyes had turned to ice. "Consider my offer," he said. "You may decide that it is not so bad."

"I won't consider it even for a second."

"Then at least do something to protect yourself and Jessymyn. Stop thinking with your heart, Penelope."

She glared at him. "It's easy for you to say that because you don't have one."

"Don't I?" He rose and pulled her from her chair. He put his arms about her, tightly so that she could not possibly pull away. She could feel his heart, then. It was beating hard against his chest, and hers.

"Maybe you do," she said faintly before he kissed her.

Her mouth was open. He invaded it. His kiss took everything from her and left her weak and helpless.

When he pushed her away, however, he seemed as shaken as she. "I . . . you . . . you should trust me. Will you listen to me now?''

Did he truly believe that unnerving kiss would make her trust him? It had had just the opposite effect, causing her to see just how weak and vulnerable she was with him. Besides, she would never give up Jessymyn. "No," she said.

"Then there's no more to be said. Keep your little flesh-and-blood borrowed baby. Goodbye, Penelope. Be careful, and God bless."

He touched her face. Then he left the shop.

Penelope put her head upon the counter and sighed. Although this time there were no tears, she knew she'd never felt so bleak before in her life.

Penelope finished decorating the shop for Christmas as though her life depended on it, and in a way, it did. She knew that if she didn't keep herself very busy, she would spend her days in her bed, grieving. So she hung wreaths of evergreen from the walls and draped them around the front of the counter; she put her yule log, made gay now with colored ribbons, in front of the fireplace; she even attached a bit of mistletoe just inside the front door. She also put a few more babies in the window, her rarest and loveliest ones.

Quite a few people came into the Baby Shoppe in the last few days before Christmas. It was as though everyone realized at the same time that gifts had to be purchased right away or not at all. Babies and other toys—tea sets, baby furniture, small trunks filled with exquisite, handmade clothes—fairly flew off the shelves. People seemed to be willing to buy anything and everything.

Indeed, two well-dressed matrons nearly came to blows over an English wax baby with blue eyes and soft blond hair. Penelope had to use all of her tact to separate them.

The frantic rush helped Penelope even more. Now she only thought about Lord Treymaine every hour instead of practically every minute.

Then, too, she was occupied with worrying about what Mr. Jones might do. Although he had not returned to her shop since his last encounter with her and His Lordship, there were a number of other men about, burly, rough-looking types, who did not seem to belong in the neighborhood. Every time she went out in the street, they were there. Sometimes she even thought one or two were following her. She wondered if they'd been sent by Mr. Jones to wait for their chance to snatch Jessymyn.

That didn't seem very likely since he surely did not have the money to pay them. Therefore, she attempted to put the idea from her mind.

At last it was Christmas Eve. "I never thought we'd see this day," Nanny grumbled. "Look at them shelves. They're practically bare."

"I had to step on a lady's foot to get her to give up my baby," Jessymyn said. "I told her it was mine, but she said she was going to buy it, anyway."

Penelope ruffled the child's blond hair. "I'm very proud of you," she said with a grin. "Why don't you close the shutters? I'll lock the door, and then we can go into the kitchen for a lovely meal."

"Don't have no lovely meal. Too bus—"

Nanny's mouth dropped open. The word was never finished. "It's 'im."

Penelope grabbed Jessymyn and thrust her behind her. She knew she would defend herself and her little family against Mr. Jones and his thugs to the last ounce of her strength. She also knew she couldn't do it. Where was Lord Treymaine? She needed him. Oh, how she needed him.

"You," she said foolishly when she realized that Nanny's "him" was not Mr. Jones, or even Lord Treymaine, but Lord Randolphe, her erstwhile fiancé. "It's only you." She began to giggle.

Lord Randolphe's beautiful face flushed. "Is that you, Penelope? Are you laughing at me?"

She looked him over assessingly, from the top of his fine, curly brimmed beaver, which he hadn't thought to doff, to his shiny black boots. He'd make a gorgeous baby, she thought scornfully. Thank heaven he wasn't one of hers.

"Come in, Charles. Shut the door. What do you want?"

"Well, really, you needn't be so curt. I've never done anything to you to deserve that sort of treatment."

No, he'd just abandoned her when she needed his support the most.

"I apologize," she said, "but it is late, and I'm tired."

He looked apologetic. "Yes, I'm sorry, but I didn't know where else to turn."

"Indeed?"

"Yes, it's very simple. Penelope, I need a gift, a baby, for . . . um . . . a friend's little girl. She's Lady Arthur. You may have heard of her. She's a widow with . . . with a little girl."

"How nice. How did you know to come here?"

"Oh, well, I've heard people talk about this place; and when they described you, I knew it couldn't be anyone else. Besides, that Lord Treymaine person said you were here. I think he expected me to visit you."

Penelope's lip curled. "How foolish of him."

"Yes. You're as beautiful as ever, Penelope."

"Thank you. You aren't."

He started to laugh. "Oh, Pen, you're just saying that because you're a little peeved with me for not coming to your shop any sooner. But, really, you aren't thinking. I couldn't come. I didn't want to embarrass you."

"Embarrass her?" Nanny Minster growled. "What are you talking about?"

His Lordship smiled diffidently at Nanny. Penelope could see that he was afraid of her. "Why, certainly. I knew it could only shame her in her present position to be called on by a lord. I was thinking about her, you must see."

Penelope had been called on by a lord many times. True,

Lord Treymaine had come in anger and had left because of
thwarted designs, but he'd always been honest and more
than helpful.

"So kind of you," she said. She picked up a wooden
baby. It was one of the ones with which Jessymyn had
walloped Lord Treymaine. "Here, Charles, is a baby. Buy
it. It's very special, and it costs twenty pounds."

"Twenty pounds! That's outrageous. I'll give you one
pound, although I'm certain that's too much."

She put the baby down.

"Ten," he said.

"Jessymyn, finish closing the shutters."

"All right, twenty." He grabbed the baby. "I don't think
you have an ounce of Christmas spirit, Penelope. Something's happened to you since you've become a shopkeeper.
It's coarsened you. I was right not to come by before."

Nanny Minster grabbed his arm. "Lord Randolphe, if
you don't go away this minute, I'll have to punish you."

His mouth opened. He gulped. Then he fled out the door.
To Penelope's surprise, with him went any residual longing
she might still have felt, and all of her anger against him.
How lucky she was, she thought, that she hadn't married
him. It was almost worth it to have lost her inheritance.

She jingled the twenty pounds. "Let's celebrate," she
said.

It was late when they finally got to bed. Indeed, in a few
hours it would be Christmas, a day of hope and joy for the
whole world. Penelope had hope that her shop would
continue to flourish and that she could provide a good life
for Nanny Minster and Jessymyn.

What she lacked was joy. Without Anthony Treymaine in
her life, joy was a stranger. It would continue to be.

Although she was exhausted, sleep did not come easily to
her. When she did finally sink into slumber, it was so deeply
that she did not hear anything, not the sounds of a door

being forced open or the sounds of objects being moved about in the shop below.

Then there was silence again.

A short while later she woke up, roused by an acrid smell that permeated her room. Penelope threw back her patchwork coverlet and got out of bed.

What was that smell? she thought, still groggy from sleep. Then she identified it. It was smoke. The building was on fire.

She looked about for a robe to cover her nightrail, then forgot about modesty. "Nanny, fire!" she screamed, rushing into the hall in her bare feet. "Jessymyn, wake up."

Like a demented person, Penelope ran to the one door, then to the other, and flung them open. "Wake up. Wake up."

Already her throat hurt, and it was painful to talk. Still she kept going from one door to the other, calling to them.

First Jessymyn, then Nanny Minster stumbled into the hall.

"Follow me," Penelope called and ran down the stairs to the kitchen with them behind her.

The kitchen was not on fire, not yet, at least, but it smelled strongly of smoke. "We're doomed," Nanny wailed. "We're going to cook like bacon. Dear God, have mercy."

"Quick," Penelope called, pushing the mesmerized Jessymyn before her, "out the back door."

The door stuck. For a second Penelope felt panic overtake her. Then she pushed and beat upon it as though it were a mortal enemy. The door swung open.

The three ran into the empty mews in back of their shop. They drew in hungry breaths of cold, damp air. It felt wonderful, even though Penelope realized that in a minute or two they would be shivering.

"It's all right, love." She hugged a sobbing Jessymyn. "We're alive."

"And poor and homeless," Nanny Minster added.

Penelope put a finger to her lips. "Never mind, Nanny. Come, let us all walk to the front of the building."

"We're not dressed," Nanny said, scandalized.

Penelope knew they looked dreadful—but they were unharmed. She began to laugh. "We are dressed. We're not decent. Come along."

They made their way to the front of the shop and stood looking at their future burn.

All of a sudden Jessymyn pulled away from Penelope. "My baby is in the shop. I can see it." Without another word she ran into the smoky building.

There was no time to think, no time to be afraid. Penelope ran after her.

It was like the torments of hell inside: heat, smoke, crackling noises, confusion, terror! Penelope's lovingly placed holly swags were burning. Her pretty babies were being consumed by fire.

None of that mattered. "Jessymyn!" she cried. "Jessymyn!"

She tripped over something and looked down. A pile of babies had been removed from their shelves and stacked in the middle of the floor. How had they gotten there? Was it possible that someone had deliberately started the fire?

The smoke seemed thicker; the licking flames were higher. There was no time to think about how the fire had started. "Jessymyn!" she shrieked. "Can you hear me?"

Blindly she put out her hands. They touched something warm and alive. "Oh, Jess," she sobbed. "Hurry, child, hurry."

Then something struck Penelope, and she lost consciousness.

When she came to herself, she was in a carriage. The air was cold around her, but she was not cold. She was cradled in a thick greatcoat, still warm from its owner's body. She knew it was Tony's coat. There was that stimulating yet comforting masculine odor composed of starch, cigars, and bay rum that was particularly his. She stirred and smiled.

"Have you decided to come back to us?" she was asked by a harsh voice that could not quite conceal the speaker's worry.

"Only if you let me keep this greatcoat," she croaked. She put her hand to her aching head. The skin underneath felt oily. It was sore to the touch in places. "What happened to me?" she asked.

"Part of the ceiling fell on you. You could have been killed." Again Tony's voice was harsh. "Slowly," he said as she attempted to sit up. He adjusted the coat more snugly about her.

"How did I get out?"

A smile lightened some of the grimness. "Did you know," he said, "that in America, or some barbaric place like that, the natives believe that if you rescue someone, you are responsible for that person for the rest of your life?"

Penelope looked at him and frowned. He was dirty and disheveled. There was a smut on his narrow, high-bridged nose. She had never seen him like that before. She thought he looked beautiful.

"You rescued me," she said. Then she began to laugh.

"And what is so funny?"

"Nothing. I'm sorry. It's just that you look so awful, all sooty like Jessymyn's father."

"Ah, yes, Mr. Jones. It was he who started the fire, you know. My men caught him lurking about afterward."

Her blue eyes widened. "What men?"

"The men I hired to guard your shop. They didn't do a very good job tonight, did they? They went off drinking and left only one person behind. Apparently, Jones had no trouble overpowering him and knocking him unconscious.''

Penelope let out a cry.

''Don't worry,'' he said fiercely. ''He won't bother you anymore. Nor will he trouble you about Jessymyn.''

She looked up at his dear face, both hope and doubt in her eyes. ''How can you know that?''

His large hands went to the sides of his ruined coat. ''Do not ask me; but if you get a letter from Australia, don't open it. Throw it away.''

He put his arms about her. ''Any more questions?'' he murmured.

''Yes.'' She pushed him away so that she could think. ''Where is Jessymyn, and where is Nanny?''

''They're fine. I sent them to stay with my mother.''

''You didn't.'' Light-headed, Penelope giggled. ''Will she accept them?''

''If she wants to remain my mother, she will.''

''You're a dreadful dictator,'' she said admiringly. Then her forehead wrinkled in lines of thought. ''How did you come to rescue me?''

She could have sworn he blushed. ''I happened to be passing by and stopped for a minute outside the shop.''

When she eyed him askance, he said, ''Don't ask me anymore now. That's all I shall say about that.''

''Very well. I have one more question.'' She sounded as though she did not truly want to ask it but could not help herself. ''What is the condition of the shop and my babies?''

Lord Treymaine looked as though he did not want to answer. He took her hand. In a low voice he said, ''There is nothing left. I'm sorry.''

Penelope stared at him, as though his words had been spoken in some ancient, lost language. ''My poor babies,'' she whispered. ''They're all gone.''

''You still have Jessymyn.''

"So I do. And Nanny Minster. Somehow, we'll have to start over."

She looked up at the sky. She saw a gorgeous, blazing star above her. She caught her breath. It was the Christmas star.

The watch called the hour. "It's Christmas morning," she said. Her rich voice was filled with emotion.

His Lordship's large hands tilted her head, so that she was looking into his eyes. Tenderly he wiped a smudge from her dainty nose. "I'm sorry that I don't have a gift for you, here and now. All I have at this moment is me. Is that enough?"

"For what?" she asked, suddenly wary.

"For the rest of your life. I'm asking you to marry me, Penelope. Will you?"

Penelope was thrilled, but then reality struck. "You can't marry me. I own a shop."

"Not anymore." He stroked her dirty face. "Well?"

"Would you marry a female who used to have wealth but now is poor?"

He smiled. "Only if the female were you."

She started to return his smile, but then hers disappeared. She shook her head. "It's impossible."

He was his old, arrogant self once more. "And why is it impossible?"

"I was in trade, Tony, even if I'm not now. You can't marry someone who's been in trade."

"You think not? Who would dare to stop me?"

Penelope smiled sadly. "Your mother, your sister, your friends in the *ton*. They'd give me the Cut Direct, I'm certain of it, and they'd cut you, too."

He slipped his arms about her and held her against him. She could hardly breathe, but she didn't care. "You're wrong, you know. My mother and sister would welcome you. They've been begging me to marry for as long as I can remember, and, besides, they were quite impressed with you. As for the rest, my mother is Mrs. Drummond-Burrell's godmother. Mrs. D. will take care of the *ton*. I discussed the matter with her this evening, and she gave me her promise that you'd have nothing to fear." He paused, then added, "Besides, with your beauty . . ."

"And your toploftiness . . . ?"

"And my toploftiness—and fortune—there's not a person in the world who would dare snub you. You'll be the most sought-after matron in England. Will you say yes now?"

She hesitated.

"What is it?" he asked quietly.

"What will happen to Jessymyn and Nanny Minster?"

He smiled at her, his teeth perfect and white in the dirtiness of his face. "We'll have Nanny Minster take care of our children, of course. As for Jessymyn, why, we'll raise her. I'd never try to take one of your babies away again, Penelope."

It was her turn to smile. "Thank you. Thank you for everything."

"And will you marry me?"

She put out her hands in a gesture of surrender. "Yes, Tony, I will."

The aristocratic features softened. "Tell me," he said in a gruff, unsteady voice, "would you really marry a man who's been a fool and could not see a treasure under his nose?"

"Only if the fool were you," she said with a mischievous grin.

"Minx!"

In the distance someone began singing, "God rest ye merry, gentlemen . . ."

Tony chuckled. Then he bent his dark head. "Happy Christmas, my love," he said huskily before he kissed her.

As his lips came down on hers, blotting out the world, Penelope knew that no matter how many more years she lived, however many more Christmases she celebrated, she would never have a Christmas more wonderful than this. She would remember it as the time she had lost all—and gained everything she could possibly desire.

Nationally bestselling author

JILL MARIE LANDIS

___**COME SPRING** 0-515-10861-8/$4.99
"This is a world-class novel . . . it's fabulous!"
                                    —Bestselling author Linda Lael Miller
She canceled her wedding, longing to explore the wide open West. But nothing could prepare her for an adventure that thrust her into the arms of a wild mountain man. . . .

___**JADE** 0-515-10591-0/$4.95
A determined young woman of exotic beauty returned to San Francisco to unveil the secrets behind her father's death. But her bold venture would lead her to recover a family fortune—and discover a perilous love. . . .

___**ROSE** 0-515-10346-2/$4.50
"A gentle romance that will warm your soul."—Heartland Critiques
When Rosa set out from Italy to join her husband in Wyoming, little did she know that fate held heartbreak ahead. Suddenly a woman alone, the challenge seemed as vast as the prairies.

___**SUNFLOWER** 0-515-10659-3/$4.99
"A winning novel!" —Publishers Weekly
Analisa was strong and independent. Caleb had a brutal heritage that challenged every feeling in her heart. Yet their love was as inevitable as the sunrise. . . .

___**WILDFLOWER** 0-515-10102-8/$4.95
"A delight from start to finish!" —Rendezvous
From the great peaks of the West to the lush seclusion of a Caribbean jungle, Dani and Troy discovered the deepest treasures of the heart.

From the *New York Times* bestselling author
of <u>Forgiving</u> and <u>Bygones</u>

LaVyrle Spencer

One of today's best-loved authors of bittersweet
human drama and captivating romance.

___THE ENDEARMENT	0-515-10396-9/$5.99
___SPRING FANCY	0-515-10122-2/$5.99
___YEARS	0-515-08489-1/$5.99
___SEPARATE BEDS	0-515-09037-9/$5.99
___HUMMINGBIRD	0-515-09160-X/$5.99
___A HEART SPEAKS	0-515-09039-5/$5.99
___THE GAMBLE	0-515-08901-X/$5.99
· ___VOWS	0-515-09477-3/$5.99
___THE HELLION	0-515-09951-1/$5.99
___TWICE LOVED	0-515-09065-4/$5.99
___MORNING GLORY	0-515-10263-6/$5.99
___BITTER SWEET	0-515-10521-X/$5.99
___FORGIVING	0-515-10803-0/$5.99